WITHDRAWN

HARVARD LIBRARY

WITHDRAWN

GOD AND THE SECULAR

GOD AND THE SECULAR

A Philosophical Assessment of
Secular Reasoning from Bacon to Kant

Robin Attfield

University College Cardiff Press

Copyright © Robin Attfield 1978

First published 1978 in Great Britain by
University College Cardiff Press,
P.O. Box 78, Cardiff, CF1 1XL, Wales,
in association with
Christopher Davies (Publishers) Ltd.,
52 Mansel Street,
Swansea
SA1 5EL.

Printed in Wales by Salesbury Press Ltd.

*All rights reserved. No part of this publication may
be reproduced, stored in a retrieval system, or
transmitted, in any form or by any means,
electronic, mechanical, photocopying, recording
or otherwise, without the prior permission of
the Publishers.*

ISBN 90142692 X

PREFACE

Thanks are due to my colleagues in the Department of Philosophy at University College, Cardiff, for discussion and encouragement, and also to Robert Young, who read an earlier version and from whose criticisms I have benefited. To Professor H. Cunliffe-Jones of the University of Manchester I am grateful for the supervision of research there, as to Professor J. L. Evans for supervision of research at Cardiff. Professor Basil Mitchell also gave invaluable help and advice. David Attfield's 'Christ is of God' must have given rise to a number of ideas incorporated in Chapter 5: I am also grateful for discussion of an earlier version of the present text with him, and also with Leela Attfield, but for whose care of the author and his children this book would not have appeared.

ACKNOWLEDGEMENTS

The author and publishers are grateful for permission for quotations from the following:

Paulo Rossi, 'Francis Bacon, From Magic to Science', Margery Purver, 'The Royal Society: Concept and Creation' and G. Leibniz, 'Theodicy', edited by A. M. Farrer, by permission of Routledge and Kegan Paul Ltd.; Volume I of 'Correspondence of Isaac Newton', edited H. W. Turnbull, by permission of The Royal Society; 'Freedom and Prediction', by J. R. Lucas, quoted from 'Proceedings of the Aristotelian Society' Supplementary Volume for 1967 (© 1967 The Aristotelian Society), by permission of the Editor; David Hume, 'Dialogues Concerning Natural Religion', edited by Norman Kemp Smith, by permission of Thomas Nelson and Sons Ltd.; 'Spinoza Selections', edited by John Wild, by permission of Charles Scribner's Sons; R. H. Kargon, 'Atomism in England from Hariot to Newton' and 'British Moralists 1650-1800', edited by D. D. Raphael, by permission of Oxford University Press; 'Early Seventeenth Century Scientists', edited by R. Harré, by permission of Pergamon Press Ltd; Thomas Hobbes, 'Leviathan', edited by M. Oakeshott, and John Plamenatz, 'The English Untilitarians', by permission of Basil Blackwell and Mott Ltd.; 'Kant and the Cosmological Argument', by Peter Remnant, quoted from 'Australasian Journal of Philosophy', 1959, by permission of the Editor; Benjamin Farrington, 'The Philosophy of Francis Bacon', by permission of Liverpool University Press; 'The Argument from Design', by Richard Swinburne, quoted from 'Philosophy', 1968, 'The Philosophical Works of Descartes', translated by Elizabeth S. Haldane and G. R. T. Ross, S. Mintz, 'The Hunting of Leviathan' and 'Unpublished Scientific Papers of Sir Isaac Newton', edited and translated by A. R. and M. B. Hall, by permission of Cambridge University Press; I. Kant, 'Critique of Pure Reason', translated by Norman Kemp Smith, by permission of Macmillan and Co. Ltd. and of St. Martin's Press, Inc.; Sir Isaac Newton, 'Mathematical Principles of Natural Philosophy and His System of the World', translated by Andrew Motte, revised by Florian Cajori, (Copyright © by Florian Cajori), by permission of the University of California Press; 'The Clarke-Leibniz Correspondence', edited by H. G. Alexander, by permission of Manchester University Press; 'Newton's Philosophy of Nature', edited by H. S. Thayer, by permission of Hafner Press; and 'Descartes, Mathematics and God', by Leonard G. Miller, quoted from 'The Philosophical Review', 1957, by permission of The Managing Editor and of Professor Miller.

TABLE OF CONTENTS

INTRODUCTION 9

CHAPTER 1: THEOLOGY AND METHOD IN EARLY MODERN SCIENCE
Section 1: Bacon's Theology and Method . . . 15
Section 2: Theoretical Physics . . . 33
Section 3: The Royal Society . . . 49
Section 4: Some Contrasts and Conclusions . . . 60

CHAPTER 2: THE ASSAULT ON PHYSICAL THEOLOGY
Section 1: The Nature of Physical Theology . . . 68
Section 2: Physics Deduced from Theology: Descartes and Newton . . . 70
Section 3: Supernatural Explanation in Newton . . . 75
Section 4: Physics Deduced from Theology: Leibniz . . . 80
Section 5: The Supernatural Explanation of Minds . . . 85
Section 6: Science and Miracles . . . 89

CHAPTER 3: SELF-DETERMINATION
Section 1: Introductory . . . 99
Section 2: Determinists and Objections to Determinism . . . 104

CHAPTER 4: THE SECULARISATION OF MORAL THEORY
Section 1: The Autonomy of Ethics . . . 122
Section 2: Theology and Utilitarianism . . . 130

CHAPTER 5: THE GROUNDS OF THEISM. I
Section 1: The Need for Natural Theology . . . 145
Section 2: The Ontological Argument . . . 152
Section 3: The Cosmological Argument . . . 163

CHAPTER 6: THE GROUNDS OF THEISM. II
Section 1: The Teleological Argument . . . 182
Section 2: The Goodness of God . . . 198

CONCLUSION . . . 211

BIBLIOGRAPHY . . . 216

INDEX . . . 227

INTRODUCTION

Secularisation is the process of the progressive assertion of human independence from religious authorities and influence. This book concerns some of the theories, claims and arguments underlying this process, and how they should be assessed. Whether or not these ideas and arguments undermined religious belief and practice or helped social and economic forces to do so, it is worth asking whether they should have: whether, that is, they show various religious beliefs to be false, inconsistent or meaningless, or whether by contrast they are consistent with religious beliefs or even possibly implicit in them, as the theologian Bonhoeffer has suggested.[1] A philosophical investigation is required to see how well the philosophers of secularisation made their points, how far religious beliefs remain tenable in face of the critique of history, and whether religion and this critique are really irreconcilable or not.

Yet care is needed to ensure that the above definition does not define secularisation out of existence. If the term 'religion' is so understood that what it names cannot decline, secularisation as defined above is a mirage. If religions are shared attitudes to nature, human nature and society as expressed in and reinforced by communal rites, then every cohesive society has a religion, and though religions may change, religion, except where societies disintegrate, cannot decline.[2]

Yet there has been a decline in the hold of religious belief and observance on individuals and of religious domination over society and its institutions.[3] Fewer people go to church. The impact of churches on the community continues to decrease. Wide diversities of religion and irreligion are socially tolerated. Public policy is seldom defended in religious terms, while religious apologists accept a defensive stance. So long as religion is understood as belief (and practices inspired by belief) in God, gods or the soul, it is not co-extensive with social bonds, and it *has* declined under the impact of secularisation.

Secularisation is accordingly not just a decrease in participation in religious ceremonies. If it were, the United States of America would scarcely have been touched by it, a paradoxical conclusion in the light of the intellectual climate and social organ-

---

[1] Dietrich Bonhoeffer, 'Letters and Papers from Prison', S.C.M., London, 1953.
[2] Cf. the sense of 'religion' in A. Greeley, 'The Persistence of Religion', S.C.M., London, 1973, at e.g. p. 61.
[3] See Chapters 1 and 4 of Bryan Wilson, 'Religion in Secular Society', Penguin, London, 1966.

isation of that nation.[4] It takes a variety of other forms, including pluralism, tolerance and disbelief in another world; as pointed out by Harvey Cox, who gives as his own account of secularisation 'the deliverance of man first from religious and then from metaphysical control over his reason and his language'.[5] This definition is however unduly vague and unduly broad; nor are all the features just mentioned either common or peculiar to secular societies. Indeed difficulties such as these have led David Martin to propose that *"secularisation* should be erased from the sociological dictionary".[6] Yet Martin himself finds the concept of secularisation indispensable[7], and is most centrally protesting at the view that secularisation has been a uniform and unified process; as indeed it has not. Besides, to fall under a general term, things need not display the same set of distinctive and common features. Secularisation, to take the case in point, can be social, intellectual or both. Indeed as long as 'religion' has a clear sense, we need not be troubled by conceptual scruples: for we can comprehend secularisation as the process by which autonomy has been claimed for various areas of life and thought from religion thus understood; and should thus expect secularisation to exhibit diverse manifestations.

As Vernon Pratt maintains[8], the secularisation of the mind began well before the Industrial Revolution and was well-advanced in at least some quarters before the migration to the towns began. I also agree with him that there must have been some causal connection between this intellectual secularisation and the social change from a religiously dominated society to one largely heedless of organised religion; and thus join in rejecting the view of Alasdair MacIntyre that the social changes caused by the Industrial Revolution suffice to explain social secularisation[9]. The causal connection will not be argued in detail, but abundant evidence of pre-industrial secularisation will be supplied, and it is surely implausible that secularising ideas current from the beginning of the Seventeenth Century scientific revolution onwards have had no social impact.

---

[4] As pointed out by Vernon Pratt in 'Religion and Secularisation', Macmillan, London, 1970, at p. 9.

[5] Harvey Cox, 'The Secular City', S.C.M., London, 1965, pp. 1ff.

[6] David Martin, 'The Religious and the Secular', Routledge and Kegan Paul, London, 1969, p. 22.

[7] Ibid. p. 23.

[8] Op. cit., pp. 10f.

[9] Alasdair MacIntyre, 'Secularisation and Moral Change', Oxford University Press, London, 1967.

If so, secularisation has not been entirely a function of social change, and theory and practice have not historically been entirely dissociated. Further the decision to discuss Seventeenth and Eighteenth Century thinkers will have been justified not just by their intrinsic interest or because intellectual secularisation took on new life at that time: their thought will also have exercised a significant historical influence. Also the diverse features of secularisation cannot be quite as devoid of connection as Martin supposes.

Secularisation can, of course, be traced back to medieval thinkers such as Averroes and Maimonides, and even to the Old Testament claim that, being created, nature is not itself sacred or to be worshipped. But shortly after 1600 the rise of modern sicence and philosophy of science gave rise to crucial new problems about religious belief, which would suffice alone to justify selecting developments of that time for assessment. Indeed most but not all intellectual secularisation (see Chapter 5 Section 1A) was causally connected to the rise of the new science. Further although later contributions have been important, by the time of Bentham and Kant the intellectual critique of religion in the name of reason had attained a certain completeness: indeed later critiques of religion often assumed the soundness of Enlightenment arguments and can often only be assessed in the light of assessments of the latter. Thus the arguments assessed all emanate from the Seventeenth and Eighteenth Centuries. Obviously much more work could be done on the more recent period: some later developments are glanced at, albeit briefly, in the Conclusion.

The philosophy of secularisation could be commended as a branch of philosophical enquiry on a level with the philosophy of education or the philosophy of mind; it is distinctive in having in part a body of philosophy as its subject-matter. The current work is principally an essay in this branch of philosophy: at the same time it also delineates in some measure the theories, attitudes and spirit of the secularisers. My approach has been to consider separately secularisation in the areas of science, of man and morals, and of the basis of religious belief; as will be seen, these diverse areas of debate unfolded in turn. For secular thought was usually interconnected, though far from concerted or conspiratorial.

Secular*isation* is not to be confused with secular*ism*, which is, as Cox points out, not an historical process but an ideology.[10] Secularism is displayed when religious doctrines are declared either false, meaningless or irrelevant to some area of discourse or of human activity (such as moral reasoning or moral action).

---

[10] *Op.cit.*, pp. 20f.

Secularism is thus of necessity anti-theological; whereas secularisation, strange as it may seem, is not. Thus a religious doctrine like that of creation may encourage an autonomous method in the study of nature such as that of modern science (see Chapter 1), whereas certain Biblical passages like Psalm 8 and Jesus' saying[11] that the Sabbath was made for man and that the Son of man is Lord of the Sabbath suggest that in Jewish and Christian teaching it is God's will that men should take responsibility for their own lives and use their capacities to the full in the name both of human welfare and of the glory of God. Indeed Bonhoeffer and Cox have welcomed secularisation in the name of Christianity, while Francis Bacon (see Chapter 1) was prominent in arguing that man's "coming of age"[12] was theologically desirable. Thus not all intellectual secularisation is anti-theological: and it may remove confusion to remark that 'secular' is the adjective not only of secularism, which is anti-theological, but also of secularisation which sometimes is not. (Sometimes, it should be added, it just connotes 'this-worldly', in keeping with its derivation from '*saeculum*', meaning 'the present age'.)

The present study, as well as scrutinising the logic of secularisation, is concerned to assess the consistency of its various aspects with theology: sometimes, it is maintained, a theologian is justified in reacting favourably to secularisation, though not always. Thus secularisation is often the spiritual descendant of Christianity.[13] On the other hand as the grounds of religious belief are among the matters in dispute it is not assumed that all secularism is false: religious and secularist tenets alike are rejected only where there are at least cogent arguments against them.

The first two chapters concern the secularisation of the study of nature. Not only did the rise of modern science involve conflict with religious authority: it also posed problems about the location of divine activity and about the very concept of the supernatural, which according to Vernon Pratt[14] it has rendered redundant. It also raised radical questions about the basis of human knowledge, which are with us still. Some of the solutions historically arrived at will be assessed as both secularist and unfounded: yet a close

---

[11] Mark 2, verses 27f.

[12] The phrase is Bonhoeffer's: cf. letter to a friend, 8.6.44, op. cit., pp. 106-110. But Bonhoeffer is (perhaps unconsciously) echoing a phrase of Bacon's: cf. Francis Bacon, 'The New Organon', edited Fulton H. Anderson, Bobbs-Merrill, Indianapolis, 1960: Book Two, Lll, p. 267.

[13] For a similar conclusion, see C. F. von Weizsäcker, 'The Relevance of Science', Collins, London, 1964, chapter 10, 'What Is Secularisation?'

[14] Op.cit., pp. 13-18.

connection will be argued to hold between theistic doctrines and the feasibility of scientific method.

The new scientific method gave secularisation a new impetus in the Seventeenth Century: historically and logically the next step was and is a questioning of theological doctrines about man and morals. Accordingly in the two chapters that follow I investigate which positions are compatible with theism, which ones are inconsistent with it (including, as I maintain, determinism), and also which ones can actually be upheld on their merits.

Eventually secularisation issued in assaults on the grounds of belief in God, and appropriately the last two chapters of the book concern natural theology. Much is conceded to the objectors to the traditional arguments, but (unfashionably) it is claimed that a rational basis for belief in a good God is needed by believers and is to be found. At the same time secularising thinkers are credited with exposing specious arguments and with questioning the credentials of authorities and revelations.

As arguments about God are involved, heed should be paid to a recent writer,[15] who has contended that all terms used of God bear a qualified or analogical sense and that, as this sense is undiscoverable, all argument about God is impossible. He also requires those who propose to resort to a theory of analogy to make this clear at the outset and not in some unexposed spot where its bearing on their other claims will escape notice.

I should therefore state at once that I believe it mistaken to grant that we do not know what we mean by 'God' or therefore what the nature of God is and what talk of God implies. Let this suffice for now: in Chapters 5 and 6 it will be explained how without begging crucial questions we can take God to be an individual of some not wholly incomprehensible sort, and thus argue, as Hume and Kant did, for or against his existence, and, as Bacon did, that empirical science must be feasible in a created world.

It has not of course proved possible to supply a comprehensive assessment of even intellectual secularisation as a whole, but the attempt has been made to furnish a consistent critique of some of its more significant manifestations. The critique is neither unsympathetic nor uncritical. Counter-critiques from readers will be welcome.

---

[15] Humphrey Palmer, 'Analogy: A Study of Qualification and Argument in Theology', Macmillan, London, 1973, pp. 109f. and 18.

CHAPTER 1

THEOLOGY AND METHOD IN EARLY MODERN SCIENCE

Section 1: Bacon's Theology and Method

A. Introductory.

How secular was the scientific movement which arose out of the Seventeenth Century? Was its method hostile to Christian and other theistic doctrines, or was it their logical outcome? Were its variants the more or the less sound the more or the less they tallied with the doctrine of creation? Such are some of the questions tackled in this chapter, which begins with the advocacy of a new method by Francis Bacon.

In the first section my main concern is to show the close tie between Bacon's religion and that form of secular outlook which he advocated and pioneered. I shall not question what I take to have been established by Margery Purver[1], that The Royal Society believed itself to have been influenced by Bacon's proposals for scientific research and to a large extent was so influenced. My immediate concern will be the logical relation between theism and the scientific method of Bacon: but if, as I shall attempt to show in Section 3, the members of the Royal Society shared his belief in the doctrine of creation and also, at least broadly, his scientific method, then the same logical relation will hold; and, further, their belief that they were followers of Bacon will have been to some degree vindicated. There again, if Bacon's central reasoning was valid, so will theirs have been.

The discussion in the present section of Bacon's theology and method will be paralleled in Section 2 by a discussion of the theology and method of speculative physicists like Descartes, and

---

[1] 'The Royal Society: Concept and Creation', Routledge, London, 1967. For a different view of the origins of the Royal Society, see Charles Webster, 'The Great Instauration', Duckworth, 1975. A view more consistent with Purver's is taken by Douglas S. Kemsley, 'Religious Influences in the Rise of Modern Science', 'Annals of Science', 24, 1968; Kemsley also reviews the extensive literature on this subject. His article is reprinted in 'Science and Religious Belief, A Selection of Recent Historical Studies', edited by C. A. Russell, University of London Press Ltd., London, 1973.

also of physicists of a rather different stamp like Kepler and Galileo. This discussion, as well as making possible a theological critique of some early proposals for scientific method, will make it easier to see the relation of method to theology in the case of a man who stood on the shoulders of all these others, Isaac Newton; he is discussed alongside his fellow members of The Royal Society in Section 3. Similar comparisons of method and theology are undertaken in Section 4 in the cases of Spinoza and of Berkeley, who allow the relation which I describe between the doctrine of creation and scientific method to be tested, at least in some fashion. Certain conclusions can then be drawn about this relation.

It will be admitted in what follows that Bacon placed insufficient stress on the role of hypotheses (in the modern sense) and on the place of mathematics in science. But the differences between Bacon's approach and that of Galileo do not overthrow the centrality of Bacon's method in modern science, despite the charge, endorsed e.g. by Rossi,[2] that his concentration on "experiments" and induction mark him off from the true path of science, a path of mathematical hypothesis and deduction. Bacon has, indeed, been recently attacked from the opposite direction: by concentrating unduly on the certainty of axioms in science and on what can be deduced from them, he allegedly ends up far from the true path adopted by The Royal Society, Newton included, of empiricism and 'constructive scepticism'![3]

In contrast with these conflicting assessments, I hold that it was to Bacon's credit that he was less sceptical than Joseph Glanvill (1636-1680) and more concerned with nature as it actually is than the later Galileo or Torricelli. Indeed, the method of Newton is more Baconian than some have thought, and perhaps, but for Bacon, the entire effort of The Royal Society and members of it like Newton would not and indeed could not even have begun.

Scientific research is extremely unlikely to be conducted when knowledge about the physical world is dogmatically grounded on authority, or again when it is believed on sceptical grounds that no such knowledge is to be had. It was a part of the achievement of Bacon to supply reasons for rejecting *both dogmatism and scepticism,* reasons in fact derived from Christianity. And these same reasons enjoined a new approach to knowledge with a strong appeal to the observation of what actually happens: only thus, Bacon believed, could scientific knowledge be reached. Further,

---

[2] Paulo Rossi, 'Francis Bacon, From Magic to Science', translated by S. Rabinovitch, Routledge, London, 1968.

[3] Henry G. Van Leeuwen, 'The Problem of Certainty in English Thought, 1630-90', Nijhoff, The Hague, 1963.

knowledge was indispensable if the lot of man was to be improved. But the grounds for the belief that there was an obligation to improve the human lot were again intrinsically bound up with Bacon's religion. We therefore begin with Bacon's theological position.

B. Bacon's Religious Outlook.

On the question of Bacon's religious opinions, I accept the judgment of Thomas Fowler in the Introduction to his edition of the 'Novum Organum' (Oxford, 1878) at pp. 43-53. Fowler concludes that despite Bacon's opposition to superstition and religious enthusiasm, he sincerely believed in God, divine providence, and the teachings of Scripture, but that he was emotionally indifferent to religious controversies, in a way compatible with the religious tolerance which he favoured. In an early work, Bacon sums up his own attitude thus: "Religious controversies have become a weariness of the spirit and men are perhaps more ready to contemplate the power, wisdom and goodness of God in his works."[4] Bacon's real concern is expressed by Fowler as follows: "What he really cared for was the advancement of science, the knowledge of nature, the extension of the kingdom of man." And to this end, as well as in the interests of religion, he advocated the separation of religion and science: a view which was to bear fruit in the science of the future.

It may then seem surprising that I am claiming a close tie between the scientific method and the religion of a man so lukewarm towards many of the religious controversies of the day. But Bacon's stress on the ethical implications of religion[5] makes this link more plausible: within his religion it was the ethic of Christianity which most inspired him. At the same time the conclusions he drew from this ethic were only possible because of his adherence to other doctrines, such as that of creation.

I have already endorsed Fowler's judgement that Bacon's true concern was the kingdom of man. This concern is borne out by the subtitle of the 'Novum Organum', 'Aphorismi de Interpretatione Naturae et Regno Hominis'. And, as the first four Aphorisms of Book One reveal, nature is to be understood with a view to forwarding the 'Regnum Hominis' or 'Kingdom of Man'. Now granted the Scriptural learning of Bacon and his readers, it is not at

---

[4] 'Cogitata et Visa', 17. Translated by Benjamin Farrington in his 'The Philosophy of Francis Bacon', Liverpool University Press, Liverpool, 1964, at p. 95.

[5] As at De Augmentis VII, I, in 'Works', edited by Ellis, Spedding and Heath (7 Vols., Longmans, London 1887-92) Vol. V, p. 7.

all fanciful to see in this latter phrase an allusion to Psalm 8, of which verses 5 and 6 read,

> "For thou has made him (sc. man) but little lower than the angels,
> And hast crowned him with glory and honour.
> Thou madest him to have dominion over the works of thy hands;
> Thou hast put all things under his feet:"

The Kingdom of Man would involve the establishment of man's 'dominion' for the common good of mankind: and this is what Bacon sees as the obligation and the promise which religion involves.

This granted, it is easy to see how Bacon holds that without understanding of nature man's dominion of it is impossible: and that what stand in the way of this dominion are the errors to which mankind is prey. For in matters of the understanding man has fallen from grace as much as he may ever have fallen into sin: while at the same time the divine purpose both shows that human learning has miscarried and offers the hope that it may be amended. Were sterile learning to give place to humble reading of the book of nature, 'the volume of God's works' (The Advancement of Learning, 1.V.6) the great restoration (the literal sense of 'Instauratio Magna') would occur, not only of knowledge but also of mankind. The following passage is a good example of Bacon's ideology:

> "We copy the sin of our first parents while we suffer for it. They wished to be like God, but their posterity wished to be even greater. For we create worlds, we direct and domineer over nature, we will have it that all things *are* as in our folly we think they should be, not as seems fittest to the Divine wisdom, or as they are found to be in fact; but we clearly impress the stamp of our own image on the creatures and work of God, instead of carefully examining and recognising in them the stamp of the Creator himself. Wherefore our dominion over creatures is a second time forfeited, . . . "[6]

The more hopeful side of the same ideology may be illustrated by the prayer from the 'Distributio Operis' of 1620, itself intended as a preface to the Six Volume 'Instauratio Magna'.

> "God forbid that we should give out a dream of our own imagination for a pattern of the world; rather may he

---

[6] Historia naturalis et experimentalis ad condendam philosophiam (1622), 'Works', Vol. II, 14.

graciously grant to us to write an apocalypse or true vision of the footsteps of the Creator imprinted on his creatures."[7]

Two of the questions raised by this ideology are the following. What precisely is the nature of the errors which have frustrated human endeavour after knowledge? And what grounds are there for supposing that, even if purged of errors, knowledge of nature is possible for us? As the answers to these questions emerge, the reasons why Bacon's 'Novum Organum' or 'New Logic' took the form it did, and why Bacon so strongly advocated the method of induction, will also come to light.

C. The Anatomy of Error.

Bacon's account of error is summed up in his exposure of "the four classes of Idols" at Novum Organum[8] I, 39-68. In part his complaints include among their targets such allegedly innate evils as prejudice and credulity, for Bacon is supplying a psychology and a sociology of error just as much as an account of error in philosophy and in logic. But under the heading 'Idols of the Market Place' or 'idols which have crept into the understanding through the alliance of words and names', he introduces a failing of both logic and philosophy, and one which is also relevant to his attacks on Aristotle and scholasticism in the section on 'Idols of the Theatre'. This problem is that of vague, unclear or ambiguous classificatory terms: not so much in the case of the 'names of substances' (like 'chalk' and 'mud', though 'earth' is bad), as in that of the words for what have been called in our day 'characterising universals', like 'humid'. Clearly those who expect all or most knowledge to arise through syllogistic reasoning will be living in a fool's paradise if the concepts of the premisses of their syllogisms are unclear: no useful conclusions about humidity will be attained if 'humidity' covers several different things at once. Bacon puts all this epigrammatically at NO I 14.

> "The syllogism consists of propositions, propositions consist of words, words are symbols of notions. Therefore if the notions themselves (which is the root of the matter) are confused and overhastily abstracted from the facts, there can be no firmness in the superstructure . . . "

Now no doubt this aphorism needs some conceptual tightening-up itself (see J.J. MacIntosh, pp. 30-32, in his chapter on 'Francis

---

[7] Works, Vol. V, pp. 32f.
[8] Henceforth abbreviated as NO followed by Volume and Aphorism numbers.

Bacon'.)[9] It may further be granted that Bacon probably underestimates the problems of attaining satisfactory classifications,[10] although he sometimes supplies aids for avoiding unsatisfactory ones (e.g. at No. II 35). Bacon's main point, however, is that we should survey the widest possible set of phenomena before being satisfied with our classifications, and then employ only what seem to be the most important. To be less scrupulous is to commit ourselves to dogmatic and ill-founded conclusions. Bacon probably supposed, in fact, that the corpuscular structure of substances would supply a finite set of entirely clear and unproblematic classifications: but if he did so think, few of his successors were likely to be misled, whereas his main point was vital if science was to get off the ground.

The point about classification then boils down to a plea for a more exhaustive, painstaking and intelligent survey of phenomena: how else will the creatures of God be adequately distinguished? A similarly grounded attack on dogmatism occurs when Bacon criticises philosophical systems, as at NO I 61-3. The main trouble with philosophical systems is that on the basis of only a few phenomena they affirm hypotheses or 'anticipations of nature' which at once purport to be the truth, discourage discovery proper, and at the same time are little better than stage-plays. Further, the founders tend to be treated with unquestioning authority by their successors, as if their tenets and methods will supply definitive answers to all problems. And as a result nature is not understood, and cannot therefore be pressed into the service of man.

In 'Novum Organum' Bacon divides systems into three kinds, the Rational or Sophistical, the Empirical and the Superstitious (I 62.) The Rational School of philosophers, he says, 'snatches from experience a variety of common instances, neither duly ascertained nor diligently examined and weighed, and leaves all the rest to meditation and agitation of wit.'' The chief fault of the Empirics is to "leap or fly" from a few experiments to "universals and principles of things': whereas Superstitious schools confuse theology and natural philosophy and attempt to do physics on the basis of Scripture. (I 64,65).

The most prominent Rationalist is Aristotle, for whom Bacon has both respect and contempt. He sees use for the syllogism in many practical spheres of life, and in proposing a new logic himself refuses, at least in his more mature works, to argue with

---

[9] In R. Harré (ed.), 'Early Seventeenth Century Scientists', Pergamon Press Ltd., Oxford 1965.

[10] But see NO II 19.

Aristotelianism on the ground that there are no common rules. "To attempt refutations in this case would be merely inconsistent with what I have already said, for since we agree neither upon principles nor demonstrations there is no place for argument." (I 51) And even in his earlier works, Bacon is unprepared to ridicule Aristotle (cf. Cogitata et Visa, 13). His ridicule is reserved for the laziness and "the pride innate in human nature" which takes the view "that all that now remains to be done is to preserve and polish the system of Aristotle."[11]

Nevertheless in the sphere of natural philosophy, Bacon finds Aristotle himself a baneful influence, and is not at a loss for standards to which to appeal. "There can be no dispute that by his logic . . . he corrupted the philosophy of nature."[12] The sign of this corruption is the fruitlessness of natural philosophy: but this fruitlessness is only to be expected. The classificatory notions employed by Aristotelian physics have already received mention. Further, the premisses of Aristotelian syllogisms are in Bacon's view not, or not adequately, based on induction, and the conclusions of course altogether depend on the premisses. Aristotle certainly describes induction, but the Aristotelians of Bacon's day, except perhaps at Padua, never went beyond induction by simple enumeration, and therefore neglected negative instances and a quantitative study of variations. Bacon also remarks that metaphysical concepts like 'act' 'potency' 'substance' and 'matter' cannot, and should never have been expected to yield results in physics or biology.

Nor is this all. Among the detailed list of complaints about Aristotle at NO I 63 Bacon alludes to the doctrine that "single bodies each have a single and proper motion, and that if they participate in any other, then this results from an external cause". This is not only an attack on Aristotle's views on motion but also part of a general complaint against explaining phenomena by the behaviour *proper to species*.[13] For Bacon sees no reason why explanations should be restricted to given kinds of thing, or why the behaviour of different kinds of thing with similar qualities should not be explained in a similar way, i.e. by the conditions necessary and sufficient for cases of the same quality to arise. (This is part of Bacon's doctrine of forms.) Those who assume arbitrarily particular limits on interspecific explanations accordingly block the progress of science.

Aristotle is also accused of pretending to reason from empirical

---

[11] 'Refutatio Philosophiarum', as translated by Farrington, op.cit., p. 112.
[12] 'Cogitata et Visa', 12.
[13] NO I 66 (first paragraph).

evidence: no weight should be given to this, "for he had come to his conclusion before". (I 63). But the main objection that remains is that at doing physics by a search for final causes. In 'Novum Organum' Bacon goes so far as to imply that final causes are not to be found: for "they have relation to the nature of man rather than to the nature of the universe; and from this source have strangely defiled philosophy". His considered view, however, is found in the 'De Augmentis' of 1623, at Book 3, chapter 4. Here he remarks that final causes have a proper place in Metaphysics, but none in Physics. Men like Aristotle and Galen have by their "handling of final causes in physics . . . overthrown the diligent inquiry of physical causes, and made men to stay upon these specious and shadowy causes, without pressing the inquiry to those which are really and truly physical; to the greatest prejudice and arrest of science."[14] Aristotle in particular is censured for assigning final causes as the purposes of Nature and then having no further need of God, whereas a natural philosophy of purely physical causes must in the end accord God his due place. Bacon does not therefore doubt that there *are* divine purposes behind nature, but implies that men are very unlikely to discern them, at least until nature is adequately described by independent means. This granted, there is in Bacon's view no incompatibility between explanations by final and by efficient or by formal causes: but the search for the former is no substitute for science, and is in general fruitless.

The Empirical School also, however, comes under the same criticism as Aristotle in that (NO I 19) it "flies from the senses and particulars to the most general axioms, and from these principles, the truth of which it takes for settled and immovable, proceeds to judgement and to the discovery of middle axioms". Bacon frequently accuses Gilbert of such premature theorising, as well as the Alchemists (in whose cases there are the other charges of pretentiousness, secrecy and fruitlessness.) It is these prematurely affirmed theories which Bacon dubs 'Anticipations of Nature', as opposed to findings based on a more painstaking and modest approach, which he calls 'Interpretation of Nature' (NO I 20). Rival such 'anticipations' are usually equally compatible with the more accessible phenomena, and Bacon justifies his right to criticise any such theorising by showing how to devise 'instantiae crucis' in the light of which alone one theory may rightly be held as superior to its rivals (II 36). It was Bacon's desire not just to 'save the phenomena' but to attain uniquely well-grounded knowledge

---

[14] 'Works', Vol. IV, p. 363

of nature. Accordingly (like Newton after him) he was compelled to reject hypotheses, at least when put out as truth: and, although his practice did not always live up to his theory, it was in this spirit that he would accept neither the Copernican nor the Ptolemaic astronomies (on which the evidence was inconclusive, prior to the mature work of Galileo); this is also the probable reason for his rejection, in his mature phase, of Democritean atomism.[15] (NO I 66, II 8).

Superstitious Natural Philosophy was, however, a more prevalent kind of dogmatism than that of the Empirical School. Bacon accuses both Pythagoras and Plato of deriving their physics from their theology (NO I 65, Cogitata et Visa 13), but his particular scorn is reserved for moderns who "have with extreme levity indulged so far as to attempt to found a system of natural philosophy on the first chapter of Genesis, on the book of Job, and other parts of the sacred writings, seeking for the dead among the living; which also makes inhibition and repression of it the more important, because from this unwholesome mixture of things human and divine there arises not only a fantastic philosophy but also a heretical religion." Hooykaas[16] tells of the work of Richard Bostocke, who in 1583 boasted to have built a philosophy exclusively on experience and the Bible, rejecting pagan influences: in fact his system was a version of hermeticism. Another hermetic writer whom Bacon may have in mind is Robert Fludd. In 'Cogitata et Visa' Bacon sets out his reasons for opposing such a "disastrous confusion between the human and the divine." "In this intimate contract only what is already received in Natural Philosophy is included; all fresh growth, additions, improvements are excluded more strictly and obstinately than ever before" (Section 7). As Bacon rightly saw, such "Physical Theology" (which is the subject of Chapter Two) leads to bad science and arrests scientific advance.

But if all these forms of dogmatism show an undue arrogance before creation and the ideas of the divine mind (NO I 23), the opponents of claims to certainty are equally detrimental to science and guilty of premature despair. Such are the Platonists and Pyrrhonists, who "allow of some things to be followed as probable, though of none to be maintained as true." Once the human mind despairs of finding truth, its interest "grows fainter" and is easily distracted (I 77). Bacon admits the proness of humanity to error

---

[15] Cf. Kargon, 'Atomism in England from Hariot to Newton', Clarendon Press, Oxford, 1966, pp. 47f. As Bacon remarks at NO I 116, the time was not yet ripe for universal theories.
[16] 'Christian Faith and the Freedom of Science', Tyndale Press, 1957.

and the fallibility of all methods of enquiry hitherto devised. But "the holders of that doctrine assert simply that nothing can be known. I also assert that not much can be known in nature by the way which is now in use. But then they go on to destroy the authority of the senses and understanding; whereas I proceed to devise and supply helps for the same" (I 37). Bacon both sees that only in abnormal cases is sensory perception misleading, and further believes that in the light of sensory evidence the forms of natures (i.e. the causes of qualities) and thus the structure of natural objects can be inferred. And he also believes that, as induction is a valid mode of reasoning, whenever it has been properly conducted with due regard to negative instances and a wide enough range of phenomena and quantitative changes, the structure of natural objects can be inferred with certainty. To this view there are grave theoretical difficulties: yet unless Baconian induction is *invalid* as a mode of reasoning, Bacon at least had ample grounds for contesting general scepticism about scientific knowledge.

D. Why Knowledge of Nature is Possible.

We already have a part of the answer to the second question posed at the end of Section 1B above. The errors Bacon castigates all either prevent or deny the possibility of a knowledge of creation through intelligent scrutiny. But why should it be supposed that any such scrutiny will bring either 'light' or 'fruit'? Might not natural objects be but imperfect copies of Reality, as the Platonists supposed, and therefore not the proper objects of knowledge? Or might not man be unable to attain such knowledge, even if nature itself is no obstacle? As opposed to the Platonists' doctrine of Acatalepsia, "a denial of the capacity to understand", Bacon propounds a doctrine of Eucatalepsia, one of "provision for understanding truly". (NO I 126) But is such provision possible?

Bacon himself supplies ample reasons why science had made little progress, yet why there was hope that it would begin to do so. For example, his predecessors had lacked both the goal, "that human life be endowed with new discoveries and powers" (NO I 81)[17] and the method for bringing that goal about (I 82). Science had never been given a try, so there was no reason to believe that, if tried, it must fail (I 94). The question should however be taken at an epistemological and metaphysical level, rather than as an his-

---

[17] Compare the College of the Six Days Works in 'New Atlantis', of which it is said (Works, Vol. III, p. 156) "The End of our Foundation is the knowledge of Causes, and secret motions of things; and the enlarging of the bounds of Human Empire, to the effecting of all things possible."

arrives at the most general axioms last of all" (NO I 19). A plausible example arises in connection with methanics: only when Kepler's laws, whose application is limited to the planets, were available, was it possible for Newton to devise laws describing the motion of all bodies whatever. This example shows that Bacon's prescription makes its accomplishment easier. For scientific hypotheses are unlikely to be satisfactory unless framed in full awareness of a wide range of intelligently sorted data: this granted, the devising of an elegant and simple explanatory theory itself admitting of further testing is at least a compassable project. Further, while what most obviously follows from Bacon's position is the possibility of *testing the truth* of theory by the observation of nature, his theology, suggesting as it does that knowledge of nature is possible, also implies that there is a rational procedure for the *devising* of theories.

The immediate aim of the method proposed was the discovery of forms, not in the Aristotelian sense but in the sense of the necessary and sufficient conditions for the instantiation of the 'natures' or qualities investigated.[21] Although Bacon occasionally implies that the relation of forms and natures is a logical one, like that of essences and essential properties, it is in general clear that statements of formal causes are not mere spellings-out of what we mean by the name of the nature in question, but rather contingent truths in which notions whose relation is external and contingent are employed. Bacon rejects essentialist explanations at NO I 63.

Statements of formal causes have to be such that the form can never exist without the nature, nor the nature without the form. For these requirements Bacon is indebted, though he does not acknowledge the debt, to Ramus, as Rossi has shown (pp. 197-201). We may remember that, granted these requirements, unless disjunctions are admitted into the description of the form, it is unlikely that there is some formal cause in the full Baconian sense for every 'nature'.

Bacon also shows some inclination to support the view that statements of formal causes would include mathematical quantification.

> "Nothing duly investigated, nothing verified, nothing counted, weighed or measured, is to be found in natural history; and what in observation is loose and vague is in information deceptive and treacherous."

Here, at NO I 98, Bacon complains at the lack of quantification in the reports of the observations of his predecessors, and at least

---

[21] The most plausible interpretation of NO II 17.

opens the way to a mathematical requirement in the conclusions of his successors. Bacon is more explicit at II 8:

> "And inquiries into nature have the best results when they begin with physics and end in mathematics."

and further shows awareness of the importance of mathematical quantification at NO II, 40, 45, 46, 47. The greater stress of Galileo on mathematics will be discused in the Section following. Nevertheless as is shown by 'De Augmentis', Book III, Chapter VI, Bacon himself regards mathematics as indispensable, so long as it is not allowed to usurp the place of empirical physics. It is (as Bacon sees) Applied Mathematics which is necessary for scientific progress.

The actual procedure is to begin with as widespread a survey or 'natural history' of the phenomena as possible, and then to proceed with the devising of a Table of Essence or Presence, against the items of which a Table of Deviation must be composed, showing instances of the absence of qualities which the first Table shows sometimes to accompany the nature under discussion. Next, intensities and quantities of the nature and concomitant qualities are set out in a Table of Degrees or of Comparison. A scrutiny of these tables (with the help of the 'Prerogative Instances' which Bacon sets out in the later part of NO II) is then to lead, by gradual stages, to the discovery of the form in question, though this may be assisted by a "first vintage" or interim conclusion on the strength of the tables, so long as it is subjected to further testing. Indeed this is where hypotheses, in the modern sense, enter the method.

It is also at this stage of forming interim conclusions that insight would come in. Bacon's emphasis, however, is on the accessibility of induction as a method for those lacking special insight or genius: induction is represented as mechanical and certain to lead to progress if enough pains are taken. The charge usually levelled here is that scientific progress does in fact require special gifts: a point Bacon partially anticipates and meets by remarking that even negative results bring light (NO I 99). Thus even the unimaginative may demonstrate the falsity of proposed theories, and this ability to eliminate at least assists scientific colleagues in the successful construction of theories, even if it does not guarantee it. The main plea in mitigation is, however, that Bacon is guilty of overemphasising a very important point: namely that neither he nor his successors ought to ascribe glory to their individual achievements, that he is not founding a school of Baconism (NO I 122), and that unlike the esoteric investigations of cabbalists and alchemists his method is open to anyone and everyone and requires, if it is to succeed, the cooperative and often humdrum efforts of many researchers. Collaboration and communication are indeed essential to the method proposed, and were taken up with appropriate seriousness by The Royal Society when Bacon's ideas were first put into application.

MacIntosh (op. cit., p. 45), after describing Bacon's method, remarks, "It will be obvious without further comment that, and, to a large extent, why, Bacon's method is unworkable." This scathing charge is only made plausible by quoting some of Bacon's own scientific efforts. Bacon, however, declared that it did not matter if his own results miscarried (NO I 118); and further that the art of discovery must itself advance as discoveries advance (I 130). Thus even if no scientist has employed precisely Bacon's method, those who, while indebted to his proposals, used a slightly different approach have still been true to Bacon's spirit, and Bacon would have been glad to see such modifications occur. Moreover The Royal Society did quite certainly acknowledge a debt not only to Bacon's arguments but also to his directions.[22] And whether or not Bacon's method guaranteed incorrigible results, his logic in combination with his method certainly supplied a valid mode of reasoning to trustworthy scientific generalisations by way of induction and verification combined, which is a great deal more reliable than the method of 'induction by simple enumeration' of Bacon's predecessors.

Margery Purver (in 'The Royal Society, Concept and Creation', at pp. 51f.) waxes lyrical about what was new in Bacon's ideas. She rightly remarks that Bacon was not contrasting experiment and random knowledge, but science properly so-called with both; and that 'the inductive method' does not sum up the whole of his originality (probably because this phrase might suggest e.g. the method put forward in NO II and that alone). According to Purver, Bacon's originality lay in advocating "new, live *sciences* for old, dead *sciences*". This way of putting it is clearly unsatisfactory: everyone claims their own proposals have the makings of life, and no criteria apart from that of what Bacon *thought* was live science are supplied. Nevertheless I endorse Purver's view that Bacon's achievement has been underrated both by his detractors[23] and his own admirers: his concept of science was unprecedented,

---

[22] Cf. Thomas Sprat, 'History of The Royal Society', ed. Jackson I. Cope and Harold Whitmore Jones, Routledge, London, 1959, p. 35.

[23] A variety of writers, including Koyré, Medawar and Popper, hold that Bacon's methodology was radically deficient. (See Alexandre Koyré, 'Metaphysics and Measurement', Chapman and Hall, London, 1968, pp. 17,90; P. B. Medawar, 'The Art of the Soluble', Methuen, London, 1967, *passim;* Karl Popper, 'Conjectures and Refutations', Routledge, London, 1963, pp. 15f.) This is not the place for a blow for blow reply; but many of their actual points are answered in the various Sections of Chapter One.

combining as it did a new goal, a reformed logic, a taxing but rewarding method, the discarding of previous systems of natural philosophy, proposals for open and collaborative research, a burning ethical purpose and a gospel of hope; and Bacon was correct in taking it to be so. Moreover once the need specified by Bacon for such a new body of science was taken up, no replication of Bacon's proposals was necessary or even possible: no new methodology besides that of science can seriously be proposed for the study of nature.

F. Theology Indispensable.

It is opportune to ask whether Bacon's methodology *could* have been proposed without the sort of theological reasonings he appealed to. And my claim is that in Bacon's day and in the setting of natural science in the Early Modern Period in general there was no other way to break the stranglehold of dogmatism and scepticism on the infact of scientific progress than by appeal to God's creation and his purposes in creation. First, a ground for rejecting dogmatism was needed. Now of course once dogmatism is recognised as such, there is no problem. But why should anyone distrust inferences about the nature of the world based on the principles of Aristotle, or Gilbert or, come to that, Moses? The only plausible reply was that the world was created by God, and could not be recreated in thought by the speculations of limited human minds. The thoughts of God necessarily exceeded and differed from human notions, unless the latter were based on the most scrupulous possible attempt to identify the former. This was not only a plausible reply: no other reply was available. It is accordingly not surprising that a parallel argument or assumption is to be found in the otherwise very different approach of Kepler and Galileo: granted that nature must, on their assumptions, conform to some mathematical pattern, it was all-important to crack the *particular* code which the Creator had employed. Had there been no Creator, then observation would have been less important: for nature might not have "lived up to" whatever mathematical paradigm it most closely resembled.

Secondly, only if a ground for rejecting scepticism were found could scientific research proceed with rationality or even hope: for otherwise there would be no guarantee of any results at all, either of light or of fruit. Here again only by appeal to the regularity of God's creation, and hence the regularity of nature, could the need be met — *at least at Bacon's time*. And further the belief that man's dominion of nature and the increase of human powers and welfare were God's will was the only firm bastion at the time against scepticism about human knowledge. The point is not just the Cartesian one that our senses are reliable as God would not deceive us: indeed no sceptical problem about the senses can be set up unless they are at least somewhat reliable. But *at the time* it could still have been disputed whether any form of induction would ever achieve reliable results in science: and the only ultimate answer was that there must be *some* such mode of reasoning, or God's will was impossible of fulfilment.

It is not claimed that at no time could a satisfactory scientific methodology have developed without theological assumptions, or that (granted sufficient faith in the regularity of nature and in human powers) science itself could not have thus got under way. But it is contended that in the light of the prevalence of the philosophical systems which Bacon saw as among the leading hindrances to science, an appeal to Christian theism was as indispensable as it was valid.[24]

G. Bacon's Secularity.

Nevertheless the methodology thus supported was secular through and through. Bacon holds (Novum Organum I 89) that the tutelage of religion over natural philosophy has been to the detriment of the latter, both among the Greeks, in the age of the Church fathers and in the Middle Ages. Neither philosophy nor theology benefits by "mingling (things divine) with things human".

There follows a valuable critique of the reactions of theologians to signs of independence on the part of natural philosophers, (a critique which in several respects anticipates that of Dietrich Bonhoeffer in his Letter to Bethge of 8.6.1944).[25] Some simply misquote Holy Writ against "a deeper search into nature" out of weak fears that is may "transgress the permitted limits of sober-mindedness", but there is no such prohibition intended in Scripture. "Others with more subtlety surmise and reflect that if second causes are unknown everything can more readily be referred to the divine hand and rod, a point in which they think religion greatly concerned — which is in fact nothing else but to seek to gratify God with a lie." We notice how Bacon protests both in the name of unfettered research and in the name of true religion. These features attach also to his comments on other theologians.

"Others fear from past example that movements and changes

---

[24] For a similar view, cf. M. B. Foster, 'The Christian Doctrine of Creation and the Rise of Modern Natural Science', Mind, N.S. XLIII, 1934, pp. 446-468.

[25] Translated at p. 108 of the Fontana edition.

in philosophy will end in assaults on religion. And others again appear apprehensive that in the investigation of nature something may be found to subvert or at least shake the authority of religion, especially with the unlearned. But these two last fears seem to me to savour utterly of carnal wisdom: as if men in the recesses and secret thought of their hearts doubted and distrusted the strength of religion and the empire of faith over the sense, and therefore feared that the investigation of truth in nature might be dangerous to them. But if the matter be truly considered, natural philosophy is, after the word of God, at once the surest medicine against superstition and the most approved nourishment for faith, and therefore she is rightly given to religion as her most faithful handmaid, since the one displays the will of God, the other his power."

Although scientific investigation has often shaken "the authority of religion", Bacon is basically right here in holding that men of religion should not and indeed cannot consistently oppose it. Two further points should be picked out; one is that, though science is the handmaid of religion, Bacon's whole argument is that it can only progress if autonomous, both in respect of a methodology of its own and in respect of freedom from theological assumptions either about what it must find to be the case or about what it may investigate and what it may not. The other is that Bacon holds that a true theology favours such an autonomous scientific enquiry, and indeed supplies good reasons for his view.

We have already seen how Bacon's methodology involves purging natural philosophy of a search for final causes, and of the custom of deriving conclusions from Scriptural passages. All this is because natural philosophy needs an independent methodology: and, until someone like Bacon himself set one down, it is not surprising that natural philosophy made so many concessions to religious dogma as to be unable to make progress of any appreciable sort in its search after truth.

The other point to note about the secularity of Bacon's approach is its goal, the furtherance of human powers and welfare. This goal is paralleled in Descartes, who declares in Part VI of his 'Discourse on Method' that he had felt constrained to publish his works because of the practical benefits he saw accruing from his physics, and because of "the law which obliges us to procure, as much as in use lies, the general good of all mankind."[26] The pursuit of this goal could, of course, be detached from a religious approach, and often has been.

---

[26] 'The Philosophical Works of Descartes', Translated by Elizabeth S. Haldane and G. R. T. Ross, Cambridge University Press, (Cambridge, 1967, Two Volumes), Volume I, p. 119.

Nevertheless no such distinction was in the mind of either Bacon or Descartes: the furtherance of the good of mankind meant for both of them the glorification of God.[27] Once again, then, the secular approach Bacon advocates is one he views as blessed by religion: it is God himself who calls man to be independent of mind, that God's purposes may be fulfilled.

Section 2: Theoretical Physics

A. Introduction.

I now turn to the presuppositions of a number of physicists who differed at least in emphasis from Bacon. The common feature among them is a stress on the place of theory in scientific work. Some of them Bacon would have criticised for producing anticipations of nature, but it is uncertain whether he would have applied this stricture to the hypotheses of Kepler and Galileo, granted their willingness to revise their hyoptheses if the world turned out not to be as they described it.

All the physicists to be discussed introduced *a priori* elements into their work, but not all hoped to arrive at the truth about the physical world entirely by *a priori* reasoning. The less place a physicist had for experimental tests, the more he fell under the disdain of the Royal Society. The chief fault in the eyes of the 'virtuosi' of that body consisted in contriving ingenious descriptions of the world which 'saved the phenomena' through being consistent with the sorts of phenomena hitherto observed, but which did not admit of being tested against phenomena, being instead compatible with whatever happened.

The builders of physical systems open to this charge were Gassendi, Descartes and Hobbes. On other principles of classification, Descartes would instead be classed with those who saw the importance of mathematics for science, and on this count would be compared with the Kepler, Galileo and Newton. But Descartes' assumptions are rather different from these others', despite his employment of mathematics and his contributions to the conceptual structure exploited by Newton. There again, both Gassendi and Hobbes have a considerable place for experiment, Gassendi in particular having taken the trouble in Marseille harbour to find out what would happen to weights dropped from

---

[27] Thus in 'New Atlantis' the College of the Six Days Works was instituted... "for the finding out of the true nature of all things, (whereby God might have the more glory in the workmanship of them, and men the more fruit in the use of them) . . . "

on the evidence of the senses.[35] Nevertheless Gassendi inevitably employs *a priori* premises in arguing for the truth of atomism, and thus displays a qualified confidence in the powers of human reason so long as it does not stray too far from experience. Carré points out that Gassendi's chief contribution to the scientific work of the century was his atomic theory, eventually to be accepted and used by both Boyle and Newton: nevertheless his empiricism was a support to the (more experimental) empiricists of The Royal Society; and we know that his disciple Bernier was friendly with Locke,[36] who is held by a leading expositor to have been much indebted to Gassendi.[37]

As one who was converted to philosophy by reading Euclid, Hobbes set much more store by rational demonstration. Hobbes was well-aware of the dangers of confused terminology, and required that premisses should be clear enough to answer to experience, so that only to material objects would the properties of substances be ascribed.[38] Hobbes believes that, granted adequate definitions and sober statement of fact, all will be well: his method suffers, perhaps, from failure to confront the challenge of philosophical scepticism, (except his own variety.) Despite his lack both of mathematics and of understanding the need for experimental testing, the rigour of his logic showed how far natural philosophy, if equipped with an autonomous method, might one day proceed in the biological and social sciences.

Descartes is distinctive both in taking philosophical scepticism seriously, and in his confidence that certain 'eternal verities' are irrefutable and indubitable however severe the sceptic's challenge. These eternal verities, including the nature and existence of God, enable us to be certain about the truths of mathematics and the existence of material objects:[39] and, this granted, our intuitions of 'simple natures', when cast in mathematical form, are thought to supply a secure basis for scientific reasoning. Scientific problems may therefore be solved by suppressing our previous opinions, and resolving the problem into a question about the simple natures concerned. We can intuit the truth about simple natures; and so long as we arrange our information in the right order, argue validly back to the level of our original problem and leave out nothing relevant, we can make as much progress as our clear per-

---

[35] 'Opera Omnia', Lyon, 1658, 4 Vols., I, pp. 79-80.
[36] Carré, Philosophy, 1958, p. 120
[37] R. Aaron, 'John Locke', O.U.P., 1937, p. 34
[38] Leviathan, ch. 5.
[39] Meditation VI. Haldane and Ross I, 185-199.

ceptions of simple natures allow. Such is the pattern of scientific method in the 'Rules for the Direction of the Mind.'

Simple natures within the realm of extended substances include extension, shape and motion, and also light, if we are to judge by the example supplied in Rule Eight of the Regulae.[40] We are exhorted to arrive at the relations between simple natures by pure acts of intuition, since to do otherwise is to appeal to authority, or else to turn to conjecture (to which Descartes seems to assimilate reliance on experience).

We at once note, as negative and positive elements in an autonomous and secular approach, the suppression of preconceived opinions and the way problems are to be analysed into their more tractable components. Nevertheless the striking feature of Descartes' account of scientific method is that so much can be achieved by intuition and deduction.[41] No doubt experience is held in reserve as an extra check, for, as Deutcher says, [42] "Surely if a theory which seemed intuitively acceptable failed to be consistent with observation, even a rationalist would say that he had intuited wrongly, or had not really intuited, or something": nevertheless Descartes held that theories could be known to be true *without resort* to this procedure of checking.

With the details of Descartes' physical system we are not here concerned. It was a triumph to devise a scheme of cosmology which seemed to account for the present positions and behaviour of earth, sun and planets, and only brought in God as the creator of matter and motion at the start. It was also an achievement to see the need for mathematics in science, even though Descartes seems to have wished to import into science not only mathematical precision and constructs answering to mathematical descriptions but also mathematical apriorism. Nevertheless Descartes' laws of motion (Principles of Philosophy, Part II) yield false predictions.[43] Descartes in fact derives his laws of motion from the changelessness of God, an example of doing physics by theology (to be discussed in Chapter Two.) Autonomous as Descartes' method was of the Aristotelians, his application of it could not dispense with God.

In a paper in Philosophy, 1955, Meyrick Carré suggests that Descartes' science is an extreme form of mathematical Platonism,

---

[40] Haldane and Ross I, p. 24
[41] Rule 3, 'Rules for the Direction of the Mind', Haldane and Ross I, pp. 5-8
[42] M. Deutcher, 'René Descartes' in R. Harré (editor), 'Early Seventeenth Century Scientists', Pergamon Press, Oxford, 1965.
[43] As shown by Deutcher, p. 174

Descartes is of course particularly clear that extended substances lack purposes and mental qualities in general, these being proper to thinking substances only.

The other aspect of teleological explanation is explanation by the purposes of God, on which Bacon's mature view, as expressed at 'De Augmentis', Book 3, chapter 4, has already been discussed. As an empiricist, Gassendi is opposed to such modes of *a priori* explanation, but he is eager to leave room for the doctrine of providence and tone down the ancient Epicurean denunciations of teleological explanation.[32] Hobbes' theory of religious language enables him to dispense altogether with references to God's purposes: according to Hobbes no predicate ascribed to God is ascribed in any intelligible sense at all.

> "For the nature of God is incomprehensible; that is to say, we understand nothing of *what he is*, but only *that he is*; and therefore the attributes we give him, are not to tell one another, *what he is*, nor to signify our opinion of his nature, but our desire to honour him with such names as we conceive most honourable amongst ourselves.[33]

Arguments about God's purposes will be discussed in a separate chapter: but this much must at once be granted to Hobbes; that unless we know what sort of thing God is, we can explain nothing by allusions to his purposes; for, unless we know *that*, we have no idea at all what it is for God to have purposes, and may for all we know be talking nonsense. Hobbes' theory of religious language, together with his mechanism, enabled him to exclude the action of God from the physical world (except in the case of certain miracles), but if the theologian can give him a reply on what it is to talk of God, he himself can be accused of unjustified scepticism and unjustified secularism in philosophical theology.

Descartes also argues to a view on final causes from the incomprehensible nature of God, but in Descartes' case "God is incomprehensible" is not a contention about meaning, since Descartes has already given some account of what it is to be God in the course of his Meditations at a stage before he adverts to the incomprehensibility of God's purposes in Meditation IV.[34] Descartes is rather thinking of the limits of our knowledge, and continues . . .

---

[32] Carré, 'Philosophy' 1958, p. 115: for some ancient Epicurean denunciations of teleology, see Lucretius, 'De Rerum Natura' I 1030ff, II 177ff, VI 43-95.

[33] Leviathan, ch. 34: Oakeshott, p. 257.

[34] Haldane and Ross translation, Volume I, p. 173.

"... I have no further difficulty in recognising that there is an infinitude of matters in his power, the causes of which transcend my knowledge; and this reason suffices to convince me that the species of cause termed final, finds no useful employment in physical (or natural) things; for it does not appear to me that I can without temerity seek to investigate the (inscrutable) ends of God."

In effect Descartes' view is the same as Bacon's: God certainly has purposes, but they are hard or impossible to know, and it is better for the natural philosopher to enquire into other sorts of causes instead.

The refusal to look for final causes on the part of the founding fathers of the new philosophy in both France and England was an important contribution to the autonomy of natural philosophy and to the possibility of its conduct as an empirical discipline. This refusal effectively declared that theology and physics were to be kept apart, a principle so effectively adhered to both in Cartesian and Newtonian physics that by the time Leibniz urged the reintroduction of teleological explanations in physics (Discourse on Metaphysics, 20-22) natural philosophy was too firmly founded as an autonomous discipline to be diverted from its course. Moreover the instinct of Bacon and Descartes was a sound one: for our knowledge of God's purposes must, to be well-grounded, be based on observation of how created bodies behave: so to predict the behaviour of created bodies from divine purposes closely resembles arguing in a circle. We cannot predict events as yet unknown by this method.

Mechanism and the abandonment of final causes in physics certainly have secular implications, and eventually exercised a profound influence on Enlightenment thinkers such as La Mettrie and Diderot. Nevertheless more important still was the claim that natural philosophy can be pursued by a new *method*, independent of scripture and other authorities. Mechanistic conclusions might prove insufficient — as Newton found (see Section 3D) — but if natural philosophy could be supplied with an autonomous method, its potential for exciting and disturbing discoveries was far greater than that of mechanism.

Gassendi is here distinct from both Descartes and Hobbes because of the strength of his appeal to experience. He inherits from Epicurus and Lucretius a tradition which maintains that all factual knowledge must be based on sense-experience, so the attacks of sceptics on sense-experience in general must miscarry; and he also opposes dogmatism where it exceeds what can be based the masthead of a ship.[28] Even Descartes is famous for his experiments on animals. Nevertheless experiment, as opposed to experience, has a crucial place in none of their systems.

This does not mean, however, that their attitudes and assumptions are devoid of a secular spirit. To some degree the reverse is true: for the followers of Newton saw fit to accuse Descartes of having banished God from the world.[29] Speculative physics can make greater claims for human reason than experimental physics, and be equally opposed to dogma. If wedded to a rationalist epistemology it can even lead towards a secularism which simultaneously denies the free agency of God in creation, and the need for experiment to discover what that agency issued in. Neither Gassendi, Hobbes nor Descartes adopted such arguments, yet they can all be seen as making a plea for the autonomy of natural philosophy from dogmatic preconceptions, whether ecclesiastical or Aristotelian.

B. Speculative Physics and Autonomy.

We have already seen how Descartes shares Bacon's belief that the point of science is the furtherance of human welfare, and how the failure of the Aristotelians to produce results is one of the charges Bacon makes against them. Hobbes shares Bacon's and Descartes' view of the goal of science: in his chapter of Leviathan on 'Reason' he declares that "increase of *science*" is "the *way:* and the benefit of mankind, the *end.*" But its aim was not the only respect in which the new philosophy was secular.

Gassendi, Descartes and Hobbes join in strong attacks on the dogmas of the Aristotelians.[30] In place of explanations of the behaviour of bodies by natural places, essences and final causes, they put forward in different forms mechanistic theories, by which change could be explained by matter and motion, or by matter, motion and weight, alone. It was thus claimed that the world could be succinctly and fruitfully explained without employing the notions normally favoured by the ecclesiastical and lay establishment. But apart from the secularity of outlook with which mechanism was propounded, it can also be secular in outcome; first in that the need for the postulation of divine initiatives and particular purposes within the created order is eliminated (though Gassendi is careful to safeguard the doctrine of providence), and secondly in that a mechanistic doctrine of man (like that of

---

[28] Koyré, 'Newtonian Studies', London, 1965, p. 176.

[29] Koyré, Ibid., pp. 95, 112.

[30] Gassendi in 'Exercitationum paradoxicarum adversus Aristoteleos libri septem, Grenoble, 1624, 'Opera Omnia', t. III; Descartes in 'Meditations', *passim;* Hobbes e.g. at Leviathan chs. 1, 4, 5.

Hobbes) is liable to clash with theological anthropology (see Chapter 3: Self-Determination.) It should be conceded that Gassendi, despite his atomism, is not consistently a mechanist.[31] Hobbes, however, is unremitting in his attacks on clerics for their inculcation of a sense of mystery which could be cured by a clearer use of terms, more rigorous thought and mechanist explanations. (e.g. Leviathan, ch. 2.)

In the more consistent mechanist systems of physics, those of Descartes and Hobbes, there is indeed little room for God. In Cartesianism God is, like the human mind, consigned to the realm of thinking things, while in the thorough-going materialism of Hobbes, God only figures at all because he is material! For Hobbes' materialism is applied not only to the created world, but to the universe, God included. Thus Leviathan ch. 46:

> "The universe, that is, the whole mass of things that are, is corporeal, that is to say, body; and hath the dimensions of magnitude, namely length, breadth and depth; also every part of body is likewise body and hath the same dimensions; and consequently every part of the universe is body, and that which is not body is no part of the universe, and because the universe is all, that which is no part of it is nothing; and consequently nowhere."

The mechanistic physics of Descartes is by contrast applied only to the realm of created matter, and Descartes is consistent enough, having required the Creator to supply the matter and motion needed, not to ascribe to him a position or function within it, which, being timeless and placeless, he could scarcely occupy. Descartes' physics and metaphysics are thus fully consistent with the doctrine of creation, but this did not prevent the Newtonians accusing him of diminishing God's power (See Koyré, 'Newtonian Studies', p. 112 and *passim.)*

Another corollary of mechanism is denial of the belief of the Aristotelians in final causes. If the behaviour of material bodies is predictable from their prior states by means of causal laws, explanation of their behaviour by their purposes is at least redundant, since their behaviour can be predicted from independent information. There is no room for explanations by final causes in the system of Hobbes, nor should there have been in that of Gassendi: though to explain motion Gassendi felt obliged to ascribe purposes to his atoms (Carré, Philosophy, 1958, p. 116).

---

[31] Cf. Carré, 'Pierre Gassendi and the New Philosophy,' in 'Philosophy', January, 1958, pp. 112-120, at pp. 116-7.

which contrasts strongly with the method of Galileo. This form of Platonism assimilates science to mathematics, and maintains that the proper objects of science are ideal mathematical ones, and that these objects bear little relation to the imperfect and changing phenomena of our experience, so that it is unnecessary to attempt a comparison between the two sorts of objects. By contrast Galileo realised both the need for mathematics in science and the need to test the hypotheses of mathematical physics against experience.[44] This aside about Descartes is not entirely fair; for it was also Descartes who criticised those who neglect observation and experience and "imagine that truth will spring from their brain like Pallas from the head of Zeus",[45] and Descartes who praised Bacon for his natural histories. Nevertheless the method of Descartes has such tenuous links with the test of experience that there is some justification in the charge that he remained influenced by the scepticism of the Platonists and did not remark the implications of the doctrine of Creation as consistently as Bacon. But this overvaluing of the possibilities of reason against those of experience was not secularism, for there was no denial intended by Descartes that God could create a physical world intelligible and thus amenable to scientific understanding.

It is here appropriate to remark, though only briefly, that neither in physics nor metaphysics is Descartes either as firm a rationalist, or consequently as firmly secular in assumptions, as might appear. It has frequently been charged against Descartes that he argues in a circle, not only grounding the existence of God in clear and distinct ideas, but also grounding the truth of clear and distinct ideas, whether physical, mathematical or metaphysical, in the will of God. Anthony Kenny[46] holds that the clear and distinct ideas could not be false for God if true for us, and thus that there is no circularity. But this solution is unconvincing, because of what Leonard G. Miller[47] calls Descartes' "firm conviction" that, being all-powerful, God "is indifferent" to "'every reason of truth and goodness" in the sense that all truths, contingent, necessary and moral, are alike His creatures and might very well have been other than they are if He had so chosen." Descartes gives us the impression that, if God so desired, 'two and two make four' would to-

---

[44] 'Platonism and the Rise of Science', pp. 340-343.
[45] Haldane and Ross I. p. 15 (Rule V).
[46] In 'Descartes, A Study of His Philosophy', Random House, New York, 1968, pp. 190-9.
[47] 'Descartes, Mathematics and God', reprinted in 'Metameditations', ed. Sesonke and Fleming, Wadsworth Publishing Co., Inc., Belmont, California, 1965, p.45. The inner inverted commas are Miller's.

morrow become false: and, this being so, what is necessarily true for us is not necessarily true for God.[48] We have to conclude, then, that the clear and distinct ideas depend on God for their truth-value, and that accordingly truth is simply a function of the will of God. This means not only that the charge of circularity sticks, but that intuition is vulnerable and that the human intellect cannot with certainty intuit or deduce all truth.[49] Here another form of scepticism lies hidden within Descartes' system: and in this case it is anything but calculated to inculcate confidence in the practitioners of natural philosophy as an autonomous discipline.[50] The passages of Descartes that point towards scientific progress on the basis of assured principles of reasoning are rather the passages in which he stresses that what the 'light of nature' teaches us we *can* be certain about: only if mathematical knowledge, for example, is invulnerable can precisely quantified predictions in science reliably be made.

Such then were the bases of the systems of speculative physics of the period 1600-1660: it will be valuable to note the reaction to them on the part of The Royal Society before turning to the mathematical physics of Galileo and Kepler.

We might have expected The Royal Society to embrace as allies Gassendi, Descartes and Hobbes, because of their common reaction against forms of ecclesiastically entrenched dogma and opposition to autonomous methods in natural philosophy. Certainly all the new philosophers had much in common, and often profited by each others' ideas. Thus Newton employed Gassendi's notions of atoms and void, and Descartes' notions of motion and rest as *states*.[51] Such borrowings, however, were compatible with a radical disagreement about method. It was the *speculative* nature of the work of the systematic physicists that proved objectionable.

We have already seen above how Bacon abandoned atomism, probably on the grounds that such theories were premature and constituted 'anticipations of nature'. Similarly Joseph Glanvill, perhaps the most sceptical of the earliest members of The Royal Society, refuses to accept either Gassendi's or Descartes' systems as

---

[48] Thus Haldane and Ross II, p. 248, pp. 250-1; also I 220.

[49] See further David C. Goodman, 'God and Nature in the Philosophy of Descartes' pp. 13-14, in 'Towards a Mechanistic Philosophy', Block II, Units 4-5 of 'Science and Belief: from Copernicus to Darwin', The Open University Press, Milton Keynes, 1974.

[50] *Pace* R. Hooykaas, 'Religion and the Rise of Modern Science', Scottish Academic Press, Edinburgh and London, 1972, p. 42.

[51] On Gassendi, see above. On the Cartesian notion of inertia, see Koyré, 'Newtonian Studies', pp. 65-79.

> "These, however, are merely assumed by mathematical astronomers in order to facilitate their calculations. They are not retained by philosophical astronomers who, going beyond the demand that they somehow save the appearances, seek to investigate the true constitution of the universe — the most important and admirable problem that there is. For such a constitution exists; it is unique, true, real, and could not possibly be otherwise . . . "

This passage is notable partly because of its entirely laudable empiricism and concern for truth, and partly because of the last phrase, which seems to imply that the Creator was constrained by his own mathematical reasoning. Indeed Galileo's early concern for empirical verification, as here expressed, decreased as he became more of a theoretical physicist.

Eventually, Galileo can praise the Copernicans of the period before the invention of the telescope as follows:

> "Nor can I sufficiently admire the eminence of those men's intelligence who have received and held it (sc. the Copernican system) to be true, and with the sprightliness of their judgements offered such violence to their own senses that they have been able to prefer that which reason dictated to them to what sensible experiences represented most manifestly to the contrary."

Now certainly the faith of the Copernicans had at last been partially[64] confirmed by observations made through the telescope: nevertheless had they had in their day the same concern as the young Galileo for "the true constitution of the universe" they would have rejected Copernicanism, despite its elegance. Galileo is in fact prepared by this stage to praise *a priori* science even where it does not save the appearances. And this, despite his denials that we can understand the Creator's purposes,[65] is surely to maintain that we can determine by reason alone what the Creator had to create.

But Galileo, and his pupil Torricelli, go even further. Here it is necessary to consider two passages oddly cited by Rossi[66] as para-

---

[64] But only partially. See David C. Goodman, 'Galileo and the Church', pp. 102 & 118-9 in 'The 'Conflict Thesis' and Cosmology', Block I, Units 1-3 of 'Science and Belief: from Copernicus to Darwin', The Open University Press, Milto Keynes, 1974.

[65] 'Dialogue Concerning the Two Chief World Systems', (1629), translated by Thomas Salusbury (1661), University of Chicago Press, 1953. Day Three, p. 378.

[66] Rossi, p. 221.

digms of seventeenth-century scientific thought. A letter of Galileo is first cited (Opere VII, 156):

> "I argue *ex suppositione,* imagining a movement towards a given point, starting from immobility, gathering speed, and increasing in velocity proportionately with the passage of time; and from this movement I demonstrate conclusively a number of phenomena. I then add that if experience reveals similar phenomena occurring in the movements of weights naturally falling we can truly assert that the movement is the same as that which I had defined and foretold. If this should not be, my demonstrations, based on suppositions, will have lost nothing of their force and conclusiveness; as the conclusions demonstrated by Archimedes on the spiral were in no way invalidated by the fact that no spiral can be found in nature to move in such a way."

Now Galileo may only be saying at the end of this passage that unverified scientific reasoning remains *valid* reasoning: yet his tone implies that he means more than this. He may, instead, only be saying that although nothing in nature has *quite* the sort of constant acceleration he describes, yet what he describes could be used, with adjustments for air pressure etc., to predict the movements of actual weights; but again he seems to imply more. He seems to imply that what is properly worth studying is mathematics, whether nature complies with it or not, and yet still to suppose that he is doing science.

These strictures may be unfair in the case of Galileo, but they are not unfair in the case of the more explicit Torricelli:[67]

> "I imagine or suppose that a certain body moves up and down according to the given law, and with similar motion horizontally. When this is done I say that all Galileo and I myself have said will follow. If balls of lead, iron, and stone do not then follow the supposed direction, it is their loss: we shall say that we are not concerned with them."

Now, as Rossi points out, such retaining of a theory in face of contradictory sense-experience is the very thing castigated as unscientific by Bacon at NO I 125. But does this make Bacon a defective philosopher of science? Certainly much is to be gained by the practice of theoretical physics and by a largely deductive procedure, granted that the structure as a whole is underpinned by

---

[67] Again quoted by Rossi at p. 221. No reference is supplied.

of Aristotelian physics, was much indebted to the Aristotelians of Padua with whom he had studied, and who had long been debating the logic of induction.[57] Galileo's readiness to test theory by observation is owed to these Aristotelians: his own contribution to scientific method was his introduction of ideal mathematical bodies into physical theories, but, till his later writings, he always stressed that theory must be verified by experience.[58] And in this respect he was much less a Platonist than was Descartes, and much less a Platonist than he himself supposed.[59]

Both Galileo's theology and his assumption that things answer to mathematical description are expressed in the following much-quoted passage from 'The Assayer' of 1623.[60]

> "Philosophy is written in this grand book, the Universe, which stands continually open to our gaze. But the book cannot be understood unless one first learns to comprehend the language and read the letters in which it is composed. It is written in the language of mathematics, and its characters are triangles, circles, and other geometric figures without which it is humanly impossible to understand a single word of it; without these, one wanders about in a dark labyrinth."

The reference to the writing of the book of nature is clearly a reference to the creation of nature by God: and it is this belief in creation which, as in the case of Bacon, spurs Galileo to science. The recognition that mathematical ideals are necessary in science is certainly correct, and it must be conceded both to Knight and to Rossi that Bacon was less well aware of this than Galileo; I can only repeat that a reading of Bacon's 'De Augmentis', Book Three, Chapter Six suggests that Bacon's appreciation of the place of mathematics was more considerable than they seem to think.[61] Mathematical ideal objects allow such factors as friction and air resistance to be neglected while the bones of an explanation are assembled: these factors can then be allowed for when particular phenomena are being explained or predicted.

Galileo's belief that nature is an intelligible book enabled him to

---

[57] Cf. J. H. Randall, 'The Development of Scientific Method in the School of Padua', 'Journal of the History of Ideas', Vol. 1, 1940.

[58] Carré, Philosophy, 1955, p. 340.

[59] Thus Carré, ibid: also T. R. Girill, 'Galileo and Platonistic Methodology', J.H.I., October, 1970; a valuable corrective to Koyré's 'Metaphysics and Measurement'.

[60] Quoted by D. Knight, 'Galileo', in the Harré collection at p. 64 and by Rossi, 'Francis Bacon', at p. 220.

[61] See Section 1E of this chapter.

take a stance paralleled to Bacon's over the deriving of conclusions in physics from the Bible. It is absurd, he says, for theology to dictate in advance the conclusions the sciences are to arrive at: "this would be as if an absolute despot, being neither a physician nor an architect but knowing himself free to command, should undertake to administer medicines and create buildings according to his whim — at grave peril of his poor patients' lives, and the speedy collapse of his edifices."[62] His confidence that the physician and the architect genuinely *are* independent of the despot, and natural philosophy of scripture, rests on the belief that nature is itself a book written by God.

Several features of Galileo's method are brought out by another passage from 'The Assayer', the famous passage where Galileo concludes that the cause of the ability of the Babylonians to cook eggs by whirling them in slings, when we cannot, is that unlike us they are Babylonians. The most obvious point here is Galileo's contempt for the citing of authorities in scientific argument: the fable about the Babylonians is to be believed, Galileo holds, because the ancient authority Suidas reports it: — or it should be believed if appeals to authority like those made by his opponents are in general legitimate. But it is also interesting to note Galileo's method and assumptions. If a phenomenon occurs in one set of circumstances and not in another similar set, there must be a difference, and the scientist must search by inspecting and varying the initial conditions till he finds it. Yet more interesting is the assumption that if there is no difference in initial conditions, the same phenomena will crop up. For this assumption is closely similar to that of Bacon when he holds that each nature (i.e. quality) has a single form (i.e. is always produced in the same and only the same conditions). Certainly Bacon here goes further than Galileo, for Galileo's principle is consistent with one and the same quality emerging from different conditions: yet Bacon (who is usually berated for what he says) is *at least* asserting the crucial methodological principle also asserted by Galileo.

Galileo, like Newton after him, contrasted the sort of physics which merely 'saves the appearances' and the sort which gets to the truth, a comparison we have already encountered in connection with The Royal Society's members' reaction to speculative physics. Referring to the eccentrics, deferents, equants and epicycles of anti-Copernican astronomers, he says (in the 'Letters on Sunspots')[63]

---

[62] From 'The Letter to the Grand Duchess', quoted by D. Knight, op.cit., p. 61. This striking letter is included in full in D. C. Goodman (ed.) 'Science and Religious Belief; A Selection of Primary Sources', John Wright & Sons/The Open University Press, Milton Keynes, 1973. For an illuminating discussion of Galileo's position, see Hooykaas, op.cit., pp. 124-126.

[63] Quoted by D. Knight, op.cit., p. 57.

'the *certain* account of Nature', and contrives to praise Descartes only through taking seriously the latter's profession that he is only describing "how things possibly *may have been made* consonantly to sensible nature", not "how *they truly were effected*".[52] The much firmer condemnation of "hypotheses" (as opposed to the conclusions of true induction) on the part of Newton (in the General Scholium of the 'Principia') is intended to condemn the speculations of such as the Cartesians, and here Newton reflects the theory (if not the practice) of Bacon in opposing unsubstantiated theorising.

A similar, but more stringent, attitude was adopted towards Hobbes by Seth Ward, another founding member of the Society, on the occasion of the appearance of Leviathan. What Hobbes really cherished, said Ward, was "the desire that Aristotelity may be changed into Hobbeity, and instead of the Stagyrite, the world may adore the great Malmsburian Phylosopher". (This passage is quoted by Margery Purver, who argues in a footnote for its authenticity.)[53] The point here is that Hobbes is setting up yet another *a priori* system, whereas what is needed is patient collaborative research and the restraining of men's speculative imaginations.

The position could be expressed in two ways. Both The Royal Society and the speculative physicists advocated an autonomous and therefore secular method; but the system-builders had constructed what could be seen either as a secularised structure of dogma, or alternatively as a natural philosophy not yet secular enough, because of the refusal to accept observation of the created order as a test and to construct only theories falsifiable by that test. For this failure issues in doing physics by the methods of metaphysics. Nevertheless not even Descartes, the most rationalist of the system-builders we have considered, goes as far as to deny that the created order could have been otherwise or to imply that it is unnecessary to inspect it in order to do science: these implications attend rather the strongly rationalist system of Spinoza, (little as Spinoza would have endorsed them.) Descartes' stress on the will of God saves him from the secularism of extreme rationalism; but, as pointed out above, is itself taken to such extremes as to render his entire method insufficiently secular.

---

[52] 'Scepsis scientifica', London 1665, pp. 211-2, quoted by Kargon, 'Atomism in England from Hariot to Newton', Oxford, 1966, at p. 113.

[53] Purver, p. 65, and footnote 12, p. 66.

C. Mathematical Physics and Creation.

Once again my concern is not with the physical theories of the thinkers concerned. Nor am I concerned with Kepler's (very unsecular) interest in the occult; nor even with Galileo's conflict with the ecclesiastical authorities, even though it was in the case of Galileo of all the thinkers to be discussed that secularisation was most vehemently opposed by the church. Rather I am concerned with their philosophy of science and its relation to their beliefs about God. Like Bacon, Kepler and Galileo saw the need for an autonomous method for science, and, again like Bacon, both the premisses they assumed and the motives which spurred them to scientific enquiry were, in part, theological. Thus again the pursuit of natural philosophy as an autonomous discipline turns out to be consistent with and even to issue from theological beliefs.

Both Kepler and Galileo assumed that scientific knowledge must be mathematical and were adept at devising mathematical models of how the world could be arranged. That they were not content to stop at this stage was due to their conviction that God must have created the world according to some mathematical paradigm, and accordingly that nature must answer to one mathematical ideal or another. This granted, the problem was to test their theories against observation to find if they describe "the true constitution of the universe"[54] or need to be revised in face of it.

Harré well sums up Kepler's scientific method.[55] "He believed that the world was an orderly construction and that its order was discoverable by man. But it was no satisfaction just inventing some order or other and imposing it on the facts, for the order was truly there if only it could be found. Every hypothesis as to what harmony prevailed was to be subjected to the strict test of fact, and if there was a discrepancy then it is the hypothesis which must be rejected, to be replaced by another devised along the same lines." An example of the use of this method is his rejection of the sine law of refraction, despite its elegance, because it failed to fit some of his observations.[56] The integrity of his methods allowed Kepler to found two new sciences, astronomy and optics; and this he achieved despite the fact that his motive was to discover the ratios which he felt must exist between the nature of man, the motions of the planets, and the celestial music which would please a mathematical God.

Galileo's method, paradoxically enough in the arch-opponent

---

[54] From Galileo's 'Letter on Sunspots', quoted by D. Knight, 'Galileo', in Harré (ed.), op. cit., p. 57

[55] R. Harré, 'Johannes Kepler', ibid., p. 84.

[56] Id., ibid., p. 93.

empirical evidence or that the purpose of the enterprise is understood to be the description of observable phenomena which therefore constitute ultimately the criterion of success (granted that classificatory problems have been solved). But, though Bacon is not fully aware of all this, what Torricelli affirms is altogether different again. Torricelli has ceased to be interested in how physical objects actually behave, and is only interested in how the ideal objects of mathematical physics would behave. It is as if the only world *worth* creating were the mathematical one which mathematical physics describes, and if God happens to have created another one, it is of no intrinsic interest. For he abandons (at least in this passage) the ultimate test of experience on which Bacon rightly insists, and at the same time he implicitly abandons Bacon's theological arguments against dogmatism in natural philosophy. It is no longer realised that the original creation cannot be imaginatively created by the notions of finite men unless they attend to and learn from what confronts their senses. In short, the present passage in an instance of a new secular dogmatism, secularist in implication because of its neglect of the doctrine of creation. (This alone is not of course to say that it is false, but only that the two positions are in conflict.)

Like Bacon, Kepler and Galileo were able to avoid the Scylla and Charybdis of dogmatism and scepticism because of their belief that empirical nature was an orderly construction, a book written by God. It is thus interesting to note that when (perhaps) the late Galileo and (more certainly) his pupil Torricelli lapse into dogmatism, they have thereby at least partially forfeited this belief. It is not contended that science is impossible without that belief; (perhaps the world just happens to be orderly). But it is contended that when science becomes based on a radically unsound method, it is inconsistent with that belief.

Mathematical physics is, however, compatible with that belief, as the passages of Galileo cited earlier show: and this was also the opinion of Isaac Barrow and the young Newton. Newton and Barrow, by whose Mathematical Lectures he was strongly influenced, combined Bacon's search for certainty in science to be attained through experiment with *mathematical rigour*. What Barrow wished to combat was the accumulation of merely possible hypotheses, after the manner of Gassendi, Descartes, Hobbes and indeed of some members of The Royal Society. Experimentation was to remain the basis, but disputation and uncertainty were to be eliminated by the mathematical quantification of theories and the mathematical analysis of what they predicted.[68] This method was

---

[68] Barrow's lectures and Newton's method are ably discussed by Kargon, op.cit., pp. 118 ff.

adopted by Newton, who found it fully compatible with the compilation of Baconian tables.[69] Indeed Newton's method probably reflects a broader understanding of Bacon than that of the 'vulgar empirics' who found little room for mathematics in natural philosophy.

The methodology of The Royal Society and of Newton is to be discussed in the next section: but enough has been said to show that the theoretical element in mathematical physics can be combined with respect for experimental verification, and not only need not imply an entirely *a priori* approach for science but can positively be employed in the criticism of speculative or purely hypothetical physics. In general, mathematical physics can profitably be pursued only when deployed in a way compatible with taking the doctrine of creation seriously, and not when deployed to further a purely rationalist and *a priori* methodology.[70]

Section 3: The Royal Society

A. Introduction

My purpose in this section is to investigate some aspects of the method of various members of The Royal Society, including Locke and Newton, and the relation of method to the religious beliefs of those concerned. This investigation will allow of a comparison with the method and the theology of Bacon.

All those to be discussed in this section, like Bacon and like the theoretical physicists, favoured the pursuit of natural philosophy by an autonomous method, and opposed both the method of the Aristotelians and the assumptions which lay behind it. They were alike opposed to explanations by formal causes (in the traditional sense) and by essences, and in addition they held in common a commitment to observation and experiment. They differed, however, about the role of theory and of mathematics in science; and also about the kind of certainty obtainable: they also differed in point of the consistency of their beliefs with the doctrine of creation. Once again, therefore, there is opportunity for theological and philosophical assessment of arguments and conclusions alike.

---

[69] Kargon, p. 123.

[70] Koyré similarly concludes that Newton's commitment to induction was required by belief in a voluntary creation ('Newtonian Studies', pp. 113-4).

The members of The Royal Society selected are those whose ideas significantly contributed to the secularisation of natural philosophy and those whose arguments admit of a comparison between their theology and mthod. Locke is primarily an instance of the first (though his religious writings are, of course, considerable), Glanvill of the second; whereas Newton is an example of both. At the same time it is possible to see if some of the most typical views of Royal Society members tally with those of Bacon. (There is in fact further discussion of Newton in Chapter 2: The Assault on Physical Theology.)

B. The Empirics.

Thomas Sprat, the historian of The Royal Society, declares that its aim is "to overcome the mysteries of all the Works of Nature" and alludes to its ultimate goal as "the Benefit of humane life, by the Advancement of Real Knowledge." The Royal Society thus cherished the same secular aims for science as Bacon and as Descartes.

But Sprat does not expect the benefits of science to emerge suddenly or quickly. There must be "Experiments of Light" as well as of "Fruit." just as Bacon said. The task called for patience and collaboration, and ideas were welcomed from all quarters. Basically it rested on observation of particular phenomena, the cautious formulation of principles, the demonstration of what would follow, experimenting, and yet more domonstration and experimenting, and so on. All experiments were to be carried out by members of the Society, for the sake of 'exactness', and results were to be recorded with great caution. The time for theories had not yet come, and theories should be avoided while initial observations were being recorded: but later generations should not be prohibited from 'speculations' once they have an adequate store of results to go on.[71]

The most sceptical of the earlier members about arriving at indubitable theories in science was Joseph Glanvill, who wrote, in 'Plus Ultra' (1668)

> "This (sc. the vanity of the talk of the Schools at Bacon's time) being considered, the *deep* and *judicious Verulam* made the *complaint,* represented the *defects* and unprofitableness of the *Notional* way, proposed *another* to reform and inlarge *Knowledge* by *Observation* and *Experiment,* to *examine* and *record Particulars,* and so to rise by degrees of *Induction* to

---

[71] See Sprat, 'History', pp. 2, 31, 64, 83, 107, 245.

THREE SORTS OF BACONIANS 51

general Propositions, and from *them* to take *direction* for *new Inquiries,* and *more Discoveries* and other *Axioms;* that our Actions may have a *Foundation* upon which a *solid Philosophy* may be built, that may be *firm, tite,* and close *knit,* and suted to the *Phaenomena* of things: so that *Nature* being *known,* it may be *master'd, managed* and *used* in the services of human Life."[72]

It is notable here that Glanvill acknowledges not only the aim but also the method of Bacon, despite Bacon's conviction that certainty can be attained, and also that he is prepared to speak in the same sentence of natural philosophy conforming to observed phenomena and at the same time of 'Nature' becoming *'known'.* This shows that there were limits even to Glanvill's scepticism, and that he did not always contrast appearances, which science could study, with reality which, some think, the Royal Society members believed it could not.[73]

Kargon argues that all the members of The Royal Society accepted Bacon's call for *certainty'.*[74] Kargon's valuable summary of the different ways this call was interpreted and the different reactions to the hypothetical physics of Gassendi, Descartes and Hobbes merits quotation.

"Yet, the revolt against the hypothetical physics took several forms; there was a spectrum of Baconians opposed to the excesses of the hypothesizers (although not necessarily to their mechanical principles). First, there were those in The Royal Society who rejected all theories, and fell back upon elaborate 'natural histories' after the fashion of some of Bacon's treatises. These 'empirics' claimed it was too early to utilize or pretend to theory (sic); collections of facts were all that at present could be attained. Secondly, there were those, like Robert Boyle, who (despite concessions to the empirics) attempted to *test* the great systems of Descartes and Gassendi. Boyle was not satisfied with the *a priori* nature of the systems of the French philosophers, and wished, through experimental investigations such as the *Experiments, Notes, etc. about the Mechanical Origins . . . of Qualities,* to investigate the manner of their conformity with experience. Finally, there were those like Isaac Barrow and Isaac Newton,

---

[72] Quoted by Purver, at pp. 95 f.
[73] Thus Henry G. Van Leeuwen, 'The Problem of Certainty in English Thought, 1630-1690', Nijhoff, The Hague, 1963, passim.
[74] Kargon, p. 109.

who accepted Bacon's demand for certainty, and, not finding it in the hypothetical physics, emphasised the necessity for what they called 'mathematics' and what today would be called 'mathematical physics'."

If this three-fold classification is accepted, Glanvill and, to some extent, Sprat are clearly amont the 'empirics'. Though, as we have already seen in the previous Section, Glanvill was at times tolerant of hypotheses so long as they were only regarded as possible, his later emphasis was on the worthlessness of scientific theories as opposed to the systematic recording of observation. Thus in his 'Essays on several important subjects in philosophy and religion' of 1676 he wrote of the scientists of New Atlantis,[75]

"They did not set down any *System* or *Body of Principles* as *certain* and *established:* They consider'd the *incomprehensible* wisdom that is in *the works of God;*... and therefore gave but *timerous* assent to any notions in *Natural Philosophy:* They held no *infallible* Theory *here*: Nor would they allow any speculations or accounts of Nature to be more than *Hypothesis* and probably conjecture . . . So that they thought with much reason, that best *Foundation* for *Natural Philosophy* would be a good *History of Nature:* This they saw to be very defective in their Time."

Such theological grounds for scepticism are typical of Glanvill: yet what is set out here is a sceptical position which would have prevented scientific progress as effectively as the Platonism opposed by Bacon.

It must certainly be allowed that Glanvill was as opposed to extreme scepticism as he was to dogmatism, something he had in common with John Wilkins, the founder of The Royal Society.[76] In reply to the Aristotelian, Thomas White, Glanvill denies that he holds nothing more probable than anything else:[77] rather he holds that science attains the kind of certainty where assent is proportioned to the evidence. On the other hand the claims of the speculative scienctists to understand nature are so uncertain as not to be science at all. What science can achieve is information which

---

[75] 'Essays', p. 15. The title of the present essay is 'Antifanatical Religion and Free Philosophy, in a Continuation of the New Atlantis'. The present passage is quoted by Kargon at p. 114.

[76] Cf. Wilkins' posthumously published 'Of The Principles and Duties of Natural Religion', London, 1675.

[77] In 'Of Scepticism and Certainty', one of his 'Essays' of 1676, pp. 45ff.

there is no reason to doubt, as opposed to information which could not possibly be otherwise.

Glanvill appears here to be distinguishing between logically necessary and logically contingent truths, and to be affirming that there are procedures for arriving at the latter, scientific procedures included. This however would be over-generous. On the one hand he treats logical necessities like the law of non-contradiction as merely indubitably certain, not as infallibly and necessarily certain, this on the ground that human faculties are at all times fallible. Again he believes it is indubitably but not infallibly certain that the faculties do not always deceive. On the other hand (and more seriously) the validity of some of his arguments would gravely limit the procedures and the method open to scientists. Thus he sensibly denies that the conclusions of science are of a sort that could not be otherwise, a proposition of rationalists like Spinoza which both conflicts with the doctrine of creation and discourages empirical enquiry. But one of the reasons given is that as no tenet is true on every philosophical system's principles, none is necessarily true:[78] as if necessary truth required universal consent. Nevertheless Glanvill's point here is theologically sound and methodologically vital.

Sometimes Glanvill anticipates Hume. He holds that "the real causal connections among natural events are not discoverable".[79] Causal connections are not perceptible, for only sequences can be observed, and "to argue from a concomitancy to a causality, is not infallibly conclusive."[80] In any case events are so interrelated that to understand any event one would have to understand every event, and this is beyond human capacities.[81] The second argument here implies that no causal predictions in science are possible, but neglects the possibility that implicitly conditional theories of the form, "In conditions C, E will occur" may be propounded, tested and secure rational acceptance without all relevant cases being investigated first. Nor is the first argument conclusive. For the fact that we are able to distinguish between mistaken and correct causal theories shows that true (though not incorrigible) causal theories can be attained: yet this is the very fact on which Glanvill relies.

Glanvill employs Bacon's idea that human error results from the Fall, and sometimes shares Bacon's confidence that it is possible for this fall into error to be rectified.[82] But at other times he is more

---

[78] 'Scepsis Scientifica', London, 1665, p. 194.
[79] Van Leeuwen, p. 76.
[80] 'Scepsis Scientifica', p. 190, quoted by Van Leeuwen at p. 77.
[81] Ibid., pp. 217 f.
[82] Cf. 'Of the Modern Improvements of Useful Knowledge', 'Essays', p. 23.

doubtful.[83] The difficulty probably stems, as with Descartes, from holding that the truth of what we take to be indubitable always depends on God.[84] This view implies that, as God could have altered the truth-value of even apparently necessary truths, no human belief is necessarily true: and, this being so, those conceptual and logical truths on which scientific investigation depends are imperilled, and with them scientific investigation itself.

Glanvill's caution was no doubt salutary in its day, when sober science was in its infancy: but his scepticism implicitly denies the possibility of prediction in science, and this despite his belief in the organisedness of nature (from which he hoped a belief in the existence of God would emerge).[85] If God's act of creation is purposive and its outcome orderly, there is good reason to do science with an ampler method than Glanvill's views allow of.

Robert Boyle is often thought of as an empiric, despite his preparedness to take seriously and test mechanist theories like atomism. Granted some ingenuity, this was clearly a possible direction for the Baconian search for certainty to take, and one probably more in keeping with Bacon's hopes than the path of the empirics was. But my current interest in Boyle is rather to discuss his reasons for opposing Aristotelian explanations in science and for preferring explanations of a new sort.

C. The Poverty of Essentialism.

Had a Seventeenth Century Aristotelian been asked why fire rises or why planets travel in circles, he would as likely as not have replied, "Because of their substantial forms as fire and as planets." Objects' behaviour was explained as being due to their being things of the kinds they belonged to. It would usually be assumed, in conjunction with this view, that particular objects were exhaustively distributed between mutually exclusive natural kinds, whose names were the names of species.

To such views, Boyle replied in his major theoretical work about science that explanations by forms or by essences were entirely unilluminating and therefore redundant.[86]

---

[83] Cf. 'Against Confidence in Philosophy', 'Essays', p. 17.
[84] Cf. 'The Agreement of Reason and Religion', 'Essays', p. 21: Van Leeuwen, p. 85.
[85] 'Philosophia Pia', to be found in 'Collected Works of Joseph Glanvill', George Olms Verlag, Hildesheim, 1970, Volume 5; pp. 17-22.
[86] Robert Boyle, 'The Origin of Forms and Qualities', 1666. In Thomas Birch, 'The Works of the Hon. Robert Boyle', 6 Vols., London 1772, Vol. 3, pp. 46-7. My attention was drawn to this passage by a paper of Roger Woolhouse.

"I do not think, but that natural philosophy, without being for that the more defective, may well enough spare the doctrine of substantial forms as an useless theory; not that men are arrived to be able to explicate all the phenomena of nature without them, but because, whatever we cannot explicate without them, we cannot neither explicate by them."

Such explanations leave us no better equipped to understand the world, or therefore to control it. Boyle requires instead explanations at once more particular and more general. He wants an explanation, which the Aristotelians could in any case not provide by appeal to a substantial form, why saltpetre produces cold when placed in water, but heat when placed in oil of vitriol. And he also wants an explanation of heat which transcends the boundaries between species or kinds of material.[87] And if the cause of heat in two sorts of thing is to be the same, it is at least likely that they have a common subsensible structure, as Boyle supposed. Boyle is confident that the size, shape, motion and texture of subsensible particles will explain all the properties of objects, including those in virtue of which we classify things into kinds.

The failing of explanations by substantial forms is that the connection between the explicandum and the explanation is not contingent, empirical and informative, but necessary, conceptual and tautological. This is the core of Boyle's point, and he was entirely right; if science was to make progress, it had to produce explanations which linked things externally and not internally related. But the main philosophical and theological interest in his protest at Aristotelian essentialism lies in the arguments about classification with which both he and Locke supported his point.

The common element in their reasoning is that things just happen to be assigned by humans to particular species, in accordance with arbitrarily selected sets of their qualities. Since essences attach to species, we cannot explain the behaviour of individual objects by what we call their essence, for they could without difficulty (at least in many cases) have been allocated to different species with distinct essences.[88] And if so, of course, there are no natural kinds: things are not of such a character that we are obliged to classify them one way rather than another, and are not arranged into sorts till arranged by us.

There is probably at least one philosophical mistake here: for we can only pick out things to classify them under some description,

---

[87] 'Of the Mechanical Origin of Heat and Cold', 'Works', Vol. 4, p. 232.
[88] Thus Boyle, 'Works', Vol. 3, pp. 27, 50: also Locke, 'Essay Concerning Human Understanding', III. VI. 4.

and therefore when we classify we can only classify things *of some sort* as being (also) of some further sort. We cannot pick things out simply as 'things', for 'thing' is not a genuine sortal term, and supplies no principle of identification or reidentification. But this is not to say that there is a most natural initial classification for any and every object: only that if we are even to be able to raise the question "Of what sort is this *x*?" we must be willing to give some sortal term *or other* as a value for the variable "*x*". Nor, *a fortiori*, is this to settle what the secondary classifications of objects shall be. We shall have to be willing to use the term 'whale' if we are to ask of some whale "What class does this belong to, fish or mammal?" but there may be a considerable element of discretion involved in actually answering the question.

Though Boyle perhaps went too far in regarding classification as arbitrary,[89] he was right to the extent that classification is at least sometimes relative to human interests. Thus a giant mallow may be classified by one set of gardeners as a weed, though by others as a bedding plant. And if so, which classification is adopted will depend on which of an individual object's qualities are of interest, and which side of interspecific boundaries a particular individual falls will often be a matter of some uncertainty. This being so, it cannot be assumed, as the Aristotelians tended to assume, that every object in creation was created as if labelled with the specific name of some species, much less that its behaviour can be prdicted from the behaviour proper to that species.

This conclusion would also seem to be the corollary of the belief of the new philosophers (Bacon, Descartes and Glanvill included) that we cannot know God's purposes. For to claim that an individual, being necessarily of one sort, is therefore necessarily of no other sorts, is to claim to know what God created it *as*, a question which, on Baconian principles, is a matter at least partly for observation, and certainly not for dogma, to settle.

It is sometimes thought that Bacon himself was Aristotelian over explanation:[90] for he too explains by 'forms', not by laws. But Bacon himself attacks explanations of the behaviour of bodies by the behaviour proper to their species:[91] and his 'forms' are not the essences of sorts of things, but the explanations, in terms of conditions necessary and sufficient, for the incidence of qualities. (If anything Bacon is vulnerable to the opposite danger, of disregarding what it is to be of a certain type: for his doctrines seem to leave open the possibility of realising the alchemists' dream and

---

[89] Ibid., p. 27.
[90] Thus Larsen, 'Journal of the History of Ideas', 1962.
[91] NO I 66 (first paragraph).

superimposing the qualities of gold on base metal.) Bacon would accordingly have agreed with Boyle and Locke that the divisions between species are not (or not entirely) God-given; and that it is legitimate to look for the explanation of the various qualities of things separately, and indeed at a subsensible level if some possibility of experimental verification is allowed of.

The Lockean view on classification could (just) be divorced from that on explanation, so long as the explanations a scientist adopts refer beyond natural kinds. Nevertheless the attack on the doctrine of created natural kinds was salutary both for science and theology. For theorists like Newton were encouraged by attitudes like those of Boyle and Locke to seek for interspecific explanations of motion: and in theology the claim to know *a priori* what men cannot know, namely as what, and for what function, any and every object was created, was tacitly undermined.[92]

D. Newton.

Newton's hatred of hypotheses issued in his exclusion of theological and metaphysical remarks from the body of his scientific writings, a secularising demarcation in the spirit of Bacon. Yet Newton's sytem is underpinned by metaphysical and theological beliefs. To quote Koyré[93]

> "It is his acceptance of two absolutes — space and time — that enabled him to formulate his fundamental three laws of motion, as it was his belief in an omnipresent and omniactive God that enabled him to transcend both the shallow empiricism of Boyle and Hooke and the narrow rationalism of Descartes, to renounce mechanical explanations and in spite of his own rejection of all action at a distance, to build up his world as an interplay of forces, the mathematical laws of which natural philosophy had to establish. By induction, not by pure speculation. This because our world was created by the pure will of God; we have not, therefore, to prescribe his action for him; we have only to find out what he has done."

---

[92] Boyle did nevertheless hold that we could infer the functions of many organs and organisms, and thus desired to resuscitate the Argument from Design in opposition to the followers of Descartes, a fellow-mechanist who however had no place for such reasoning. See the extracts from Boyle's writings in D. C. Goodman (ed.), 'Science and Religious Belief: a Selection of Primary Sources'. A similar position was adopted by Newton and is assessed in Chapter 2, Section 3.

[93] 'Newtonian Studies', pp. 113-4.

In the chapter that follows, a theological motive is suggested for the metaphysical belief in absolute space and absolute time. The present section is more narrowly concerned with the relation between Newton's method and his theology.

Kargon relates[94] how fiercely Newton responded to Pardies and Hooke when they dared to suggest he was devising hypotheses. 'Hypothesis' connoted to Newton (at most periods) 'speculation' or 'conjecture', whereas Newton was concerned, like the young Galileo, to discover "the true constitution of the universe", i.e. to ground theory securely on observation and experiment, and not to speculate, at any rate while doing science, on what *could have* caused the regularities thus discovered. Newton's concern for certainty based on experimentation is expressed in a letter to Oldenburg, secretary of The Royal Society.[95]

> "For what I shall tell concerning them (sc. the colours) is not an Hypothesis but most rigid consequence, not conjectured by barely inferring 'tis thus because not otherwise or because it 'satisfies all phaenomena' (the Philosophers universall Topick) but evinced by the meditation of experiments concluding directly and without any suspicion of doubt."

And as Kargon remarks,[96] such a method is more Baconian even than Boyle's, for Newton attempts to reach a theory inductively from experience, not to begin with a theory and try to devise relevant experiments. In such a way does Newton argue for his own theories of subsensible particles and their qualities.

What Newton can be seen as claiming, both above and in his 'Regulae Philosophandi' (which form the start of book III of the 'Principia',)[97] is that physical science has a procedure both autonomous of external authorities and *a priori* speculation, and adequate to attain truth. For if it is possible to distinguish truth from error in science, as Newton certainly believed, then science must be able to attain truth, — and not only by accident. Inductive inferences will not admittedly justify us in being certain about our conclusions or taking them to be incorrigible, but if scrupulously conducted according to the best experimental methods can issue in knowledge. Or at any rate this will be so, so long as we can rely on the tenet of Bacon and Galileo that like conditions produce like

---

[94] Op. cit., pp. 125-7.
[95] Isaac Newton, 'Correspondence', ed. H. W. Turnbull, Cambridge, 1959-61, Vol. I, pp. 96-7.
[96] Ibid., p. 132.
[97] More fully, 'Philosophiae Naturalis Principia Mathematica'.

effects, a tenet which in the looser form of 'like bodies have like qualities' licenses the kind of analogical reasoning endorsed by Newton in the 'Regulae' (Hypotheses II and III). Newton himself accepts that later experiments may show inductive conclusions to be false: but would no doubt hold that the perpetual possibility of being wrong does not mean that we are never entitled to believe we have found the truth.

None of this is to deny that, in the modern sense of the term, Newton does employ hypotheses. It is into his hypotheses that his mathematics enters: Newton predicts what will happen if the motion of bodies is governed by a precise mathematical relation between their masses, and finds that experiment justifies his theories. Indeed Newton assumes, like Galileo, that nature is both regular and explicable by relatively simple ratios: he therefore undertakes not to stop till he has discovered the one true set of ratios that obtain. And to see this is to see a good part of the connection between his theology and his method.

Throughout the present chapter the implications of belief in a Creator who purposefully creates order have been followed up. Here it is appropriate to add a comment on the limits to the benefits for science of such a belief. I have traced the benefits for science in the consistent critique by such as Bacon of both dogmatism and scepticism in the light of this doctrine, and we have also seen its value in the connection of mathematical physics. Benefit may also flow in the opposite direction if teleological arguments from the worlds's order to its divine creation can be sustained — like the following one of Newton.

"This most beautiful system of the sun, planets and comets could only proceed from the counsel and dominion of an intelligent and powerful being."[98]

Such arguments will be discussed in Chapter Six.

But Newton looked for the purposive presence of God in Nature beyond the endowing of Nature with its ordered regularities even though this theological belief is unquestionably the mainstay of his scientific endeavours. The passage in the General Scholium that follows ("a being, however perfect, without dominion, cannot be said to be "Lord God" ") probably reflects adversely on what Newton regards as the *lack* of divine dominion in Cartesian physics. Nature must be shot through with divine purpose, and

---

[98] 'Principia' (1713). Book III, Scholium Generale, pp. 481-2. In 'Newton's Philosophy on Nature' ed. Thayer, (Hafner Library of Classics), Columbia, 1952; p. 42.

particular phenomena must be found to reflect it. Here Newton seems discontented that divine purposiveness should occur in God's creative purposes only: and the outcome is his half-reluctant discoveries of roles for God *within* the physical world, some of which will be discussed in the chapter following. Such discoveries clearly take Newton beyond anything the doctrine of creation implies.

Nevertheless its genuine implications certainly encouraged him to seek the mathematical description of creaturely matter, in which search he was so conspicuously successful.

Section 4: Some Contrasts and Conclusions

A. Spinoza

Though I am not contending that science is only possible for believers in creation, I am contending that doctrine is compatible with, and suggests the viability of, a certain method for discovering truth in natural philosophy, intermediate between dogmatism and scepticism, and more or less delineated by Bacon. Besides arguments in its support, this contention can also be sustained (up to a point) by being tested. For we could expect that philosophers who do not believe in creation will not, unless perhaps by accident, endorse the method of Bacon and of the Royal Society: and that philosophers whose notion of method is far separated from this method may not believe in creation too seriously, if at all. Of the two expectations mentioned above, the second is by far the more important. The discovery that non-believers in creation endorsed or exhibited a method close to that of Bacon and of The Royal Society would in no way falsify what I am claiming. What might seriously tell against what I am claiming would be the disappointement of the second expectation and thus the discovery that a philosopher whose notion of method was far different from that of The Royal Society *did* take Creation seriously: and what would tell conclusively against what I am claiming would be that such a philosopher was consistent in so doing. This is because, if p implies q, then $-q$ implies $-p$: therefore to discover that $-q$ and p can be consistently held by the same man proves that p does not imply q.

The philosophers to be specially considered are Spinoza and Berkeley. Both were interested in science, as Spinoza's corres-

SPINOZA REJECTS CREATION 61

pondence with Oldenburg[99] and Berkeley's investigations in optics[100] testify. Yet neither can take either the notion of empirical science or that of creation with full seriousness. This was pointed out in 1934[101] by M. B. Foster, to whose stimulating writings I am much indebted.

The flavour of Spinoza's system is well illustrated by the following passage:

"In Nature there is nothing contingent, but all things are determined from the necessity of the divine nature to exist and act in a certain manner."[102]

Now, as Foster points out, if nothing is contingent, there is no place for observation: at best observation will be redundant, since demonstration can always supersede it, granted enough definitions and axioms; at worst it is harmful because liable to mislead. No consistent Spinozistic scientist could propound hypotheses on the understanding that if experimentally refuted they would have to be revised or rejected. To put it another way, there can be no empirical science for a consistent Spinozist.

But how does Spinoza draw the above conclusion? Spinoza is only able to draw it because of premises concerning God. The relation between natural objects and God is that between the modes of an attribute and the substance to which the attribute belongs. Thus natural objects have no independent existence: "Whatever is, is in God" (Part I, Proposition 15). And there is therefore no creation: for no existence independent of the one Substance has been, or could have been made. *Or could have been*. For God's activity is not voluntary: it is entirely conditioned by and deducible from his nature. (Proof of Proposition 29). This is why whatever is true is necessarily true, and there is no scope for observing what could have been otherwise. Once again belief in creation is exluded. In fact Spinoza regards nature when passively conceived as simply the logical consequence of nature as actively conceived, or God, a God whose infinite attributes include extension. It is, indeed, peculiarly hard to see how, granted Spinoza's views on necessity, his view of God could have been

---

[99] 'Correspondence of Spinoza', Translated and Edited by A. Wolf, London, 1928: especially Letter VI.
[100] 'New Theory of Vision', Dublin, 1709.
[101] M. B. Foster, 'The Christian Doctrine of Creation and the Rise of Modern Natural Science', Mind, N. S. XLIII, 1934, pp. 446-468, especially at pp. 466-8.
[102] 'Ethics' Part I, Proposition XXIX, 'Spinoza Selections', Ed. John Wild, New York, 1930, p. 125.

different: or how, granted his view of God, he could also have consistently championed empirical science.

A man who wishes to pursue empirical science must, in consistency, believe that there are physical objects to investigate which are epistemologically and metaphysically independent existences, — even if he holds that their 'real essences' are unknowable.[103] He must also hold that they could have been otherwise. If he believes in God and in creation he will be encouraged by the belief that creation is orderly and intelligible, but (it still being assumed that he believes in God) he will believe neither in divine creation nor in contingency in nature unless he also believes that God is free in creation, and could create otherwise (or not create at all.) Most of these crucial tenets were, as we have seen, denied by Spinoza.

B. Extreme Empiricism.

A difficulty now arises over Berkeley, the same difficulty as arose for Foster. Berkeley gives preeminence to the will of God: but for God's gracious provision of a Natural Language of arbitrary signs, we could not as much as pick out one thing from another.[104] Yet it will be argued that Berkeleianism is inimical to scientific method. In what way, then, was Berkeley committed to beliefs incompatible with that in divine creation?

In the 'Principles of Human Knowledge', Berkeley capitalises on Locke's scepticism about secondary qualities and on Locke's belief that the real essence of things is unknowable, and concludes that the same reasoning shows that even primary qualities are not real as qualities of things, let alone essential to them, but "are only ideas existing in the mind."[105] And at once he attacks the idea of matter as an idea involving a contradiction: for matter will now be a substance all of whose possible qualities are unreal. It is thus a redundant notion.

Not that Berkeley ceases to use the ordinary sortal terms, like 'table' and 'chair' for what are normally supposed to be physical objects. He denies, however, that tables are material. For them, to exist is to be perceived: they are in fact ideas, or appearances accessible to our senses such as sight and touch. It will follow that their existence is not independent, but dependent on the mind of

---

[103] The view of Locke (Essay IV, VI, 6) and of Newton (General Scholium, 'Principia' (1713 edition), Book III). Newton of course holds that things' nominal essences *are* knowable.
[104] 'Alciphron', Dialogue IV, 'Works', Edited Luce and Jessop, 1950, Vol. III, p. 157.
[105] 'Principles of Human Knowledge', 9.

the person or persons who perceive. They are *his* or *their* ideas, (not ideas which just *happen* to be perceived.)

We have already seen enough to see that Berkeley denies the independent existence of created objects: and it is accordingly not surprising that the doctrine of a Natural Language has to be produced to account for the appearance of there being persistent public objects whose behaviour is relatively regular, and to account also for the difference between the stability of such 'ideas' and the instability of the 'ideas' of our imagination and of our dreams. It might be suggested that this doctrine is itself a doctrine of Creation: certainly the ideas depend on the activity of God. But *as what* do they depend on God? Only as the ideas of various minds. They have no independent existence and cannot, in consistency, have real causal relations between themselves, much less be intelligible through the causal explanations of Newtonian physics. (Much less still can they be explained by hypotheses about subsensible particles: for if only ideas and minds exist, and subsensible particles are necessarily imperceptible and non-mental, then there can be no such particles.)

Berkeleianism is thus incompatible with modern science,[106] but this no contingency. For, on Berkeleianism, it is futile to seek for a rational understanding of physical objects. For the regularity which we perceive is not a quality of natural objects, but a regularity of God's resolve to produce ideas which are mutually coherent.[107] One implication of this is that the empirical study of nature is, properly, empirical theology! But, more important, God's choice to produce ideas at all must be newly made for each successive moment, — a disincentive to attempts at scientific prediction.

These difficulties stem from the denial of the independent existence of everyday objects, i.e. of their independent indentifiability and reidentifiability as the objects that they are, and of the logical possibility that they could exist were nothing else to exist. But this is to deny that God creates objects whose existence is independent of people's minds.

Thus, though Berkeley's intention was to scotch the atheism which he believed to be implicit in the theories about matter in Newtonian science, he ends up committed to beliefs incompatible with the doctrine of creation.[108] And had Galileo or Newton shared his philosophical beliefs, it is most unlikely that they would have

---

[106] A point effectively made by Berkeley himself at 'Principles', 107.
[107] Thus J. D. Mabbott, 'The Place of God in Berkeley's Philosophy', 'Philosophy', 1931, pp. 18-29; especially at p. 21.
[108] On *both* points, see 'Principles', 92.

had the confidence to devise theories for verification against *future* phenomena.[109]

C. Conclusions.

The relevance of the present chapter to the subject of secularisation has lain principally in discussion of the ways in which the doctrine of creation encourages a particular autonomous and thus secular method for science and in which various proposed secular methodologies turn out to be as dubious methodologically as they are theologically. But what are the grounds for the claim that natural philosophy needs an autonomous method? That only on an autonomous method are independently chosen topics likely to be investigated and independent as opposed to preconceived results likely to be achieved; that only such results are likely to be of value; and theologically that the doctrine of creation suggests that science is feasible and that this combined with the Jewish and Christian beliefs that creation has been subjected to man's dominion and that men ought to seek each other's welfare, renders its pursuit positively obligatory on any society which holds these beliefs.

Recently it has been claimed that these very beliefs about dominion over nature are the source of undue exploitation of the environment.[110] No doubt they have sometimes been an excuse for self-aggrandisement, and for the exploitation of other *people*, on the part of a few. But the objection to pollution and the depletion of scarce, non-renewable resources is the harm done worldwide to humans both in this and coming generations; and is thus itself both Baconian and Biblical. The roots of the ecological crisis thus lie elsewhere; while its solution lies not in the abandonment of technology but in a technology genuinely suited to human needs, the end of science proposed by Bacon.[111]

---

[109] A partially similar point about the extreme empiricism of David Hume is made by John Hedley Brooke at pp. 45-46 of 'Natural Theology in Britain from Boyle to Paley' in 'New Interactions between Theology and Natural Science', Block IV, Units 9-11 of 'Science and Belief: from Copernicus to Darwin', The Open University Press, Milton Keynes, 1974.

[110] Thus Lynn White Junr., 'The Historical Roots of Our Ecological Crisis', in 'The Environmental Handbook', edited John Barr, Pan Books Ltd., London, 1971, pp. 3-16. This analysis receives heavy qualification in John Passmore's 'Man's Responsibility for Nature', Duckworth, London, 1974, chapters 1 and 2.

[111] Thus in the Praefatio of 'The Great Instauration' ('Works', Vol. IV, pp. 20f) he urges "that they (sc. men) consider what are the true ends of knowledge, and that they seek it not either for pleasure of the mind, or for contention, or for superiority to others, or for profit, or fame, or power, or any of these inferior things; but for the benefit and use of life; and that they perfect and govern it in charity." For proposals for solving the ecological crisis, see Barry Commoner, 'The Closing Circle', Jonathan Cape Ltd., London, 1973, chapter 11.

In any case, however, it is now clear both that Bacon was substantially right in finding grounds to combat both dogmatism and scepticism in the doctrine of creation, and that the method and attitude most compatible with this doctrine was the method adopted both by Bacon and by most members of The Royal Society. This, in fact, is why it has been important to sustain the view that The Royal Society really did adopt Bacon's method, and did not merely say they did (i.e. through Sprat's explicitly saying so in the 'History').

Bacon derived from his belief in creation both a healthy scepticism about speculative physics, dogma and unquestioned assumptions, and a confidence that the book of nature was orderly and intelligible enough to be legible. These same conclusions were crucially important in the work both of Galileo (who seems to have arrived at them independently) and of members of The Royal Society like Newton. Those philosophers who forgot the first were led into a-priorist physics like that of Descartes, while those lacking confidence that the objects of sense experience were both reliable and regular would in the course of time have been deterred from physics altogether.

The mathematical method of Barrow and Newton, which echoed that of Kepler and Galileo, was certainly an improvement on that of men like Glanvill and Boyle, as well as on that of Gassendi and Hobbes. But it was fully compatible with the Baconian belief that observable nature is comprehensible, and would have had Bacon's approval.

Further, both in their support of systematic observation and in their belief that nothing short of knowledge is satisfactory in science and that merely possible theories are inadequate, the members of The Royal Society were being true to Baconian theory and to Baconian theology. For on the one hand while systematic observation prior to the devising of hypotheses is not logically necessary, it is unlikely that even plausible hypotheses can be built up without it: intelligent reasoning based on systematic observation is the only rational procedure for devising hypotheses (as the cases of Kepler and Galileo attest). And on the other hand the quest for knowledge of observed nature is precisely what the doctrine of creation seems to encourage. Again, if knowledge of nature is possible it is likely not only that hypotheses can be rationally verified but also that they can be rationally devised.

It is alleged by Van Leeuwen that Bacon and The Royal Society had different notions of certainty. But the term "certainty" covers many sins. Neither Bacon nor The Royal Society were seeking, or expected to attain *psychological* certainty. Rather they sought for knowledge. But neither men like Glanvill *nor Bacon himself* sought withing science for knowledge of what was logically necessary. They realised alike, as Descartes did not, that if science is to be based on intuition and demonstration alone it can say nothing of nature, and that if it is to be empirical, its truths must be contingent. For God could have created otherwise. But this is no reason against investigating how the created world in fact is. The necessities Bacon looked for were what we might call 'contingent necessities': nature being what it is, such and such conditions must produce such and such effects. Bacon may have been less aware than Newton that scientific findings are never incorrigible: yet this hardly detracts from his achievement, granted his belief in verification by observation.

Nor can we place too much stress on the denial by Newton and Locke of the knowability of real essences, in contrast with Bacon's hope of attaining the truth about nature. For Newton shared this hope, and attempted to find the real causes of real qualities, whatever metaphysical doubts he was induced to share about the inner nature of those substances to which the qualities belonged.

Bacon's aspirations to knowledge were, in short, shared by the members of The Royal Society. The least Baconian was probably Glanvill, who sometimes argues against any theorising however closely based on observation: and in addition Glanvill shared with Descartes some very unBaconian doubts about apparently necessary truths, doubts which were scarcely encouraging for science.

Other objections to Bacon, or to the view that his method and that of The Royal Society are similar, have been discussed in earlier passages. But even if Bacon's logic were valid only over the grounds for rejecting dogmatism and scepticism, so will be the logic of the members of The Royal Society: for their premises and conclusions were the same. And what follows is that the doctrine of creation implies that science is feasible, but only if a critical and cautious method, like that of the young Galileo and that of The Royal Society, is followed. Accordingly an entirely theoretical method will be open to theological as well as philosophical strictures: as will be one on which reliable verification is despaired of, or on which things are not believed to have powers or to be of a sort such that causal relations are possible between them.

It should be emphasised that the doctrine of creation, while historically indispensable for getting natural science off the ground, cannot without circularity be employed to defend the assumptions of science about the regularity of nature.[112] Yet, for all that, a

---

[112] Thus Hume, 'Enquiry', Section XII, Part I, in 'Hume's Enquiries', ed. Selby-Bigge, Oxford, 1894, p. 153.

theological critique of scientific method remains possible. Besides, whatever other grounds we may have for confidence in the method just described, *if* the doctrine of creation can itself be shown to be probable (i.e. on cosmological and teleological grounds), then the mistakenness of incompatible methods for natural philosophy, like that of rationalism, is thereby shown to be at least as probable. Whether this can be shown remains to be seen.

In the present chapter there has been little scope for discussion of the attack which was made in the course of secularisation on the intrusions of theology within philosophy whether natural or metaphysical. This attack was made in precisely the same critical spirit as that advocated and embodied by the founders of early modern science as essential to all scientific work — a point which to some degree extends also to secularisation in other fields. But this particular attack, on what I shall call 'physical theology', is the concern of the next chapter.

CHAPTER 2

THE ASSAULT ON PHYSICAL THEOLOGY

Section 1: The Nature of Physical Theology

In this chapter, some incursions of theology into physics and some secularising attacks on such incursions will be considered. What is meant by 'physical theology' must therefore first be explained, it being the purpose of this chapter to explore the form which physical theology took and why it was necessary to attack it.

> "It is physical theology; that is to say, it treats divine action as one factor among the factors which together constitute the working of the natural system. And this appears to be perhaps unscientific certainly blasphemous: God's action cannot be a factor among factors; the Creator works through and in all creaturely action equally; we can never say 'This is the creature, and that is God' of distinguishable causalities in the natural world. The creature is, in its creaturely action, self-sufficient: but because a creature, insufficient to itself throughout, and sustained by its Creator both in existence and in action."[1]

Despite the advocacy of autonomous method in natural philosophy on the part of the new philosophers of the seventeenth century, and despite the mechanist assumptions of many of them, the explanations they from time to time adopted of the world around them were frequently theological in character. Sometimes explanations or descriptions were derived from beliefs about God held *a priori:* while sometimes, when human ingenuity gave out before a gap in physical knowledge, the activity of God was invoked as the only possible explanation. It is to the latter practice that the passage of A. M. Farrer, quoted above, alludes: but both practices could appropriately be termed 'physical theology'. In both cases the natural philosopher was implicitly stipulating some feature with which the physical world had to conform: instead of

---

[1] A. M. Farrer, Editor's Introduction to 'Theodicy', by G. W. Leibniz, translated by E. M. Huggard, London, 1957: p. 28.

letting the phenomena speak for themselves, instead of striving until an adequate analysis of the world in terms of its own powers and qualities was arrived at, he would bring in God.

Now if the arguments for the existence of God could establish the Creator's character, and establish it with enough detail to allow of the confident inference that one form of possible creation would be preferred to another; were all this the case then some physical theology would be not wholly unreasonable. Even then there would be a constant need to check that the world was indeed of the character which had been inferred and that metaphysical arguments had not led us astray. But all this is to argue *per impossibile*. Arguments from the world to the character of God cannot disclose further information about the world which was not available without them. Such knowledge, therefore, as we may come by about God will not allow us to hold that the world is thus rather than thus.

Moreover to detect a divine presence in some natural phenomena while regarding natural phenomena as, for the rest, self-sufficient involves grave liabilities. From the side of theology, it is to diminish God, both as representing his workmanship as deficient and in need of repair, and as conceiving of God himself as on a level with creaturely agencies. Meanwhile from the side of physics there are dangers for the theologian just as great. In time, more thorough investigation is likely to show that divine agency is redundant: and if new arguments for the existence of God should be devised on the strength of the allegedly indispensable intervention, the existence of God itself may be declared a redundant hypothesis, if so grounded.

Thus wherever theological physics crops up, there are both theological and physical grounds for a secularising protest. The protest that theological explanations are irrelevant within physics[2] is therefore one in which the theist is likely to be able to share. But the protests will normally be grounded in notions of scientific method such that both inferences from theology and supernatural explanations are inadmissible.

Examples of physical theology and of secularising protests will be considered and assessed in the four Sections which follow. Physical theology will be detected both among the Newtonians of

---

[2] One such protest was made by Denis Diderot in his 'Lettres sur les Aveugles à l'usage de ceux qui voient' of 1749; he adopts the Epicurean view that, given long enough, particles moving at random could form any world-state, including the present one. See David C. Goodman, 'The Enlightenment: Deists and 'Rationalists' ' in 'Scientific Progress and Religious Dissent', Block 3 of 'Science and Belief: from Copernicus to Darwin', The Open University Press, Milton Keynes, 1974, pp. 61 and 63f.

England and among the Cartesians and Leibnizians of the Continent, and it will be observed how each party criticised the physical theology of the other: for lapses from a properly secular study of nature were easier to observe away from home than close at hand. Nevertheless by the time of Newton's death the progressive elimination of theology from natural philosophy was irreversible: and it is perhaps unsurprising to find an opponent of the trend of the times in the person of Berkeley, devising a last ditch metaphysic in which God was once again indispensable for explaining every natural occurrence. By this time there was less need for secularising attacks on physical theology (except in the realms of biology and geology): and secularising attacks are soon found directed not at the role of God within nature but at the very existence of God himself. These attacks will receive separate discussion.

Finally in a Section on miracles the question is asked whether, as both Spinoza and Hume believed, belief in miracles is itself a form of physical theology. On mechanist assumptions there is little room for miracles: yet miracles appear to be within the power of the Creator, even of the Creator of a world explicable to a considerable degree on mechanist principles. Despite this, important doubts are raised over whether we have grounds for miracles, or could use or be expected to regard miracles as grounds for anything beyond themselves.

Section 2: Physics Deduced from Theology: Descartes and Newton

The first kind of theological physics mentioned above is that in which some law of nature or natural fact is derived from God's character. Thus Descartes, true to his *a priori* method, derives all three of his laws of motion and impact from God's immutability and the immutable manner of his acts. (This is pointed out in Koyré's essay 'Newton and Descartes'.)[3] Indeed his allied assumption, that both motion and the rest are states whose change but not whose continuation requires explanation, was put to use by Newton. Nevertheless Newton was firmly opposed to physical laws being grounded in this way. For they are mere hypotheses. "Whatever is not derived from things themselves, whether by the

---

[3] In Koyré, 'Newtonian Studies': see especially pp. 70-79.

external senses or by the sensation of internal thoughts, is to be taken for a hypotheses . . . "[4] And in his fourth and final published rule for the conduct of natural philosophy, Newton makes it clear that hypotheses have no place.[5]

"In experimental philosophy we are to look upon propositions inferred by general induction from phenomena as accurately or very nearly true, notwithstanding any contrary hypotheses that may be imagined, till such time as other phenomena occur, by which they may either be made more accurate, or liable to exceptions. This rule we must follow, that the argument of induction may not be evaded by hypotheses."

Newton's protest at Cartesian physics is a secular one in that he is defending an autonomous, experimental method against the intrusions of *a priori* speculation. Yet Descartes also supposed himself to be pursuing an autonomous method. Further, though Newton's protest implicitly extends to the method on which Descartes brings God into physics, he also holds, as we shall see, that Descartes has too *small* a place for the activity of God within the world. His protest against speculation is thus proper but not consistently sustained.

Indeed perhaps the motive for Newton's belief in absolute space and absolute time[6] (indispensable as these are for his laws of motion) and certainly the basis of some of his attacks on Descartes (see on) lies in a metaphysical and theological contention of his own, expressed in an early paper[7] but which he did not cease to hold.[8] Whatever exists is spatial and temporal, and thus God must have infinite extension and duration.

"Space is a disposition of being *qua* being. No being exists or can exist which is not related to space in some way. God is everywhere, created minds are somewhere, and body is in the

---

[4] From a draft for 'Regulae Philosophandi', Regula 5, once intended for addition to Book III of the 'Principia', but not so added. Quoted by Koyré at p. 272.
[5] Rule IV; in 'Sir Isaac Newton's Mathematical Principles', translated into English by Andrew Motte (1729) and revised by Florian Cajori, Berkeley, California, 1947; p. 400.
[6] Scholium to the Definitions, Motte-Cajori, p. 6.
[7] 'De Gravitatione et Aequipondio Fluidorum', probably from the 1660's or not much later. In 'Unpublished Scientific Papers of Isaac Newton', Edited and Translated by A. R. and M. B. Hall, Cambridge, 1962. The passage quoted is from p. 103, as translated at p. 136.
[8] This is established by Koyré, at p. 90-112.

space that it occupies; and whatever is neither everywhere nor anywhere does not exist.[9] And hence it follows that space is an effect arising from the first existence of being, because when any being is postulated, space is postulated. And the same may be asserted of duration: for certainly both are dispositions of being or attributes according to which we denominate quantitatively the presence and duration of any existing individual thing. So the quantity of the existence of God was eternal, in relation to duration, and infinite in relation to the space in which he is present . . . "

This being so, the position, time and motion of created individuals must be positions, times and motions in God's (absolute) space and time, even if we have to *measure* them relatively to observable places and clocks. Again, it seems to follow that any doctrine like that of Descartes, which ascribes extension to matter only and denies the possibility of the ascription of extension to God leads to atheism. For both if matter is eternal (as it will be on this doctrine), it will (Newton thinks) not have been created; and also God would be unable to create it, not 'containing in himself extension even in a preeminent manner'.[10] Neither argument seems valid, since to explain by cosmological reasoning the existence of something whose duration is infinite is not impossible and to explain that of something material by the existence of what could not be material is not impossible either. Nevertheless we begin to understand the Newtonians' protest at the Cartesians, whose God, at least on Newtonian principles, seems, being nowhere, not to exist at all.

It is also concluded by Newton that just as we can move our bodies throughout the range of our own physical extension simply through acts of will, so also can God bring it about by an act of will that parcels of space become impenetrable and thus create matter. Indeed Newton cites the text about man's being made in God's image in support of this parallelism of faculties.[11] It is views such as these which make the exercise of God's 'dominium' within nature a possibility, and enabled Newton, and more particularly his followers, to envisage God as the cause of gravitational action at a distance. It was in any case the view of Descartes that, despite God's perpetual recreation of the world and maintenance of its extension and motion, God is not purposively active *within* the world, which issued in Newton's condemnation of a theology

---

[9] Words reminiscent of Hobbes, Leviathan, ch. 34, but more probably influenced by Henry More: see Koyré, pp. 89f.
[10] Hall and Hall, p. 109; translation at p. 145.
[11] Ibid., pp. 107-8; translation at p. 141.

whose God was effectively absent. Thus in a draft for the Scholium Generale he wrote,[12]

> "He who shall demonstrate that there is a Perfect Being, and does not at the same time demonstrate that he is Lord of the Universe or Pantokrator, will not yet have demonstrated that God exists. A Being eternal, infinite, all-wise, and most perfect without dominion is not God but only Nature. This is in a manner eternal, infinite, all-wise and most powerful, and the necessarily existing author of all things; yet the dominion or Diety of God is best demonstrated not from abstract ideas but from phenomena, by their final causes."

The stage is thus set for Newton to look for supernatural explanations of particular natural phenomena: short of such agency being demonstrated, he is not sure if Descartes' God differs from the God of Spinoza.

The secularising protest at such reasoning was to come from Leibniz (see Section 3A). Our present concern, however, is Newton's belief in God's limitless duration and extension, as clearly expressed in the Scholium Generale,[13] and echoed by Samuel Clarke.[14] And to this also Leibniz has trenchant objections, including that in paragraph 40 of his Fifth Reply to Clarke.[15]

> "And if limited spaces are the affections of limited substances which are in them; and infinite space be a property of God; a property of God must (which is very strange) be made up of the affections of creatures; for all finite spaces, taken together, make up infinite space."

Clarke seeks to save himself from the view that God is spatially located by the claim[16] that "God is in all space" does not mean "God is in space" but rather that "space is a necessary consequence of his existence". But we here remember that this is, at least according to Newton, (whose spokesman Clarke probably is), because it is an attribute of God: what is necessary is the positing of space (as God's location) once we posit the existence of God. Thus on Newton's view God's infinity will, as Leibniz alleges, be the

---

[12] Ibid., p. 359; translation at p. 363.
[13] Motte-Cajori, p. 545.
[14] 'The Clarke-Leibniz Correspondence', edited by H. G. Alexander, Manchester, 1956, p. 47.
[15] Ibid., p. 67.
[16] Fifth Reply, p. 104.

sum of the finite extensions of creatures; and the outcome is indeed "very strange" in theology and physics alike.

The difficulties which beset Newton and Clarke seem to be due not to mistaken scientific method but to bad theology in an area where physics and metaphysics merge. For on Clarke's view, while God is incorporeal, he is also a spatial and temporal substance. And on this view it is very hard to see how he could be the creator of other spatial and temporal substances. This very reply was in fact made by Descartes, while explaining to Henry More, whose position anticipated that of Newton and Clarke, why he was unwilling to call the world infinite rather than indefinite.

> "But I dare not call it infinite as I perceive that God is greater than the world, not in respect of his extension, because, as I have said, I do not acknowledge in God any proper (extension), but in respect to his perfection."[17]

Descartes is no doubt mistaken to argue that infinity implies perfection, so the world cannot be infinite. (See Section 3B). But he is correct to hold that as God is greater than the world, he cannot be extended, whether finitely or infinitely.

Since the cosmological argument, and, with it, the doctrine of creation, require that God be non-spatial and non-temporal, the continental tradition of Descartes and Leibniz seems here to be the sounder one. Had More, Newton and Clarke been more theologically consistent they might have avoided both paradox and polemic. Sometimes theology can prevent physics being attempted by deduction from theology, more easily than a proper regard for scientific method.

None of this is intended as support for the relational account of time as opposed to the absolutist account. Indeed, the theory that time is the order of events would seem circular, it being impossible to say what an event is unless we first know what time is. The notion of time appears irreducible, however we in fact measure time, and to the extent that Newton was saying this, he was well advised. Nevertheless Newton's belief in absolute time seems to have theological overtones which made for both questionable physics and bad theology.

---

[17] From a letter quoted by Koyré, 'From the Closed World to the Infinite Universe', Baltimore, 1957, p. 122: as in Adam and Tannery, 'Oeuvres', Vol. V, p. 344.

Section 3:   Supernatural Explanation in Newton

A.   Cosmic Maintenance.

The questionable physics to which Newton's belief in God's spatiality led can now be discussed. One of Newton's motives for introducing divine agency within nature was, as we have seen, his belief that God is a provident governor, purposefully active, and not the kind of absentee deity he saw in the God of Descartes, and his friend Clarke saw in the God of Leibniz. But explanation by divine agency was in any case, in Newton's view, indispensable: certain phenomena cannot be explained otherwise.

Thus in Opticks, Query 31, after contrasting his own explanations of phenomena by principles of motion of great predictive power with the occult qualities of the Aristotelians which "put a stop to the improvement of natural philosophy", Newton goes on to argue that it is "unphilosophical to seek for any other origin" of the orderly natural world and of various particular orderly phenomena within it than one "by the counsel of an intelligent Agent". It is not just from the existence of the "laws of nature" that he argues, but also from the concentricity of the paths of the planets and the symmetry of the bodies of animals. "Also", he continues

> "the first contrivance of those very artificial parts of animals, the eyes, ears, brain, muscles, heart, lungs, midriff, glands, larynx, hands, wings, swimming bladders, natural spectacles and other organs of sense and motion, and the instinct of brutes and insects can be the effect of nothing else than the wisdom and skill of a powerful ever-living Agent, who being in all places is more able by his will to move the bodies within his boundless uniform sensorium, and thereby to form and reform the parts of the universe, than we are to will to move the parts of our own bodies."

Once again it is God's spatiality which supposedly makes possible his endowing various of his creatures with the order they have: and Newton also believes that but for divine agency the order they display would be inexplicable. (His disapproval of the Cartesian view on which the bodies of animals are mechanisms is not hard to understand.) Divine agency is also traced elsewhere. Thus in Query 28, one of the questions to be answered by appeal to a first cause runs, "What hinders the fixed stars from falling upon one another?" while in Query 31 Newton holds that the irregularities of the planetary orbits due to the influence of comets will increase "till the system wants a reformation", a reformation clearly only possible through the agency which caused their orbits' concentricity. Clarke and Leibniz also assume in their correspondence that Newton's God has to intervene to maintain constant the amount of motion in the universe; and with some justification, since, as Alexander points out,[18] Newton assigns in the Latin edition of the Opticks (1706) as the explanation of the maintenance of motion "these active principles" (i.e. the cause of gravity and the cause of fermentation) and "the dictates of a will", phrases which were, however, omitted from the second English edition of 1717.

Now arguments like Newton's from the orderliness of nature throughout space and time to an intelligent Creator will be considered in a later Chapter. But Newton also argues from the apparent contrivance of, or the restoration of order in, particular phenomena. Thus according to Clarke, who probably consulted Newton when writing his Replies to Leibniz, it belonged to God's glory and perfection that he restored the world to its pristine condition. But such divine interventions are among the most serious of the three complaints Leibniz makes in his First Paper to Clarke. For in Leibniz' system the natural order was self-sufficient, once created, and, if God works miracles at all "he does not do it in order to supply the wants of nature but those of grace." Thus Leibniz accuses Clarke of having a low opinion of God's wisdom and power.[19] The question which his protest raises is whether any explanation of particular phenomena by supernatural purposive agency is not thereby physical theology, and thereby a betrayal both of natural philosophy and possibly also of theology too.

Leibniz' final comment on the belief that God maintains the world like a clock which needs to be wound up seems conclusive. For Clarke had granted that the intervention he believed in was one which "surpasses all created powers: and that is the very thing which all men endeavour to avoid in philosophy . . . Otherwise nothing will be easier than to account for anything than by bringing in the diety, *Deum ex machina*, without minding the nature of things"[20] And this is what Clarke and Newton were doing.

Here Leibniz is true to the principles of Bacon and Galileo in holding that the created order is intelligible, and that its order can be discovered by observation and rational enquiry without appeal to mystery or despair of finding physical explanations. The motive

---

[18] Leibniz-Clarke Correspondence, Introduction, pp. XVII-XVIII.
[19] Liebniz, First Paper, paragraph 4; p. 12 (Alexander.)
[20] Leibniz, Fifth Pater, paragraph 107; pp. 90-91.

of the Newtonians, to find scope within the world of science for the action of the Lord of History, is understandable: yet they were looking in the wrong place, and only succeeded in a crude reinvocation of final causes where efficient and formal causes (in Bacon's sense) were sufficient.[21]

During the two centuries following, it became increasingly apparent that the divine interventions of Newton were unnecessary; and, accordingly, that there was no scope for arguing to God's existence from their indispensability. Leibniz' own belief in the conservation of energy was one of the principles which enabled later physicists to regard the world as a clock which did not run down: and eventually Laplace was able to discard God as an explanatory hypothesis within physics. Thus Leibniz' methodological principle was accepted into the Newtonian worldview: an adequate system of physics need not introduce the activity of God subsequent to Creation. And if the Newtonians wanted to leave room for divine revelation, Leibniz could reply that revelation can occur in the ordinary course of nature; and that it is a superior doctrine of providence in which the need for modification is foreseen and prevented.[22] There was no need to ascribe whole classes of events or kinds of phenomena directly to God.

B. The Initial Distribution of Matter.

In 1692 Bentley, who had been appointed to give the first Boyle lectures, consulted Newton on whether, supposing a uniform distribution of matter through the universe at any finitely distant past time, the planets and stars could by any known force have attained their current motion and positions, as the Cartesians supposed. Newton performed the necessary calculations and replied in the negative. It seemed to follow that God had distributed the stars and planets in a way compatible with their present positions,[23] and also supplied suitable initial inertia,[24] or the present configuration of the world would be unexplained. But this reasoning assumed that the world had an origin in time.

Now if we imagine a Laplacean universe, in which the

---

[21] See further Robert H. Hurlbutt, 'Hume, Newton and the Design Argument', University of Nebraska Press, Lincoln, 1965.

[22] A statement of Robert Boyle to similar effect, from his 'Inquiry into the vulgar notion of nature' is quoted by Anthony Collins (published in 'Letter to Dodwell, Etc.', London, 1731) in reply to Samuel Clarke's view that gravity cannot be a property of matter and therefore implies divine agency.

[23] First letter to Bentley: 'Correspondence', Vol. III, p. 234.

[24] Second letter to Bentley: 'Correspondence', Vol. III, pp. 239-40.

behaviour of every particle can be rigorously predicted from initial conditions and natural laws, at least two teleological questions are possible, one concerning whether design is evidenced by the natural laws, the other concerning whether the initial conditions were themselves chosen. That the latter question arises is not at once obvious, for each set of initial conditions would themselves be explicable by the natural laws and by yet earlier conditions of particles. Nevertheless, if such a universe had a finite temporal origin a teleological question certainly could arise about the very first positions and qualities of the particles concerned: for only one set of such conditions would be physically compatible with the present conditions of the universe, and yet myriads of other sets of starting conditions would have been logically possible instead.

Thus in the case of Newton's supernatural explanation of the initial distribution of matter appeal is made with apparent consistency to divine agency *in creation*. Moreover it is an appeal which could have been, though was not, used to vindicate Newton's belief in God as Lord of History. For even a Creator resolved to endow matter with universal regularities still has to choose between alternative initial distributions of matter. Moreover, without violations of natural laws, some initial distributions would be more likely than others to produce in the ordinary course of events natural coincidences which would bespeak the benevolence of the Creator, and some of which would convey revelations of his will. Thus a Creator who selected both the most appropriate laws of nature and the most appropriate initial conditions for the benefit of and for the revelation of his will to his creatures would without doubt be Lord of History, even without infringing the ordinary course of events.

But what if the world had no origin in time? Leibniz's belief in its spatial infinity (and in its internal self-sufficiency) disturbed Clarke, because it seemed to make the world independent of a Creator altogether. Leibniz himself probably believed what he suggests in his Fifth Reply at paragraph 74,[25] namely that the world had a finite origin but has an infinite duration thereafter; for his belief in its growth in perfection through time suggests a finite beginning. Nevertheless Leibniz points out that it is unnecessary even from the point of view of theology to maintain that the world has a finite past, and thus to set a dogmatic limit to the investigations of physics. "However", he says,

"those who have admitted the eternity of the world, or at least, (as some famous divines have done) the possibility of its

---

[25] Alexander, p. 80.

eternity; did not, for all that, deny its dependence upon God."[26]

And Leibniz is right. Even the existence of a sempiternal world is a contingency; so the Cosmological Argument does not require the world to have a chronological first point. Yet the reluctance of Newton to imagine a sempiternal world and of Clarke to admit the possibility is easy to understand. For the contrary assumption allows theologians to ask why it began at one time rather than another, and also to seek an explanation of the initial distribution of matter as Newton did. But if the world's past is endless, then almost any distribution of matter and energy (and therefore of inertia) could result after a long enough time in the present positions of material particles. Even Descartes did not (as we have seen) accept the world's infinity, which for him would have meant its independence and perfection, despite Newton's charge that he did. (See Section 2.) Thus Newton was in fact supplying a supernatural explanation for distributions of matter in the finite past which needed no such explanation: and by the time people became prepared to ascribe sempiternity to the material universe, such physical theology was no longer possible.

As for Clarke, he shared the traditional belief that what is infinite is self-explanatory: and this seemed to show that if the world was infinite, God had no choice in creating it, that he would have *had* to make it infinite, or perhaps that a Creator would be redundant.[27] These views led to physical theology of the other sort: since only God is self-explanatory and infinite, Clarke inferred that the world, not being self-explanatory, must be finite. And such a conclusion was particularly unfortunate for theology: for future generations endorsed his reasoning and concluded that since the world is probably infinite, it is therefore both internally and externally self-explanatory. (Hume's Philo, for example, takes seriously such a view.) Thus the gradual refutation of physical theology seemed to mean the refutation of theology in general.

Once again it was Leibniz's theological reasoning which pointed to the defect in physical theology. By now we have seen how the attempts of the Newtonians to find room for natural agency in a world the movements of whose particles are explicable by natural laws one by one came adrift. Theology is unnecessary for the explanation of apparent order in particular creatures or of particular universal phenomena like gravitation: nor is God needed to explain *where* particles came into existence, since the

---

[26] Ibid., para. 75, p. 80.
[27] Clarke, Fourth Replies, para. 21, p. 50: Fifth Replies, paras. 73-75, p. 108.

world may have an infinite past. Unless miracles occur, all the likely gaps for God to fill have been plugged; or would have been, had not Leibniz himself supplied others: see the next two Sections.

All that remains of the Newtonian arguments is the teleological question about the laws of nature as a whole, (to be separately discussed). Yet it would be unfair not to point out that there remains also another teleological question, the counterpart for a temporally infinite world of Bentley's question about the positions of matter in a temporally finite one. For even in an infinite world with exceptionless natural laws, the entire trajectory through space and time of each particle could have been different: thus the set of the trajectories in space and time of material particles itself raises the possibility of intelligent preference and design, if these trajectories are more beneficial, granted the same laws, than others would have been.

Section 4: Physics Deduced From Theology: Leibniz

Leibniz, the critic of physical theology among the Newtonians, himself derives certain findings about the world from the character of God in the form of his 'Principle of Perfection' and of his application of it: and this time it is Clarke who protests. Leibniz' 'Principle of Perfection' presides over contingent truths in his system rather as the 'Principle of Identity or Contradiction' presides over necessary truths. With Nicholas Rescher[28] whose account of Leibniz I follow, I would distinguish from these two principles the architectonic 'Principle of Sufficient Reason', which maintains that for every truth there is a reason such that every true proposition is analytic. Now the 'Principle of Sufficient Reason' is impartial as between sorts of reasons, so long as the reasons are themselves derivable from the notion of some substance. The 'Principle of Perfection', which tells us the sort of reason to look for in the area of contingent truths, is thus independent of the Principle of Sufficient Reason, being not a logical principle, but (in Rescher's words) "a fundamentally ethical" one (p. 29). Leibniz's point is that God, in choosing between possible worlds, chooses the world with most perfection. And perfection involves both maximal simplicity of laws and maximal variety of substances.

---

[28] 'The Philosophy of Leibniz', Englewood Cliffs, New Jersey, 1967.

In part, Leibniz was intent on maintaining the objectivity of the world's beauty. As against Descartes and others who "say that things are not good by any rule of goodness, but only by the will of God",[29] Leibniz holds that the world is not merely what God happened arbitrarily to create, but that it was created on the principle of bringing the greatest degree of perfection into existence. Like Cudworth (see Chapter 3) Leibniz insists on the conceptual independence of the notion of goodness from the notion of God, and holds that God can only seriously be held to be good if in creation his purposes are characterisable as good. This involves Leibniz in holding that God could have chosen otherwise, and that the proposition "God is good' is contingent: and if so, many propositions about creatures will also be contingent. (Leibniz also, of course, holds that by means of an infinite analysis possible only to God "God is good" and every other contingent proposition will turn out to be analytic, in accordance with the Principle of Sufficient Reason. Yet the apparent difficulty need not detain us: for Leibniz' belief in the contingency of the way the world is involves the need for empirical science rather than (exclusively) *a priori* science, and this belief if grounded in the contingency of God's goodness.)

But this is not all that the Principle of Perfection involves. It also involves a claim to understand God's purposes, and to make possible the knowledge of what counts as perfection. For example, substances which 'mirror' or 'perceive' more clearly than others are more 'perfect' (Rescher pp. 27f). Further, a universe whose substances manifest varying degrees of perfection is more perfect because more varied than one whose substances have a similar degree of perfection. (Rescher, pp. 28, 50, 51.) Accordingly there are no gaps in nature, for a world in which there was no substance of some determinate degree of perfection would be comparatively imperfect, and would not have been created.

The Principle of Perfection has other corollaries. One is that there cannot be indistinguishable items in different zones of space: and this means that God would not choose to create any two objects alike. And it would immediately follow from this that atomism is false:[30] for the atomists, such as Boyle, Newton and Clarke, held that atoms were qualitatively identical.

There is another reason why atomism must be false, issuing from the same Principle; and that is that God would have no reason to make particles of matter indivisible below any particular

---

[29] 'Die philosophischen Schriften von G. W. Leibniz', edited C. I. Gerhardt, 7 Volumes (Berlin, 1875-1890), Volume 7, p. 278; quoted by Rescher at p. 29.

[30] Leibniz 5, paragraph 22, p. 61 (Alexander).

order of magnitude rather than any other. Granted the logical possibility of particles being of any size whatever, the most perfect universe would be likely to contain particles of every size and shape. Now this line of argument may point to a serious defect in atomism. An atomist would argue that there must be particles of *some* minimal size preserved in every change, or all change would be impossible. And an opponent could reply that even if particles of *some* minimal size must persist in every change, there need not be the same minimal size of particle persisting through every change. The scientific argument, corresponding to Leibniz' theological one, would involve the enquiry why any particular magnitude of particle should be fundamental and particles of that particular magnitude physically indivisible.[31] Nevertheless Leibniz' argument is a matter of physical theology, and could be answered as such. For were God choosing between different minimal magnitudes for the particles of his world, the difference being indifferent to his purpose, Leibniz seems to hold he would be unable to make any choice for lack of a principle of preference. But if one size were as good as another, why should God be barred from selecting at random?

A similar argument actually occurs in the correspondence between Clarke and Leibniz over whether God could make two exactly similar cubes. Leibniz holds[32] that he could not: if the full picture were taken into account they would turn out not to be exactly similar. But the only difference in Clarke's example is that of position, and Leibniz is committed, believing as he did that space is not fundamentally real, to count this as no difference.

Now certainly Clarke confused the issue, for he introduced the possibility of God locating some particle arbitrarily[33] without mentioning the context in which such an act would be plausible, namely one in which God had some purpose which would be equally well served whether the particle was in one position or the other. Thus presented, Clarke's idea reasonably enough aroused Leibniz' disapproval, constituting, as it seemed, a genuine breach of the Principle of Sufficient Reason. Leibniz, however, failed to give way even when Clarke specified the example more clearly. For a God who was looking for perfection would allegedly not act as Clarke contended, even if it involved his not acting at all.[34] No universe would include constituents differing only in time or

---

[31] Leibniz 4, Postscript.
[32] Leibniz 5, para. 66, p. 78 (Alexander). Cf. Clarke 4, para. 18, pp. 49-50.
[33] Clarke 2, para. 1b, p. 21 (Alexander).
[34] Leibniz 4, para. 3, p. 37 (Alexander).

position. (And, on the other hand, all mutually different compossible substances must actually have been created.)

Here Leibniz is indulging in the first kind of physical theology mentioned above: for from a purported piece of knowledge about God's character he set bounds to the physical world. Leibniz uses the Principle of Perfection to determine which substances have been created, how many of each, and how small they might be; he also uses it to settle the extent of the matter created; which must clearly be infinite, for there could be no reason to decide between one arbitrary finite total and another.[35] The same reasoning is also used to deny that there is a void, and to assert the world to be a plenum.

"I lay it down as a principle, that every perfection, which God could impart to things without derogating from their other perfections, has actually been imparted to them. Now let us consider a space wholly empty. God could have placed matter in it, without derogating in any respect from all other things: therefore he has actually placed some matter in that space: therefore there is no space wholly empty: therefore all is full. The same argument proves that there is no corpuscle, but what is subdivided.[36]

Even Leibniz' principle of the conservation of *vis viva*, or energy, is probably so derived,[37] for God would have no reason for creating a world whose resources of motion decreased and had to be replenished. (Both here and in his opposition to atomism the parallelism with Descartes is notable. Nor is the style of reasoning dissimilar, at least in the present case.)

Clarke's assessment of Leibniz' view that God's wisdom would eschew the creation of indiscernibles seems the correct one.

"But how does he know, it could not be wise for God to do so? Can he prove that it is not possible God may have wise reasons for creating many parts of matter exactly alike in different part of the universe?"[38]

---

[35] Leibniz 4, para. 21, pp. 39f. "There is no possible reason, that can limit the quantity of matter; and therefore such limitaion can have no place."

[36] Leibniz 4, Postscript, p. 44.

[37] See Leibniz 1, paragraph 3b, p. 12 and the surrounding text. Also his 'Principles of Nature and of Grace, Founded on Reason', section 11. In 'Leibniz' Philosophical Writings', Everyman's Library, London 1934, p. 27.

[38] Clarke 5, paras. 21-25, p. 100 (Alexander). A. O. Lovejoy, in 'The Great Chain of Being', Harvard U.P., Cambridge, Mass., 1936, agrees that Leibniz' opponents had the better case over there being some features of the world not chosen for reasons which exclude all alternatives.

And these remarks of Clarke's are a typical instance of secularisation. Physics must be left to its own procedure and observations for deciding whether many objects of the same sort exist within the created world, and whether there is a void; and even metaphysical questions, like that of the finitude or infinity of matter, which observation could never in principle decide, are still not to be settled on theological grounds: for if we are uninformed about the purposes of God's wisdom, we cannot form conclusions about the nature of his handiwork except on the one hand by studying it and on the other hand by discovering which theories best fit our observations. We may be in a position to argue from the world to its Creator's purposes, but not *vice versa*.

Leibniz believed that we could so argue, but this involves questionable theology. For Leibniz claims to know that a Creator who did what he did for reasons would be bound to prefer diversity and to avoid making creatures indiscernible (whatever their place and time). But he does not pretend to have *a posteriori* grounds for such knowledge: rather he sets limits on God's possible purposes *a priori*.

Here Clarke's retort asserts the autonomy of natural philosophy on the best of theological grounds, namely the unknowability of the sum of God's purposes, grounds urged earlier by Descartes (see Chapter 1 Section 2.) Only if theological deductions could be excluded from science as effectively as Leibniz had argued against the Newtonian divine interventions was the progress of scientific explanation likely to proceed unimpeded.

But the merits of Leibniz' view should also be mentioned. In the 'Discourse on Metaphysics' he is in part opposing the dogmatic assumption that if the natural world is explainable by natural laws, no place is left for talk of God's purposes or goodness. For we can still in fact ask why any natural laws apply to phenomena, and why these particular ones do rather than alternative possibilities. Yet Leibniz would have been better advised to argue in this direction, from the world to God, than to imagine that any particular predictions, of any degree of reliability, could be made by arguing in the reverse direction.

Section 5: The Supernatural Explanation of Minds

Granted the Cartesian doctrine that minds are independent immaterial substances which interact with bodies, apparently insoluble problems cluster around the manner of this apparently impossible interaction of the material and mechanical on the one hand and the immaterial and unextended on the other.[39] This problem a succession of his followers, culminating in Mallebranche, attempted to solve by invoking divine agency, a move for which Descartes, immune as he was from explanations by final causes, nevertheless supplies a precedent.

For in arguing to the existence of God in his Third Meditation, Descartes alleges that the continued existence of a mind from moment to moment stood in need of explanation by divine agency,[40] and that in general the existence of finite substances involves a new creation in each successive instant. This theory seems to involve the denial of the powers of creatures to persist in being through finite stretches of time, and also to imply a view of causation, or at least of causation through time, by which the connection between any cause and any of its effects is divine agency. It also seems to deny the possibility of real relations between any pair of created substances over any finite period of time. And, in that commonsense assumes what theology asserts, that God can create objects able to persist through time, this is a redundant appeal to divine causality, and thus a case of physical theology.

It was, however, no great leap from this theory of Descartes to that of Occasionalism, on which there is no real connection between intentions and bodily movements, or between the impact of objects on sensory organs and the feeling of sensations. Rather God supplies people's minds with coherent sets of ideas so that, for example, steady sensations follow regular sequences of impacts on the eyes and ears of people's bodies. And even in the physical world, the relation of cause and effect was again regarded as a relation between ideas supplied to our minds by God.

This drastic solution had one advantage over the current Aristotelian theory (as described by Pierre Bayle in the article 'Rosarius' in the second edition on his dictionary). This theory, says Bayle, was "a *way of influence* of the body upon the soul and the soul upon the body."[41] By this theory, soul and body were each substances, and acted upon each other. (I am not ascribing to

---

[39] Descartes, in admitting that this interaction cannot be understood (Haldane and Ross I, p. 295), himself prepared the way for a supernatural explanation.
[40] Haldane and Ross I, p. 168.
[41] Quoted by A. M. Farrer, Leibniz' 'Theodicy,' p. 38.

Aristotle the view that the soul is a substance but only to his Seventeenth Century followers.) And the problem which the Aristotelians, like Descartes, could not satisfactorily answer was how substances so essentially dissimilar could interact at all. This problem the Occasionalists could answer, but only at the expense of abandoning natural explanations: their world was inexplicable unless divine agency intervened at every juncture.

Bayle, himself a Cartesian who sympathised with Occasionalism, protests at the objection that this system "brings in God acting by a miracle," (a phrase Leibniz had employed against it) "*Deum ex machina,* in the mutual dependence of the body and soul: for since God does only intervene according to general laws, he cannot be said to act in an extraordinary manner."

In reply to Bayle, as elsewhere to Clarke, Leibniz resorts to his sense of miracle in terms of what is only supernaturally explicable. Farrer summarises his reply as follows:

> "Cartesianism in the form of occasionalism *does* involve miracle, for though God is said by it to act according to laws in conforming body and mind to one another, he thereby causes them to act beyond their natural capacities."

Leibniz is at any rate right to hold that occasionalism treats the interactions of minds and bodies as explicable only by divine agency.

Occasionalism is thus a paradigm of physical theology, even though it is a theory in metaphysics and not in physics. It implies God could not create objects able to persist for any finite period without direct assistance, or embodied thinking beings able to initiate or perceive changes without special intervention. And sooner than this a revision was called for either in the philosophy of mind or in the philosophy of matter.

Leibniz himself, however, did not despair of a solution. His own solution was the doctrine of Preestablished Harmony. Built into the notion of every simple substance was a full description of the history of the universe including all other substances. Each substance was therefore able to mirror or "perceive" all others from its own point of view. No substance influenced any other causally, but every change in one substance was accompanied by a corresponding perception in all the others. Some of these simple, extensionless substances occupied dominant positions among their kind and constituted souls in animals and the spirit in man. Each simple substance or "monad" was made at Creation to answer to its complete description, and thus within history there was at every juncture a complete harmoney between the perceptions of different individuals.

Body itself was not fundamentally real, as extension cannot be composed of extensionless units. Nevertheless extension entered into the perceptions of the monads, nor was it illusory, for it is a phenomenon 'well founded' upon the monads and their positions. And the material world itself obeys strict mechanical laws. But there is no possible discrepancy between the movements of a body and the mind of the man whose body it is: for the behaviour of the mind in accordance with its own desires has been foreseen at Creation and the behaviour of matter so ordered as exactly to fit the operations of mind. The pre-established harmony is thus applied to the mind-body problem, in a manner which avoids God's constant intervention.

Leibniz sees in this doctrine the further merit of an extra proof of God's existence: "none but God, viz. the universal cause, can produce such a harmony of things."[42] But this very devising of a new argument for God's existence, from the only envisageable solution of a problem about one set of phenomena among others, puts us on our guard. Might not Leibniz himself be indulging in 'physical theology' (of our second kind) at htis point? Indeed Clarke accused him on introducing a miracle.[43] Leibniz' reply[44] is that the harmony between the soul and the body "is not a perpetual miracle; but the effect or consequence of an original miracle, worked at the creation of things; as all natural things are."

To the charge that his doctrine is miraculous, Leibniz has two possible replies. Like the Occasionalists he can point out that the operation of his Harmony is everyday, familiar and therefore natural. And this reply on its own rebuts the charge of a miracle, but only at the expense of opening the way to a charge of supernatural intervention. But to this charge Leibniz would make his second reply, that there is no supernatural intervention in his theory, for the only agency of God is at the stage of the original Cration. And this agency may be called supernatural, or even, on Leibniz' definition of miracle ('whatever exceeds the powers of natural objects') miraculous: but it is in no sense intervention, and accordingly not objectionable in the way in which the interventions of God in some of his opponents' theories were objectionable. In short, Leibniz would claim that he was introducing theology neither into physics nor psychology, but only into his account of Creation, where it is indispensable.

Nevertheless it is precisely at the Pre-established Harmony of Leibniz that A. M. Farrer devised and directed the phrase 'physical

---

[42] Fifth Paper to Clarke, para. 87.
[43] Clarke 4, para. 31; p. 51.
[44] Leibniz 5, paras. 89 and 90, p. 85.

theology'. Farrer holds on the one hand that, granted monads represent, (and represent each other representing), the world can only be explained if a Harmony was established from Creation onwards. And on the other hand "When Leibniz discovered that his system of mutual representations needed to be pre-established, he ought to have seen that he had come up a cul-de-sac and backed out; he ought not to have said, 'With the help of God I will leap over the wall.'" This point is, perhaps, as follows. Granted Leibniz' understanding of the world as a system of mutually representing monads, his introduction of divine agency was just as reasonable as Aquinas' introduction of a First Cause, a Cause which left nature to pursue its natural course but nevertheless constituted its supernatural ground. But this system itself was intended to explain or make sense of the character of our world, and it is this world, which, according to Leibniz, could not proceed without a certain sort of divine concurrence. Leibniz should, accordingly, instead of finding a proof of God in his system, have looked for another system wherein phenomena might have been explicable by natural agencies alone; however difficult this was for one who both lived at the turn of the Eighteenth Century and accepted the substantiality of the soul.

I therefore endorse the judgement of Farrer. Of course were Leibniz' system the only way of making sense of the world, then we should have to conclude with him that in creation God actually does bring about the existence of mutually harmonised monads: that the only intelligible world is of this character and no other. Leibniz' system certainly has certain advantages over the rival theories of dualism and occasionalism, particularly with respect to the will. Since however we could never identify people's minds or their constituent monads independently of their bodies, the very coherence of all three theories is open to question. Perhaps Leibniz' belief in the freedom of the will and the mechanical nature of matter would have prevented his ever imagining that human minds are necessarily embodied: yet this remains a viable alternative theory of mind.

Thus Clarke, though misguided in accusing Leibniz of miracle — (for one thing the Harmony of Leibniz is not one event but the explanation of many) — had a sound instinct in attacking the way in which a supernatural explanation was introduced. The suggestion that there is a supernatural explanation for all purposive behaviour and all perception would have stunted the science of human and animal psychology in its infancy and undermined the possibility of real as opposed to illusory causal explanations throughout the social sciences. Not that Clarke had a superior theory to propose, except that of dualism supported by the analogy of God's creation of matter.[45] But even this solution allowed a causality of their own to people and their purposes, and acknowledged the possibility of the creation of such agents by God.

As before, the assault on physical theology was necessary both for science to proceed unhampered, for the hopes of Bacon that its understanding would increase for the benefit of man to be capable of fulfilment, and for the theistic understanding of God to remain unsullied.

Section 6: Science and Miracles

A. The Coherence of 'Miracle'.

Theologians in our period were interested in miracles either as evidence of theological doctrines (thus Locke)[46] or as vehicles of divine grace (thus Leibniz)[47] or revelation (thus Butler),[48] or as all three (as in Paley).[49] But the rise of science led thinkers of a more secularising turn to question the very possibility of miracles (thus Spinoza) or of our having adequate grounds for believing in them, (the point made by Hume.) Such questions concerned events not merely unusual (Clarke's sense of miracle) but also which violated laws of nature: and if an event was inexplicable by physical laws it was clearly either inexplicable (period) or explicable by supernatural agency alone. This is the point Leibniz makes when he defines 'miracle' as an event which 'surpasses all creaturely powers'[47] (even though his terminology is better suited to Aristotelian than to modern scientific method.)

Accordingly I shall use 'miracle' in a somewhat narrow sense, on which a miracle is an event both which violates laws of nature and which is explicable, if at all, by supernatural agency. The term 'miracle' is often used more broadly, e.g. of very unusual events like coincidences explainable by natural laws: but there was no methodological ground for questioning the possibility of events such as *these*. It is also often used more narrowly, in that an event is only a miracle if it also has religious significance, e.g. by testifying to divine providence: but the critics of miracles did not in fact show

---

[45] Fifth Reply, to Leibniz 5, 110-116. Alexander, p. 116.
[46] 'Essay on Miracles'.
[47] See above, Section 3A.
[48] 'Analogy' in 'Works' edited by W. E. Gladstone (2 Vols.), Oxford, 1896.
[49] 'A View of the Evidences of Christianity', 1794, 'Prefactory Considerations'.

more than casual interest in the difficulties concerning the extra evidence needed for identifying events like these.[50] What interested them was whether miracles in the above sense were evidence for God's existence and/or activity, or were the media of divine revelation. And, since it was rarely denied that every event was in *some* way explicable, miracles, if miracles there were, were regarded as necessarily evidence of some supernatural agency, even if not that of the Christian God. Objections therefore concerned whether miracles did, or could occur. And the latter question is a conceptual one, posed in our period by Spinoza.

In the Appendix to Part One of his 'Ethics', Spinoza rejects explanations which take refuge in the will of God as avowals of ignorance.[51] All events proceed from the necessity of the divine nature (see Chapter 1 Section 4) and are therefore to be explained by their natural causes. With 'the removal of ignorance', wonder at purported miracles will lapse, to the discomfiture of those who profit by it. To these themes Spinoza returns in Chapter VI of the Theologico-Political Treatise, 'Of Miracles'.[52] There he purports to demonstrate the impossibility of miracles as follows:

> "Now as nothing is necessarily true save only by Divine decree, it is plain that the universal laws of nature are decrees of God following from the necessity and perfection of the Divine nature. Hence any event happening in nature which contravened nature's universal laws, would necessarily also contravene the Divine decree, nature and understanding; or if anyone asserted that God acts in contravention to the laws of nature, he, *ipso facto*, would be compelled to assert that God acted against his own nature — an evident absurdity."

Therefore nothing can contravene natural laws, which are both eternal and immutable and therefore exceptionless. Or, in more modern terms, the notion of miracle is incoherent.

Now granted Spinoza's assumptions his reasoning is successful. If however natural events are describable only by contingent statements, or if such statements are not deducible from the general attributes of nature, must natural laws remain exceptionless? It is at first sight plausible that Spinoza's conclusion will stand even without his rationalism: for if an event is irreconcilable with current descriptions of the laws of nature, this is often thought

---

[50] These observations are much beholden to Richard Swinburne's 'The Concept of Miracle', London, 1970, a work which has influenced much of this Section.

[51] 'The Chief Works of Spinoza', Translated by R. H. M. Elwes, London, 1891, Vol. II, pp. 78-9.

[52] Ibid., Vol. I.

merely to show the inadequacy of those descriptions. To put it another way, nothing that actually happens is inconsistent with the laws of nature, for laws of nature precisely concern whatever actually happens.

But this is to assume that whatever happens is predictable and regular; i.e. it is to legislate against the possibility of non-repeatable events, events which would not recur however similar the circumstances, and whose occurrence is itself therefore unpredictable by general laws however elaborate. Now it has been pointed out above that both Bacon and Galileo, despite their differences of emphasis, assumed that from like conditions like events arise. Perhaps this is true, but is it *necessarily* true? For if no law of nature could be found on which some observed event which conflicted with existing formulations of laws of nature could be predicted, yet a very wide range of phenomena were predictable, and in a simple and elegant way, from one of these formulations, we should say that the event was a counter-instance of the laws of nature because unrepeatable. Both the event and the formulation of natural law would of course need to be particularly well attested before we were prepared to acknowledge a case of such an unrepeatable event: nevertheless such an event is not conceptually impossible. Spinoza's belief to the contrary is another instance of the secularism by which he denies the contingency of statements both about God's will and about natural objects.

B. Miracles as Evidence of Divine Agency.

Spinoza goes on to claim that so-called "miracles" are in fact events *so far* unexplained, and as such of no value as evidence of divine agency. But if miracles (in our above sense) are after all possible, there may still be miraculous evidence for theological tenets. Only however, if we have evidence sufficient for believing that there are miracles: and this is what is questioned by Hume in his 'Enquiry Concerning Human Understanding'.[53]

Hume's point is that the evidence required to establish natural laws must be of a very high order — what he calls 'firm and unalterable experience'. Thus very strong evidence indeed is required to establish the occurrence of an event not only unusual but so unusual as to constitute a counter-instance to what all the experimental and observational evidence supports. Indeed we should only have such evidence if the probability of the reliability of the witness or witnesses was greater than the probability, on the basis of all the evidence for the natural law, that the event was no exception to that law.

---

[53] Chapter X, 'Of Miracles': Selby-Bigge, pp. 109-131.

As Swinburne point out, this would involve the generalisation that witnesses of the sort of the witness to the alleged miracle are reliable being better confirmed, or more rigorous, or both, than the formulation of the law of nature itself. Hume seems to have regarded this state of affairs as itself impossible; but Swinburne argues cogently[54] that it is in principle possible that the evidence should be balanced this way, but very unlikely to occur, granted the difficulties of attaining well-grounded generalisations about classes of witnesses most of whose members lived in the past.

It should perhaps be explained why Hume's principle for the assessment of evidence is, thus modified, acceptable. It is sometimes alleged against Hume that, however constant the observational evidence for a particular formulation of natural law, a well-attested piece of counter-evidence will require that formulation to be revised. But the formulation will only be revised if events like the newly attested one can be predicted by a new formulation on which the old evidence can also be predicted. If phenomena like levitation could be predicted on revised natural laws together with the phenomena predicted on conventional laws of motion, then our formulations of natural law would indeed have to be revised. But there could be events which, because unrepeatable, were irreconcilable with natural law however adequately formulated: and it is to the evidence required for belief in such events that Hume's principle applies.

Thus to establish that an event is miraculous we need good grounds for believing that events of that sort are not subsumable under formulations of natural law, and extremely strong grounds indeed for believing that the witness to the alleged miracle was a reliable one. Further if it is independently required that an event must show supernatural agency in order to be a miracle (and it cannot be assumed that what is naturally inexplicable must be theologically explicable), we should need evidence that such an event was e.g. a response to a prayer, and preferably a prayer to a named deity. The combination of these requirements is certainly unlikely to be satisfied.

All this, however, supposes that we lack independent grounds for belief in a deity predisposed to reveal himself through miracles. Swinburne follows Paley in supposing that if we had such grounds, the burden of proof would be considerably lightened, both for the believer in the occurrence of miracles, and for the believer in the providential employment of particular miracles as vehicles of particular revelations. It seems to me that the burden of proof for those desiring to identify particular miracles would only

---

[54] See his chapter 4, 'Historical Evidence'.

be very slightly lifted: for they would still need equally strong evidence that a violation of a law of nature had occurred. The only proposition about miracles which it would be easier to establish would be the proposition that miracles *sometimes* occur; but to establish this would be of little help in identifying miracles and therefore of deriving revelatory information from them. For we might then be expectant with respect to miracles, but should still need all our critical acumen for the assessment of the scientific and historical evidence relative to particular claims.

Hume's argument in Part One of Chapter X of his first 'Enquiry' is thus not only a good instance of secularisation but a perfectly proper protest at the credulity of current religious believers and of their reluctance to apply the same sort of critical spirit to religious literature as empirical scientists bring to the study of nature. This is none the less true even if, in some of the factual arguments of Part Two of that Chapter Hume somewhat overreaches himself.

It remains of importance, however, to see how far either scientific methodology or the doctrine of creation has a bearing on the possibilities that God would, and that he does, choose to work miracles.

C. Miracles and Divine Order

What is here at stake is the truth of the (contingent) proposition that from like conditions like events arise, and its corollary that for every difference between phenomena otherwise similar there is in principle a general explanation. To put it another way, the working assumption of scientists is at stake that all events are susceptible of scientific explanation.

As has already been said, it is perfectly conceivable that this proposition is false. It could be that rain falls everywhere except at Cardiff on Tuesdays, when instead heavy drops of water remain suspended in the air: and this would be possible even if there were no special feature which explained this amazing difference between what is normal and what happens at Cardiff on Tuesdays. It could be that eggs can be cooked by whirling them in slings, but only by Babylonians. The question, however, is whether God would bring such irregular events about.

Here we cannot be confident that he would not. To be confident of this would be to embark upon physical theology. Yet we could still have stronger grounds for thinking that there is a God who would not than for thinking that there is a God who would; and this on the strength of the arguments for the existence of God. Thus if the teleological argument is successful and God desires and causes order on a universal scale, the God whose existence is thus disclosed is unlikely to produce miracles. Now this would merely be an academic issue were it likely on independent evidence that miracles have been correctly identified as such: for the more the observable world displays non-repeatable counter-instances to natural laws the weaker teleological reasoning from universal order in any case becomes. But as we have seen, it is unlikely that such violations of natural laws *have* been correctly identified. Thus without assuming as a necessary truth that from like conditions like events arise, we may well have evidence against God's being disposed to work miracles.

It is instructive here to note that religious apologists are ill-advised to argue both from the world's regularity to God and from miracles to God. For (on the current sense of miracle) the evidence of either argument is counter-evidence to the evidence adduced in the other. This was perhaps not fully realised by Paley; but it was seen by Spinoza who claims[55]

> "That God's nature and existence, and consequently His providence cannot be known from miracles, but that they can all be much better perceived from the fixed and immutable order of nature."

(By this passage Spinoza is using 'miracle' in the sense of 'event *as yet* unexplained': but his view would be the same on my sense of miracle, on the grounds that there are no miracles.) It is also likely that Hume's principle for the assessing of evidence for miracles not only makes it unlikely that anyone can argue successfully from miracles to God, but also that it makes slightly stronger than Hume believed the grounds of the teleological argument, which Hume also criticises.[56]

May we not, however, have evidence supporting the belief that God is disposed to produce miracles? May there not, as Leibniz held, be "wants of grace" which can, as Paley believed, be only thus supplied? Again no confident conclusion is possible, but the following considerations are of relevance.

(1) The "wants of grace" in Paley's view depend on men's salvation hanging on their holding certain beliefs only likely to be held if they are in receipt of certain information. But this tenet is itself in need of independent support.

(2) Even if God desires to convey information through particular events, these events must be recognisable as acts of God,

---

[55] Ibid.
[56] 'Dialogues Concerning Natural Religion'. See Chapter 6, Section 1.

if the purpose of God is to be accomplished. But the recognition of violations of laws of nature is, on rational standards, unlikely to occur at all often, and is at all times hazardous in the extreme.

(3) God could supply the "wants of grace", as far as they concern men's well-being, by a less disorderly means, namely by so selecting the space-time trajectories of material bodies as to conduce to human well-being at the same time as complying with the natural laws of his choice. God would then work through coincidences rather than miracles.

(4) God could also work through the natural course of events by creating in mankind enough intelligence to discover and teach one another wherein their well-being as persons consists. In this way revelations about both ethics and salvation could be entirely non-miraculous.

(5) If God really desires men to develop their capacity to choose between alternative actions and ways of life (and if he does not, he is to blame for *moral evil*), he will be disposed to create an environment regular enough to facilitate choices. The more miracles there are, the less regular will men's environment be. And if this reasoning is valid, God will be aware that men will not believe in his goodness unless he refrains from producing more than very few miracles. (This reasoning, however, assumes God's goodness and his desire that men should believe in it: the former tenet will receive separate discussion in the Section on Theodicy, Chapter 6, Section 2.)

Such evidence as there is, then, seems to support the belief that God would not be disposed to produce miracles, or, if he were so disposed, to produce very few. And this is a weak confirmation of the underlying assumption made by working scientists. Nevertheless the main evidence for their assumption must be observational; for it is a contingent belief whose probability depends on the strength or weakness of the evidence that violations of laws of nature actually occur.

D. Conclusions.

If the above is correct it would be proper to say that Hume was opposing physical theology; in that to resort to supernatural explanations of events which his principle for the assessment of evidence does not allow us to regard as counter-instances to laws of nature is to despair of physical explanations and do theology where physics, or another of the natural sciences, is appropriate. Yet Spinoza's denial that there could be miracles is also physical theology, though of the first sort: for Spinoza derives the necessary regularity of all events from the nature of God. The position of Leibniz was, in effect, a reply to this purported derivation: for if God is free in creating, then other worlds were possible; so even if all actual events are regular they could have been otherwise, while the freedom of God means that we cannot even rule out the possibility of miracles. (Unfortunately Leibniz replaces Spinoza's derivation with one of his own, by which the created order is demonstrably maximally diverse and minimally repetitious.)

Section 6 also suggests that we lack the evidence needed to affirm that any particular events are miraculous in character, even if perhaps miracles sometimes occur: and further that, as Boyle held (see Section 3), a God responsible for the order which natural science has been able to describe is unlikely to infringe his own laws (and that even the exigencies of revelation are unlikely to constrain him to do so). Thus the basic assumption of science, that from like conditions like events arise, is a proposition against the truth of which, quantum physics notwithstanding, there is little evidence, even though no amount of favourable evidence would establish its truth to the point of certainty.

It may be objected that many scientific laws are probabilistic and therefore do not concern what invariably happens. Now clearly a law about the half-life of uranium is not infringed if some uranium remains intact after the time specified: though we may one day discover why some uranium atoms outlive others. But if the intact uranium suddenly changed not into lead but into chlorine and floated away into the clouds, the law would be infringed. For *any* law entails that a great many eventualities invariably fail to happen, and no law is compatible with every possible event. It follows that counterinstances to probabilistic laws are perfectly possible, (and could be miraculous). Such laws do not relate that such-and-such usually happens, but anything else can instead. Rather they relate what must invariably happen, nature being as it is, to a fixed proportion of items of a particular sort. So the objection is inconclusive.

In the course of the chapter as a whole, several significant kinds of physical theology have been investigated as in the thought of Descartes and, more particularly, Newton and Leibniz. The physical theology of the Newtonians most often took the form of resort to supernatural explanations when the ingenuity of the working physicist ran out, or where his theological *alter ego* wanted a niche for God's purposiveness to be displayed; whereas (at least within physics as opposed to metaphysics) both Descartes and Leibniz were more prone, as was the arch-rationalist Spinoza, to espouse the sort of physical theology which deduces propositions in physics from theology *a priori*.

The assessment of the assault on physical theology has brought out further the nature of the damage effected by physical theology both to the search of science and of theology for truth, damage whose preliminary diagnosis appeared in Section 1. Newton's belief in God's spatiality (discussed in Section 2) was of some advantage to physics, but deleterious to theology through failing to observe adequately the qualitative differences between Creator and creatures. It also issued in the physical theology of supernatural explanations discussed in Section 3.

Such explanations both derogate from God's wisdom (Section 3A); are occult in that the explanation allows of no predictions of new phenomena — a point relevant also to Leibniz' advocacy of even the most general teleological explanations in physics (Section 4); and neglect the possibility that future physicists may consolidate the phenomena thus explained, together with other phenomena, in a unifying physical theory, or may require for their theories a broader time span than is imaginable at the time of the supernatural explanation (Section 3B). Indeed the Newtonian belief in the world's temporal finitude is an example of the liability to physics his belief in God's unending duration was likely to be. The despair over physics shown by Newton's supernatural explanations was however paralleled by the equally premature despair of Leibniz over metaphysics in the matter of the Pre-established Harmony, despair of a sort equally liable to discourage the progress of science (Section 5).

On the other hand the *a priori* derivation of physics from theology in Descartes (Section 2), Spinoza (Section 6) and Leibniz (Section 4) involved a denial of the value of the very empirical procedure by which alone natural science made advances as an autonomous discipline; at the same time as implying a kind of knowledge about God unattainable by men. And whereas physical theology was an impediment to science, its demise (see Section 3B) was of course prone to discredit theology altogether.

Thus secular protests made in the name of science were frequently in keeping with theology and quite often required by it, quite apart from the extent to which a religion which promises the coming of mature humanity (Galatians 4) requires the unstinted exercise of rationality. Arguments for God's existence or agency from gaps in scientific knowledge must be rejected for the reasons explained, as must other theological intrusions into areas proper to scientific method.

At the same time further reasons have been given in Section 6 in support of the contingency both of observable regularity in general and of observable regularities in particular, a contingency in any case implied by the doctrine of creation.

98 THE ARGUMENT FROM ORDER UNASSAILED

Further, although propositions about God were rightly excluded from the explanatory theory of natural science despite all the ingenuity shown in the attempt to include them, the teleological argument for God's existence from regularities pervading both time and space is not only undisturbed by the arguments of defenders of the autonomy of scientific method; its premiss about universal regularities has even been marginally supported, since the evidence for there being more than a very few counter-instances to natural laws is unimpressive.

CHAPTER 3

SELF-DETERMINATION

Section 1: Introductory

A. Theism and the Denial of Human Freedom Incompatible.

In this and the next chapter I shall discuss secular objections to doctrines concerning human capabilities, and to the derivation of morality from theology. Human nature is treated first. What humans are is relevant to how they should act and how they should be treated. Thus if humans flourish only by exercising a capacity to choose and discriminate, there is reason to think that they should not be treated as it might be justifiable to treat automata.

Now the view that people are capable of self-determination is arguably central to both Christian and Judaic theism. The reality of human self-determination must be maintained both for theistic ethics to be coherent and also for theistic understandings both of man and of God to be tenable. There follow four arguments for the incompatibility of the denial of human self-determination and certain crucial tenets of theism.

(1) The notions of desert and creativity have application only if agents are sometimes able to choose between alternative possible courses of action.

(2) The notion of sin and the cognate one of salvation from sin are similarly dependent on that of choice.

(3) If all evils are natural evils and no evils result from human choice, the enterprise of theodicy becomes impossible.

(4) If the notion of choice has no application to humans, we can give no sense to its application to God, or accordingly to the doctrine of creation.

(1) Unless we could sometimes in the same circumstances have acted otherwise than as we actually did[1], we are never *deserving* of praise or blame, however *useful* praise or blame may be[2]. For no alternatives were open to us, and we were unable not to do what we actually did. Nor can we choose or direct our path in life, become

---

[1] In the Eighteenth Century this implication of libertarianism was most clearly stated by Anthony Collins, in 'An Answer to Mr Clarke's Third Defence of his Letter to Dodwell', published in 'A Letter to Dodwell', (London, 1731) at p. 360.
[2] See to this effect e.g. Samuel Clarke, at 'Letter to Dodwell, Etc.,' p. 433.

creative, or indeed be expected to achieve any ethical standards. Goodness and badness of character would in fact be illusory.

(2) But this is not all. For the entire Judaeo-Christian scheme of sin and salvation is gravely imperilled, for no blame would be due for sin nor praise for virtue.

(3) Indeed such a scheme is more than imperilled. For if it is held that God rewards and punishes, yet humans deserve neither rewards nor punishments, then God is inescapably unjust. Nor is this all. Someone might be prepared at this juncture to withdraw the view that God rewards and punishes. But if God is the Creator of a world in which the evils apparently resulting from human choice cannot be set to the charge of humans, God must be chargeable with all these evils: he must not merely permit them, to allow of human self-development, but ordain them: or, in traditional language, they must stem not from his 'consequent' but from his 'antecedent' will. Now the problem of evil is large enough if it is raised over physical evil, i.e. evils not issuing from human choices. But the task of theodicy becomes altogether impossible if apparently moral evils are all in fact physical evil. Or, in short, the goodness of God becomes indefensible (unless, with Hobbes and Wittgenstein, we take God's goodness to *mean* whatever God ordains).

(4) And there is yet a further corollary for the doctrine of God. For our whole notion of God's freedom in creating is founded on an analogy with human choice. Had we no concept of choice we should have no idea what God's freedom could mean. Here some words of Austin Farrer are appropriate.[3]

> "But if we do not ourselves exercise real choice in any degree, then we have no clue to what any choice would be: and if so, we have no power of conceiving divine choice, either . . ."

To this it might be objected that we should on becoming determinists retain the concept of 'acting when one could have done otherwise' but regard it as uninstantiated except in the case of God. But determinists usually hold that there is no possibility of the application of such a concept to human action. Thus human action can no longer supply an analogy for the freedom of divine action, and we should no longer have any idea what it might be for God to act for reasons (or rationally), or to choose at all. We should in fact have to adopt a theory of the divine attributes something like that of Hobbes (see Chapter 1, Section 2), by which we have no idea whatever of their meaning, but employ them simply to

---

[3] From p. 32 of 'Editor's Introduction' to 'Theodicy' by G. W. Leibniz, edited by Farrer (London, 1951).

honour God or exalt him. (But, as Hobbes' critics noticed,[4] gibberish is no compliment to anyone.) Dr Farrer's view is thus justified: granted determinism, not only would God not be good, but we could not even intelligibly think of him as choosing anything — or, therefore, as creating (in the full sense of that term).

I conclude, therefore, that Christian theism and the denial of human self-determination are incompatible. To conclude thus is not of course to accept or reject either. Nevertheless it now becomes necessary to investigate the main reasons put forward by philosophers for denying that humans are self-determining. As elsewhere, the main reasons that have been put forward on this topic were voiced in the period under investigation, an age interested not only in predestination, fate and morality, but also in the possibilities of the new approach to science and in the critical spirit fostered by it. The next Section will therefore concern early modern arguments about the freedom of the will: but it is first necessary to discuss more fully what determinism involves.

B. What Determinism Involves.

It is sometimes claimed, on the one hand, that determinism cannot coherently be formulated: whereas it is also said, on the other hand, that determinism is no single thesis but several. To the former claim I grant that formulations like 'Every event has a cause' are unclear and unsatisfactory, while holding that a formulation incorporating the notion of prediction may be more successful. To the latter view I grant that denials of human self-determination have taken several forms from actualism (the thesis that nothing that happens could have not happened, and that there are no unfulfilled possibilities) to doctrines to the effect that all human action results from the unalterable will of God. Nevertheless denials of human self-determination usually hint at a common thesis, a thesis which, though not acknowledged by philosophers such as Spinoza, Hobbes and Priestley, is consonant with what they did acknowledge and would in all probability be endorsed by them were they alive today. This thesis is that for every human action, a prediction is possible of the kind that J. R. Lucas[5] has called 'procrustean'. According to Lucas the only predictions which pose a problem for freedom are as follows:

"(1) they are based on factors other than the agent's own

---

[4] Thus Leibniz, 'Reflexions on the Work that Mr Hobbes Published in English', at 'Theodicy', p. 403.
[5] In 'Freedom and Prediction', P.A.S. Supp., 1967, pp. 163-172.

intentions, actions or attitudes[6]; (2) they are infallible, in the sense that if the prediction failed to come true it would falsify a well-attested and well-worked-out scientific theory; (3) they are precise, and do not merely establish limits within which the predicted action must lie, but specify the agent's behaviour so completely that no other action on his part would satisfy that specification."

It is in fact in the predictions of physics that Lucas finds these features most nearly instantiated.

Determinism thus holds that for any event or action E_1, there is some set of scientifically discoverable causal laws L_1 and some set of directly or indirectly observable initial conditions C_1 such that from descriptions of L_1 and C_1 the nature of E_1 can be predictively deduced to whatever degree of specificity anyone may require. Thus granted C_1, E_1 *must* take the form it does. The sense of 'must' here is not that of logical necessity, (although philosophers like Spinoza, to whom natural and logical necessity were one, might have construed the definition of determinism given as involving logical necessity). 'Must' is rather the 'must' of empirical or natural necessity. The notion of natural necessity is perhaps best explained as the familiar and probably indispensable notion that it is, by pointing to its counterpart, the notion of natural possibility. Is it possible or not for me to jump to the moon? As far as logical possibility is concerned, it certainly is: no self-contradiction is involved in claiming that I could. Yet in fact I cannot, and this 'cannot' is the 'cannot' of natural impossibility. In terms of laws of nature I cannot because my so doing would be a counter-instance to the laws of gravitation: in more medieval terms, I cannot because so to do would be to exceed my natural powers. Ultimately, then, natural possibility and natural necessity concern what is possible and what is necessary, natural laws or natural powers being what they are. Thus ultimately the naturally necessary is necessary conditionally upon nature being what it is. (This notion of necessity is reducible into the notion of logical necessity, in that it will be logically necessary that, nature having some specific character, certain types of events should occur, whenever events of some other type occur.)

---

[6] Lucas modifies his account of the first requirement for procrustean predictions in his book 'The Freedom of the Will' (Oxford, 1970). This feature becomes the requirement that to be procrustean a prediction must be based on factors outside the agent's control. The modification allows psychological determinism to be presented more plausibly as involving procrustean predictions; and in order not to exclude Priestley's psychological necessitarianism from the varieties of determinism I shall adopt this modified account of procrustean predictions for present purposes.

DETERMINISM AND SELF-DETERMINATION INCOMPATIBLE

The same 'must' of natural necessity is that employed in the expression of scientific laws (though not in that of empirical generalisations): such laws are of the form "All A's *must* B", even though there is no self-contradiction involved in the thought of an A which does not B. Such expressions of laws may be taken as claiming that A's being A's, and nature being what it is, A's lack the power not to B, or cannot but B. Further, determinism in the sense introduced above may be interpreted as involving the assertion that within the course of nature the possibility of any event being otherwise, its antecedents remaining the same, does not arise. Again, miracles, even if envisaged as merely counter-instances to laws of nature, cannot (on determinism) occur: for, nature being what it is, all events are predictable, granted antecedent states of the universe, on the basis of causal laws which lack non-repeatable and repeatable counter-instances alike. Accordingly any apparent infringement of natural laws must in fact instantiate some natural law, probably under a more adequate formulation than yet arrived at. The determinist thus effectively holds that the character of every event, past, present and future, is governed by the set of natural laws under some discoverable description. (And the same applies to all bodily movements.)

In the same article Lucas argues, to my view rightly, that if determinism in this sense is true, no human action could ever be otherwise and agents are never free to choose between alternative possibilities. If my bodily movements could not be otherwise, and depend wholly on factors ultimately beyond my control, clearly I have no choice about what action I perform, even though actions do not reduce without remainder into bodily movements. For if my body cannot be moved otherwise, then clearly I lack the capacity to move it otherwise: and the mere fact that my movements can be interpreted under diverse action-descriptions does not make me any the more free.

Nor should it be supposed that propositions about human capacities such as the capacity to act otherwise can themselves be analysed into hypothetical propositions of the form (a), "Had circumstances been otherwise, he would have performed action x", much less (b) into ones like "Had his character been otherwise, he would have performed action x". For determinism is incompatible with our ordinary beliefs about human capacities. Professor M. R. Ayers has demonstrated the inadequacy of such analyses in his book 'The Refutation of Determinism'[7]. (a) That the former analysis miscarries can be shown as follows. 'p' entails 'p is possible', but not 'p, if q'. Thus when A performs action x, it

---
[7] M. R. Ayers, 'The Refutation of Determinism', Methuen, London, 1968.

does indeed follow that A can perform action *x*, but we cannot infer on these grounds alone that *under specific circumstances* A *will* perform action x. Thus 'Can . . .' does not entail 'will . . . if . . .', as the latter can be false when the former is true. (b) That the latter analysis miscarries is also shown by its circularity. For the notion of character is itself dependent on the notion of actions performed when the agent had the capacity to act otherwise; so the notion of capacity cannot without circularity be expounded in terms of that of character. Thus the notion of character cannot figure in "procrustean" predictions.

It may of course be granted that 'could have' sometimes simply means 'had the (unexercised) ability to'.[8] But when an agent has acted freely, 'he could have done otherwise', entails not only this but also that it was within his power to want to do otherwise: and this is incompatible with his action having been causally necessitated.

Accordingly, should considerations be advanced in the light of which determinism (in the above sense) is exhibited as true, then human agents are unfree to act otherwise; and Christian theism would have to be abandoned. It is my view that no considerations yet advanced show determinism to be true; and that, on the contrary, since there is such a thing as choice not all human actions are subject to any such natural necessity as it portrays. In short, I take determinism (as stated above) to be a metaphysical thesis which is significant but false, and I take its denial to be a metaphysical truth. But these views cannot be defended without an examination of the arguments for determinism actually produced.

Section 2: Determinists and Objections to Determinism

A. Three Necessitarians

Necessitarianism is the view that everything happens necessarily and that everyone has to do what he does.[9] (Thus all determinists are necessitarians, though not *vice versa*). In the Seventeenth Century necessitarianism assumed two forms, one grounded in

---

[8] Thus Robert Young, 'Compatibilism and Freedom', 'Mind', Vol. LXXIII, 1974, pp. 19-42: also in 'Freedom, Responsibility and God', Macmillan, London, 1975, ch. 11.

[9] This definition is supplied by Ayers, op. cit., at p. 6.

construing causality as a logical relation, the other in mechanism.
For Spinoza, as explained in Chapter 1 Section 4, whatever is true is deducible from the divine nature, which is itself necessary. Thus true statements of causal relations will be necessary truths, and no event could conceivable have been otherwise. Short, therefore, of a redefinition of freedom, humans have no freedom of choice; and indeed, properly speaking, they are not individuals at all, but modes of attributes of the one and only possible self-dependent cause, God; though their ability to persist in being as the same organised systems endows them with a measure of individuality.

I shall not be concerned with an evaluation of this kind of necessitarianism.[10] Spinoza's definition of 'substance' leaves no room for discussion of human freedom as ordinarily understood, since such discussion requires a vocabulary in which the individual people of everyday experience can be treated as substances to which predicates can be ascribed in their own right: while his rejection of all contingent understanding of causality again means that there are no terms he would accept in which one could argue with him about contingency at the level of everyday objects. (The consolation is that a consistent employment of his vocabulary might well fail to cope with everyday conversation about ordinary occurrences and familiar organisms.)

The mechanistic necessitarianism of Hobbes arose more directly from physics. In his 'Short Tract on First Principles' (of around 1630) Hobbes adopted the principle that change only occurs when pressure is exerted upon a body by some external body in contact with it.[11] If so, thinking and feeling will ultimately be the resultants of mechanical motion, and nothing will be able to undergo change which is not material. This latter implication suggests (without implying it) Hobbes' contention that the phrase 'immaterial substance' lacks signification.[12] Hobbes differs from later materialist necessitarians, like Collins, Hartley and Priestley, in respect of this denial that anything but material objects and their primary qualities are real: Collins[13] and Priestley[14] in

---

[10] Spinoza's necessitarianism is quite effectively rebutted by Samuel Clarke at 'Being and Attributes of God', Vol. I, London, 1719, pp. 65-74.

[11] See J. W. N. Watkins, 'Hobbes System of Ideas', (London, 1965), pp. 40-46.

[12] 'Leviathan', ed. Oakeshott, (Oxford, 1955), Part I, Chapter 4; p. 23. As Mintz points out in 'The Hunting of Leviathan' (Cambridge, 1969; at p. 67) Hobbes impresses rather by asserting his materialism and its corollaries than by defending it.

[13] 'Letter to Dodwell, Etc.,', p. 340.

[14] 'A Free Discussion of the Doctrines of Materialism and Philosophical Necessity, In a Correspondence Between Dr. Price and Dr. Priestley', (London, 1778), p. 67.

particular affirm that God is immaterial. But these men agreed with Hobbes that within the created order all explanations were to be in terms of matter and its properties, and that, granted the mechanistic determinants of any event, it could not have occurred otherwise.

Unlike Spinoza, Hobbes and the other materialists did not hold that events, as well as being causally necessitated, could not *conceivably* have been otherwise, (even if, on a slightly more consistent nominalism than that of Hobbes', all truths are true by definition[15]). Discussion of this form of necessitarianism is thus more feasible than of that of Spinoza, but will be postponed until Priestley's debate with Price has been considered later in this Section.

The more sophisticated and later necessitarianism of Hume was also based, in a way, on the dictum that all events have causes. But, according to Hume, the only reason we talk of causes is our mental habit or custom of associating earlier and subsequent events which frequently occur together. Now if 'causal necessity' adds up simply to 'observed invariable concomitance', we can equally well contend for the necessity of physical events arising from physical causes, and for that of choices arising from human character. In any case we rely on such regular concomitance in all human dealings. Not that people are unfree, for their choices arise from their characters. Yet choices and acts, like all events, have their necessitating causes, as also do characters. Accordingly, in the only legitimate senses of the terms concerned, choices are both free and *necessary*.[16]

Hume's belief that nothing but what does happen could happen (his "actualism") thus derives from his empiricist epistemology and his analysis of the idea of necessity in terms of the mind's habit of associating ideas. Determinism, however, seems to involve more than the thesis that choices regularly flow from character and are generally predictable from knowledge of character. It involves the invariable falsity of claims that agents could have done otherwise, and there is room for doubt that Hume's reasoning shows as much as that.

The standard form of attack on determinism however, consisted in attempts to demonstrate the existence of an immaterial active substance within each man, a substance immune in some manner from causal necessitation. Yet other thinkers tackled the dissimilarities between motives and pressures in still further ways: but

---

[15] See Watkins, op. cit., p. 146 and generally pp. 144-150.
[16] David Hume, 'An Enquiry Concerning Human Understanding', Section VIII, Selby-Bigge pp. 80-103.

before their arguments are considered, that of dualism will be discussed first.

B. First Objection: Dualism.

Confronted with the stringencies of the new physics, which he himself had helped to devise and in which all explanations had to be in terms of matter and motion, Descartes argued cogently that there must be a subject of thought, granted the indubitability of the fact of his own thinking and the axiom that there can be no quality which is not a quality of something.[17] By a further argument to the effect that as we each have a clear and distinct idea of thinking substances it must be possible for them to exist alone, i.e. to be creatable in isolation, he concludes that what thinks is a substance whose essence it is to think but to lack physical qualities. This is more questionable, since thinking but unextended substances are not identifiable or reidentifiable independently of extended substances: so, of a world in which nothing else existed, it could not plausibly be said that they existed either. It is also an unfortunate conclusion, in that if minds lack position, doubt is cast on their very existence, (or rather was so cast by those who assumed that what is nowhere is nothing[18]), and consquently on human freedom also.

Descartes' doctrine of unextended substances allowed him a recess in which to locate human freedom immune from the assaults of mechanists. Thus he argues for free-will from introspecting his ability to resist deception.

> "At the same time as we tried to doubt all things and even supposed that He who created us employed His unlimited powers in deceiving us in every way, we perceived in ourselves a liberty such that we were able to abstain from believing what was not perfectly certain and indubitable. But that of which we could not doubt at such a time is as self-evident and clear as anything we can ever know."[19]

Indeed the objection which worried Descartes was not so much mechanism as that of the power and knowledge of God. Here again, however, immediate awareness of his immaterial self resists all doubt.[20]

---

[17] I here follow the interpretation of Descartes' 'cogito' argued for by Anthony Kenny in Ch. 3 of his 'Descartes, A Study of His Philosophy', (New York, 1968).
[18] A belief of Henry More. See Koyré, 'Newtonian Studies', pp. 89f.
[19] 'Principles of Philosophy' I: XXXIX; Haldane and Ross, I. p. 234f.
[20] Ibid., I: XLI.

"Yet the Power and Knowledge of God must not prevent us from believing that we have a free will; for we should be wrong to doubt of that whereof we are inwardly conscious, and which we know by experience to be within us, simply because we do not comprehend some other thing which we know to be incomprehensible in its nature."

Descartes' reply, however, miscarries even if his argument for the existence of the mind as an immaterial thinking substance were valid. As Leibniz points out, "from the fact that we are not conscious of the causes whereon we depend, it does not follow that we are independent" — a point he ascribes to Bayle.[21]

Leibniz notes two other weaknesses. It is no use pleading that omnipotence is incomprehensible: truths cannot conflict and must be reconciled if it is legitimate to regard them as truths. The other weakness pointed out by Leibniz is the claim that human action is entirely undetermined. As Leibniz remarks[22] this view is not needed in defence of human freedom. Indeed a doctrine of "liberty of indifference" makes praise and blame altogether inapplicable.

At the same time, Descartes was playing into the hands of materialism by the claim that the mind lacks extension and position. How could such an entity influence and be influenced by a body? Much better to make it redundant. What is nowhere is surely nothing. "The world . . . is corporeal, that is to say, body; and hath the dimensions of magnitude, namely, length, breadth and depth; also every part of body, is likewise body, and hath the like dimensions; and consequently every part of the universe, is body, and that which is not body, is no part of the universe: and because the universe is all, that which is no part of it, is *nothing*; and consequently *nowhere*. Nor does it follow from hence that spirits are *nothing*: for they have dimensions, and are therefore really *bodies* . . ."[23]

Accordingly the contemporary opponents of Hobbes with the best philosophical grounding, Henry More and Ralph Cudworth, attempted to find room within the extended universe for spirits, their activity and their freedom — spirits extended but immaterial. More in his 'Divine Dialogues'[24] believed he had shown the reality of one immaterial entity, — space itself: on the analogy of which spirits could more easily be credited (spirits necessarily extended,

---

[21] Leibniz, 'Theodicy', p. 111.
[22] 'Theodicy', p. 112.
[23] Thomas Hobbes, 'Leviathan', edited Oakeshott, (Oxford, 1955), part 4, Chapter 46, p. 440.
[24] London., 1668.

for More endorsed Hobbes' view that what is nowhere is nothing.) The distinctive contributions of Cudworth[25] were the inference that since matter is inert, the world can only be understood if there exist substances immaterial and active, both in nature at large, in animals and in man: and the claim that since human knowledge of universals cannot be derived from experience of particulars, the mind must have an existence independent of the body. Indeed Cudworth's original plan in writing his 'True Intellectual System' was to defend human freedom and write 'against the fatal necessity of all actions and events', but he discovered that this defence required a study of metaphysics at large.[26]

Cudworth's epistemology was largely taken over by Richard Price in the Eighteenth Century, and indeed one of Price's arguments (in his Sermon entitled 'The Nature and Dignity of the Human Soul') for the soul's existence is the inactivity of matter and therefore of the body.[27] Price also argues from the indivisibility of the self: the body is 'discerptible' but the subject of thought is manifestly otherwise.[28] The argument rapidly proceeds, along the lines of the 'Phaedo' of Plato, to the conclusion that the soul is imperishable, short of its annihilation by God.[29]

The argument from the indivisibility of the subject of thought is also employed by Samuel Clarke.[30] The body, being material, is divisible, and has no genuine qualities but ones resulting from qualities of the same sort in its parts. Consciousness, on the other hand, is irreducible and must reside in an indivisible substance: so its subject cannot be the body or anything material, but rather an unchanging soul. Anthony Collins, the deist thinker, opposed Clarke's argument, but his eventual defence was the scarcely self-evident possibility that consciousness is a mode of a physical quality, perhaps motion: the reducibility of the qualities of

---

[25] 'The True Intellectual System of the Universe', edited by J. L. Mosheim, (London, 1845). First published in 1678.

[26] For this point I am indebted to J. A. Passmore's 'Ralph Cudworth, An Interpretation' (Cambridge, 1951), p. 19.

[27] Richard Price, 'Sermons', (London, 1790 or shortly thereafter): the relevant sermon was preached in 1766 in support of educating the souls of the young at a Charity School. Predictably such views led to the adoption among materialists such as La Mettrie of an active view of matter. See his 'L'Homme Machine', Leyden, 1747.

[28] This was a telling point often made in the correspondence with the materialist Priestley: and it appears to confute, at any rate, the theory of the identity of body and mind, to which Priestley had leanings.

[29] 'The Nature and Dignity of the Human Soul', pp. 7-9. For Plato's Argument, see 'Phaedo', edited J. Burnet, Oxford, 1911.

[30] 'A Letter to Dodwell', pp. 22-4. See also his Four Defences of this argument, Collins' replies (all in the same volume), and my 'Clarke, Collins and Compounds' in 'Journal of the History of Philosophy'. XV, 1977, pp. 45-54.

composite objects he did not seriously dispute. Collins was much more successful in attacking the form which Clarke's immaterialism took: for, heedful of the Hobbesian view that what *'exists in No Place' 'exists not at all'*, Clarke somewhat reluctantly concluded that the soul, though immaterial, is extended: and Collins was therefore enabled to remark that if the body's divisibility made it incapable of consciousness, so too must that of the extended soul. The view of Price[31] was more defensible, that the soul has location but no extension.

Such dualist arguments, however, whether valid or not, left room for the claim on the part of the determinist that the soul's activity is unfree: and this was the more so for the very reason that the thinkers we have just been considering (More, Cudworth, Clarke and Price)[32] located the mind in the body, as also did Locke.[33] For localised minds, being able to act upon and be acted upon by bodies, appeared all the more susceptible of causal determination. Thinkers like Leibniz and Kant are not open to this objection, because they explicitly remove the self from the realm of causality: Kant by setting the self in the noumenal realm, and Leibniz by devising a system in which no substance acts on any other. But in both cases the principal difficulty would involve showing how the freedom enjoyed by the 'self' in these systems has any bearing on the choices in everyday experience of people as described in ordinary language. As Arnauld pointed out to Leibniz, the 'self' of Leibniz' analysis is not the same as the 'me' of ordinary discourse, and accordingly the analysis of these concepts is different too.[34] And Kant would be hard put to it to show how any noumenal choice could be correlated with phenomenal bodily movements, granted (as Kant grants) the determination of the latter by inclination in the phenomenal self.

All in all, specifically dualist objections to determinism seem to founder, probably because dualism creates more problems than it solves. I therefore turn to defences of our capacity to choose which turn on the nature of motives, but not specifically on dualism. For so far the theological reply to determinism has proved to miscarry.

---

[31] Op. cit., page 12, footnote 1.

[32] See e.g. 'A Free Discussion', p. 368, where Priestley surveys various forms of immaterialism.

[33] Ibid., pp. 266-7. Thus Locke has to produce further arguments in defence of freedom: see 'Essay', II, XX.

[34] 'Correspondence Relating to the Metaphysics, between Arnauld and Leibniz', in 'Leibniz, Discourse on Metaphysics, Correspondence with Arnauld and Monadology' translated by Dr. George R. Montgomery, 2nd edition, (Chicago, 1918), p. 98.

C. Second Objection: Motives Incline Without Necessitating.

Men like Cudworth, Clarke and Price realised that, in addition to whatever need there might be to argue for the soul's independent existence, there was a distinct need to locate human freedom in such a way as to defend it from mechanistic determinism and from the charge that it was a mere "liberty of indifference", something random, irrational and irresponsible.

Clarke's main defence of freedom was an answer to the claim (echoed by Collins in his tract 'Dissertation on Liberty and Necessity')[35] that "the Will is determined by the last Judgement of the Understanding." Clarke's reply[36] is that the guiding of choice in this matter is only a moral necessitation "and therefore no Necessity at all." But endorsing, as he did, the faculty psychology of his opponents, he could not avoid bestowing on the Will choices either random or causally explicable. Despite Cudworth's (perhaps unread) attack on faculty psychology the attraction of facultative explanations lived on long after him.

Cudworth himself had been determined to find a solution to the problem, but never satisfied himself that he had done so. Thus in an unpublished manuscript[37] he declares "If what I shall say concerning freewill seems unsatisfactory to any, I shall think it no marvel at all, for I never was myself satisfied in any discourse which I read of it."

Granted his opposition to faculty psychology and its division of personality, Cudworth was unwilling to do as Bramhall, Hobbes' opponent, had done and locate freedom in the exercise of reason. Indeed Cudworth was prepared to a much greater extent than Clarke to grant that action goes unexplained if all mention of desires and affections is omitted. Actions must be explained by reference to either our animal passions or concern for our own utility or by the spirit of love: yet none of these tendencies are usually thought to be within our control. Nevertheless there is a place for praise and blame, for the soul is not entirely passive: there is in us 'a weak staggering power' 'whereby the soul . . . doth in doubtful cases add something of its own to the moments of Reason

---

[35] London, 1729.
[36] 'Being and Attributes of God', 1, pp. 104-6.
[37] British Museum collections of fragments entitled 'Loci Communes Morales' and 'Collection of Confused Thoughts, Memorandums relating to the Eternity of Torments', 4982, 1. As Passmore shows, these manuscripts throw a new light on Cudworth's moral psychology. The unpublished ones have also been illuminatingly discussed by Samuel I. Mintz in 'The Hunting of Leviathan', (Cambridge, 1969), chapter VI, 'The Free-Will Controversy: Bramhall and Cudworth'.

and impulse'.[38] We ourselves are therefore able, in cases when motives are evenly balanced, to turn the balance towards our lower or higher inclinations.

But now Cudworth is in difficulties. *Ex hypothesi* this ulterior power is immune from motives: surely, then, as Collins was to urge to Clarke, and Price to Priestley, we are being asked to believe that human freedom lies in an arbitrary, motiveless act, and that this act is one for which no explanation may be sought.[39] To such an 'indifferency' Cudworth himself objects that it is 'the idea of such a thing or power as cannot possibly be in Nature'. Had we such arbitrary power we might change our character by *fiat* within an instant: but this does not fit the facts of experience. Indifferentism also has the consequences of absolving us of responsibility for our actions, and representing us as the less free the more our actions are moulded by our characters towards goodness.

But the view that free-will is our ability to choose the good is also unsatisfactory: for in order freely to sin, we should now need a second-order ability not to exercise our ability to choose the good. No wonder Cudworth was unsatisfied. He remained wedded to the view that there is a certain 'contingency' in human action, but unresolved as to where to locate it.

Was Cudworth's view therefore wholly misguided? J. A. Passmore criticises Cudworth's theory of freedom as metaphysical, and holds that whereas in other respects Cudworth was an innovator in secularising ethics, this theory (and also Cudworth's dualism) were required only by his theological concern that our deserving salvation or damnation should be fair.[40]

I should endorse Passmore's strictures on Cudworth's dualism, and should in fact myself hold that men like Descartes and Cudworth by their dualistic views tied a millstone about the neck of theistic orthodoxy. Indeed necessitarians like Priestley were able to make great play of the unity of personality which their anti-dualistic materialism allowed of.[41] But I do not see how an ethic of creativity such as Passmore applauds needs a doctrine of human self-determination one whit less than an ethic of divine judgement. Cudworth's ethic of the good like requires not only that the mind should not be a clockwork mechanism. It requires a man to be able to exercise discrimination and judgement. For this reason if

---

[38] These references are derived from Passmore, p. 58.

[39] 'A Free Discussion', pp. 349-351. In his footnote there, Price remarks that his own discussion with Priestley "is little more than a repetition" of Collins' objections and Clarke's replies. But Collins' point is made less in that correspondence than in his 'Dissertation on Liberty and Necessity', (London, 1729).

[40] Op. cit., pp. 85f.

[41] 'A Free Discussion', p. 240. On materialism, see Section 2E.

determinism, even of Passmore's non-mechanical variety, were true, Cudworth's theory of the good life would collapse, together with Passmore's praise of it.

I sympathise with Passmore's protest at dualism, thought not his view that dualism is essential as a basis for Christian ethics. But I do not see that only Christian ethics requires the theory that when a man acts freely it was within his control to have acted otherwise: for every morality would collapse in a similar way were it false. Indeed in the absence of such a theory (as remarked above) dualism is of no avail as a defence of freedom. Cudworth's emphasis on desert may be magnified by his Christianity, but his emphasis on freedom itself does not need secularising. Yet a problem remained about how to express it.

In 1778, Priestley was to put to Price a problem similar to that which Cudworth sets himself. A man is imagined who has a choice between two courses of action and who feels equally inclined to do either. If we say that it is the man who chooses between his motives, we are supposing a motiveless act: and this is just as absurd as suggesting that when the beam of a balance inclines in the direction of one or the other of two apparently equal weights it inclines as a result of no influence whatever. Rather, when a balance inclines, it is always swayed by a heavier weight, and when a man chooses, he is always swayed by the stronger motive. So whenever a man makes up his mind, one motive was at least marginally stronger than the other. To argue otherwise is to suppose there can be an event without a cause: and indeed to say this is to overthrow the Cosmological Argument, "the only proper argument for the being of a God."[42]

Price replies by instancing a conflict between self-interest and duty, the strength of the 'motives' being equal. And he takes Priestley to be saying, (rather as Leibniz in his letters to Clarke had said of God when faced with indifferent alternatives), that no choice can be made. Rather, asserts Price, the man is free to choose either, not neither alternative; and it is he himself who, by exercising his self-determination, sways the balance. To suppose otherwise is to suppose man to be a mechanism. Priestley's view of this account is that you might just as well say a balance sometimes inclines one way of itself and for no other reason: that the balance is the cause of its own inclination.

In holding that it is the man who chooses, Price is on the side of common sense, but in the course of his letter Price conceded to Priestley too readily that motives figure among the antecedents of

---

[42] 'A Free Discussion', p. 295. A contrary view is maintained in Chapter 5, Section 3C and Chapter 6, Section 1.

action, 'influencing' but not 'determining' it. (The phrase is reminiscent of Leibniz' favourite account of motives, that they "incline without necessitating". But in Leibniz' system, choices of the best or the apparent best are always contingent and immune from causality whereas Price was not similarly able to assume that no explanation of action is possible on which every actual action is the only action possible in the circumstances.) The trouble is that once motives are so treated, they acquire an existence of their own independent of the agent, while the agent in choosing between them is supposed to choose without volitions or desires; for all volitions and desires can be regarded as motives, and the agent is choosing between motives and therefore beyond all motives. Thus, as Price accepted Priestley's model in terms of 'influences', Priestley was able to present Price's account of choice as incoherent. Choices must be explicable, but Price was making them inexplicable. The best Price could do was to instance the case of self-movement in God; and Priestley was unable to say what kind of causes explained God's actions. Priestley, however, saw no reason why the First Cause should in this respect be similar to second causes.

Thus, despite Price's common sense view, Priestley had the better of this part of the argument: and, if motives are allowed unqualifiedly to be causes, his remark about the universal principle of causality requires an answer which Price was unable to give it as a theist committed to a form of that principle. Price was also conceding far too much in another way, as indeed Cudworth had at times done before him. For if freedom is only to be found when a man gives a casting vote between equal and opposite motives, he cannot be free at all when he acts without perplexity or conflict, and has only one desire. Thus straightforward acts of altruism or of self-gratification could never be free. Cudworth and Price were, of course, led to this position by their desire to discover what it was which is in our control in virtue of which we may deserve well or ill, something inherent in ourselves as opposed to the inclinations which occur along our way, Nevertheless by so construing the problem they were at the outset conceding the greater part of the ground to their necessitarian opponents.

D. Third Objection: Linguistic Analysis.

But not so Thomas Reid.[43] In Reid common sense is abetted by an appeal to ordinary language and its analysis. Reid rejects

---

[43] 'Essays on the Active Powers of Man', Essay IV, Chapter IV, in 'British Moralists, 1650-1800', edited by D. D. Raphael, Oxford, 1969, pp. 276-282.

Hume's dilemma,[44] that actions are either caused by motives or capricious and unamenable to the effect of rewards and punishment. For motives are not efficient causes at all. *Influence* action they may, but they do not act, and much less are they acted on. The very presence of motives supposes liberty in the agent to do or to forbear in their respect, or they could have no influence. Necessitarianism supposes that like matter, intelligent beings are inert and inactive, and directed proportionately to, and in the direction of the force of motives. But this is to fail to ask what a motive is.

Reid's strongest point is his analysis of the concept 'the strongest motive'. Necessitarians hold that we are always propelled by the strongest motive and therefore unable to determine ourselves. But if the test of a motive's strength is its prevalence, i.e. the fact that we actually *act* on it, then their claim is a mere tautology, and has no bearing on the explanation of our actions. If, however, the test is supposed to be found not in prevalence but independently, in the cause of the prevalence, nothing is established unless it is arbitrarily assumed that motives cause our actions. But this is circular reasoning, or rather a case of begging the question. Motives are rather to be compared to advocates in a lawcourt, where it is not the advocate but the judge who gives sentence, and he need not be swayed at all by a weak case.

The sense in which every action has a motive is not in any case the same as that in which an inclination we may be aware of prior to forming a decision is a motive. And as inclinations can be represented as cropping up independently of our own initiation and not subject to our control, the representation of all motives as inclinations readily leads to a kind of determinism.

The sense in which every action has a motive is as follows. For every intentional action some formula of the following sort can be devised: "He did it from a desire (to . . . /for . . .)". And by now we have a motive-explanation.

Of such motives it should be observed that, when viewed in a certain way, we have no control over them. For, once we have chosen to act, we have no further control over the motive from which we act: the motive is rather derived (when our actions are being interpreted) from the pattern of action we exemplified; and the content of this is already settled one way or the other, for better or for worse. Accordingly if the motive has been correctly identified, there is now no logical gap between the description of the motive and the description of the action: no new element of contingency allowing for a new choice. But, of course, the very suggestion that there should be is absurd. For such a desire and

---

[44] Hume, 'Enquiry', Section VIII, Part II.

such a motive are not among the antecedents of the action: rather they enter into the description of the action from the point of view of our wantings.[45] And such motives, as Read points out, will always be 'strongest' in the sense of 'prevalent': (though 'strongest' hardly applies; as, granted the action and a correct identification of the motive, there was no other motive than which it could have been stronger).

The term 'motives' is also used, somewhat unfortunately, of inclinations which are, or can be, genuinely antecedent to action, i.e. of datable episodes or spells of desire: but it is not true of 'motives' in this sense that every action has a motive. With motives in this sense, what we are not in control of is not the motive on which we act (for between such inclinations we *are* able to choose) but their occurrence and presentation to us. As, however, not all wantings are passions or thoughts beyond our control, but much of what we do is done because we ourselves, whether reflectively or not, choose so to act, we are not always at the mercy of motives in this sense.

It is probably by the assimilation of these senses of 'motive' that psychological determinism receives its cogency. If motives in the first sense, omnipresent in action yet over whose character we have no control independent of our control over the actions concerned, are thought of as chronologically prior to action, and explaining that action as antecedents do, i.e. as causes, we seem to have no control over the urges which make up our minds. These urges must therefore be caused by something beyond our control and the determinist case is complete.

Reid sees this in part when he denies that all motives are causes. His other achievement is a theory on which, even when we act from some single desire, we may act freely, where 'freely' implies that we could, had we exerted ourselves, have acted otherwise. Such a theory greatly expands the scope of freedom beyond the narrow compass envisaged by Price and Cudworth. Reid's theory also has the advantage of answering in part Hume's argument from predictability. Hume held that there is the same invariable concomitance between actions and motives as between events and their causes, and that actions are rigorously predictable. He claimed that human actions are necessitated in just the same sense as physical events. But as Reid points out, we do not reason from people's motives to their actions with the same certainty as from causes to effects. Thus actions cannot be 'necessary' in the same sense, at least where this implies 'caused by motives'.

---

[45] The kind of explanation concerned is 'formal', (in the Aristotelian sense), not 'causal'. See Levison and Thalberg, 'Mind', January 1969.

This reply needs development. The strength of Hume's case lies in the fact that human actions are often predictable; Reid's reply is, in effect, that this does not mean they are necessitated. How then are they predictable? Not from known inclinations present to the agent prior to action, but from known habits of choice, principles, or dispositions to choose in a particular manner. The full account, therefore, of that in terms of which such prediction is possible involves mention of choice, and therefore does not concern exclusively forces beyond the agent's control. Thus even if Hume's empiricist account of necessity were in general correct, yet (to use Hume's terminology) the idea which we have when we find actions flowing regularly from character and the idea which we have when we find physical effects flowing regularly from their causes are not one and the same.

The above arguments, based on those of Reid, are not sufficient to refute determinism: but they do seem to invalidate the principal deterministic arguments of Priestley and Hume. Their success as objections makes it unnecessary to discuss here objections to the empiricist theory of our ideas, and prepares the way for arguments to show determinism to be false. But it is appropriate first to return to the question of the degree of support lent to determinism by the materialism of Hobbes and Priestley.

E. The Bearing of Materialism.

Whereas determinism is a theory about prediction and therefore explanation, materialism is a theory about what really exists, and about the reducibility of talk about the apparently immaterial to talk about the material. Now if all changes in material objects are predictable on the basis of physical laws in the way that determinism requires (see Section I B), then on materialism our beliefs and actions are themselves susceptible without exception to deterministic predictions. If, however, our beliefs and actions cannot be explained without reference to earlier thoughts and desires, i.e. entirely in terms of physical laws and antecedents, then either materialism or physical determinism (or both) must be false, (although psychological determinism could still be true). Thus materialism could help in a demonstration of our unfreedom, but does not establish it alone.

Nevertheless a mechanist can argue for determinism by establishing that our motives or inclinations are in some way material. And this was the belief of Priestley.[46] Taking our inclinations to be ideas of projected goals, he contends that, being repre-

---

[46] 'A Free Discussion', p. 52.

sentations of their archetypes, ideas must, like their archetypes, be extended. And if they are extended, then, unless they are void space, they must be material. Priestley's belief in the materiality of our ideas is confirmed by his frequent expressions of support for Hartley's system, in which our ideas are (relatively) enduring minute vibrations in the nerves. And if our ideas are of this character, it is not hard to imagine their being mechanically necessitated.

To all this, Hume's (earlier) criticism of materialist accounts of mind is an adequate reply — that it does not make sense to say our ideas are extended or unextended.[47] But the point had been anticipated long before by an antinecessitarian, Cudworth, when he remarked that our ideas of relations cannot be understood as patches or arrangements of particles.[48] As Cudworth's point may be taken to imply, the materialist is obliged to supply rules for one-for-one equivalence between physical conditions and the content of our thoughts: and in fact a theory like Hartley's does not even begin to meet this obligation.[49] (And even if the obligation were met, the materialist must further maintain that the parallelism of mind and body amounts to an identity, which, in the cases of phenomena like pain and consciousness, he is perhaps unlikely to succeed in doing.) This one-for-one equivalence is, perhaps, all that is required to make determinism plausible, since every psychlogical change could then be predicted simply from physical laws and antecedents and a translation table correlating physical and psychological states. But the very difficulties of supposing that there is for every episode of human reasoning a set of physical conditions predictable from physical laws and antecedents alone has recently led to a further objection to determinism.[50]

Thus although materialism could be of help to one form of determinism, the difficulties of establishing it, either in the strong form of a reductionist theory or in the weaker form of a theory about the one-for-one correspondence of reports of the content of thoughts and reports of states of a physical system, make this help unlikely to be forthcoming. The arguments put forward for determinism thus fare poorly. It is now time to ask whether determinism conflicts with ordinary beliefs and whether there might not be arguments showing it to be false.

---

[47] Hume, 'Treatise', I, Part IV, Section V. (Everyman edition, Vol. I, pp. 228f).
[48] Passmore, op. cit., pp. 32-7.
[49] See 'British Moralists, 1650-1800' Vol. II, pp. 115-127 for a sample of Hartley's 'Observations on Man'.
[50] See the latter part of Lucas' 'The Freedom of the Will' (Oxford, 1970), a work in which the more familiar objections to determinism are also well set out.

F. Conceptual Difficulties in Determinism.

Is determinism compatible with out ordinary beliefs? Commonsense objections to determinism were produced long before Reid by two contemporaries of Hobbes, Bramhall and Cudworth. Bramhall's ethical objections are listed by Hobbes as follows: [51]

(1) That the laws, which prohibit any action, will be unjust.
(2) That all consultations are vain.
(3) That admonitions to men of understanding, are of no more use than to children, fools and madmen.
(4) That praise, dispraise, reward and punishment are in vain.
(5), (6) That counsels, arts, arms, books, instruments, study, tutors, medicines, are in vain.

None of these points left Hobbes without an answer; but his reply to (1), that laws regard only the will and not its causes, was adequately turned by Bramhall and later Reid: only on libertarian views will these laws be just. The fifth and sixth points appear to fail, as determinism does not involve a fatalist outlook: indeed if the future is going to be what it is through our (necessitated) choices, there is all the more cause (or is this ambiguous?) to bestir ourselves. As to the second point, it is better for our choices to be determined by factors good rather than bad: and considerations of utility give point to praise and admonitions even if men are unfree, so the remaining points are also unsuccessful.

Most of the same points could, however, be restated by a consideration of the concepts which would become redundant were determinism true. Thus, expanding Reid's point, there could be no *just* praise, or *deserved* praise.[52] Again, could there be the sort of admonitions that set out to *persuade*? For there is little scope within determinism for discrimination and judgement. And soon after Bramhall published his objections, Cudworth pointed out a further set of concepts which determinism can make nothing of — self-accusation, self-condemnation, guilt and repentence. (He might have added 'forgiveness').[53] He proceeds as follows:-

"No man accuses or condemns himself, nor looks upon himself as guilty for having had a fever, the stone, or the gout,

---

[51] 'British Moralists', Vol. I, p. 62.

[52] Samuel Clarke takes up the point about desert against Collins at 'Letter to Dodwell, Etc.,' p. 433.

[53] See P. F. Strawson 'Freedom and Resentment', Proceedings of the British Academy, Vol. XLVIII, (Oxford, 1962). I agree with Strawson that people can only be forgiven when they are believed to have been responsible: but not, for the reasons given, that belief in determinism would leave the notion of responsibility unaffected.

when uncontracted by vice; and if all human actions were necessary, men would be no more to *repent* of them than of disease, or that they were not born princes, or heirs to a thousand pounds a year."[54]

This telling passage at least shows that were determinism accepted, human life would have to become unrecognisably different from what it now is. Some determinists may hold that our present language and institutions are confused:[55] but are the changes which consistent determinists take to be necessary themselves possible? The issue becomes at this stage whether determinism itself can be held to be true, or can even *be* true.

But the conceptual difficulties reach even further. Were determinism true, could the determinist regard himself as having good reasons, either for holding it true, or for holding that any reforms required by its truth should be effected? For a determinist must believe that his own beliefs are the inevitable outcome of factors beyond his own control, and that he is unfree to assess or in any other way act upon the influences at whose mercy he is. No place therefore remains for the rational assessment of reasons: his own judgements and decisions will never hang on consideration of the logical merits of the reasons he is aware of, but on the fact that factors beyond his control (on some theories the very fact that these apparent 'reasons' are presented to him) constrain him so to judge or decide. The determinist, then, cannot consistently claim good reasons for his determinism or for any other belief. Granted determinism, therefore, no proposition can be believed true, at least on the basis of reason, and the very notion of truth radically changes, if it as much as survives.[56] And, if so, the occurrence of a single piece of human reasoning would suffice to show determinism to be false. Plausibly, then, our ordinary concepts, perhaps including those Cudworth mentions as well as those of belief, truth and knowledge, are indispensable.

The concepts of choice and responsibility are alike indispensable for ordinary life and for the theistic view of man. Had a man no control over his own actions and beliefs, he would be

---

[54] 'A Treatise of Freewill', 'British Moralists', I, pp. 120f.

[55] This appears to me the consistent course. Strawson, in the article cited above, holds that were determinism expressible and true, it would be rational to retain our present concepts. This would not seem to me rational (even if, in these inconceivable circumstances, it would be inevitable!)

Priestley, at 'A Free Discussion', 150f, gives a necessitarian account of what, strictly, we *should* mean by various ethical terms.

[56] This argument, which is not, of course, original, is ably defended by Lucas in 'The Freedom of the Will'. Needless to say, it remains a matter of controversy: I find the objectors unconvincing.

CHAPTER 4

THE SECULARISATION OF MORAL THEORY

Section 1: The Autonomy of Ethics

A. Secularisation and Ethics.

In this chapter I am concerned to identify the form secularisation took in the field of moral (and therefore also political) theory, and to assess it philosophically and theologically. I begin with a brief discussion of the ways in which the independence of human reason from religion can be asserted in this field.

Secularisation could concern either the content of premisses employed in moral reasoning or the way in which they are known. Thus it was an instance of secularisation when Lord Herbert of Cherbury contended that certain ethical truths were 'notitiae communes', or axioms which were, or could be, known by all independently of revelation. Nevertheless the examples he gives are of a most theological character:[1] and even if it is agreed without resort to revelation that e.g. we ought to worship God, it remains to be asked whether this is true in virtue of a definition of 'ought' in terms of God's will or independently of such a definition. Indeed questions about the grounds of moral judgements could still be asked even of judgements taken to be revealed. At the same time Lord Herbert facilitated other forms of secularisation by his contention that there is a place for natural reason in moral theory: had morality been regarded throughout the period under discussion as a body of revealed truth, little serious debate could have taken place. And as it seems always to make sense to ask, of any allegedly revealed duty, "Ought we to do what we have been told in revelation we ought to do, and if so, why?" Lord Herbert seems correct in opposing the view that *all* morality is revealed.

Nevertheless secularisation took a further step with the claim

---

[1] In 'De Veritate'. His examples are quoted by Vernon J. Bourke, 'History of Ethics', (2 Vols., Doubleday, New York, 1968), Vol. I, p. 189.

no more "made in the image of God"[57] than the lowliest member of the animal kingdom. The core of this doctrine is that man has a creative capacity, a power of choosing between possibilities and moulding his environment and his future; and that this creativity is a reflection of that of the Creator, who is free to create or not to create, and to bring into being whichever of an infinite set of possible worlds he chooses.[58] Only then if notions like self-determination have application may man be made in God's image; both because mechanisms lack the creative ability to bring about something altogether new, and also because, as argued in Section 1, unless we can know what it is for creatures to choose, we cannot begin to know what choice would be in God, nor therefore coherently claim that in point of choice and creativity man in some measure resembles the Creator.

Thus necessitarianism, actualism and determinism turn out to be secularist doctrines, and also to have been, in all probability, misguided. Though the 'image of God' doctrine has not been shown to be true, the objections to it from human capacities miscarry. Yet the objectors themselves reflected the creditable spirit of those who never despair of seeking explanations (even though they made the mistake of requiring exclusively causal explanations at all points); and both sides exhibited a candour, tolerance and openness to debate typical of secularisation at its best, as well as of the kind of maturity encouraged by the New Testament.[59]

---

[57] Genesis I, verse 26.
[58] Descartes saw this as the nub of the 'image of God' doctrine: see Meditation 4, Haldane and Ross, Vol. I, p. 175.
[59] At e.g. Ephesians 4, verse 13.

that certain moral notions were irreducible. Not that the view that God's will was good simply because it was God's will had at all times been a predominant one: yet the reasoned denial of this view was vital for the secularisation of moral and political theory. For, were it true, disputes about moral and political principles would ultimately turn out to be disputes about theological fact, i.e. about what God actually wills.[2] But if it is false, the principles underlying moral judgements at least *may* be irreducibly moral: and in any case moral reasoning will in large measure be independent of theology. The refutation of theological naturalism will therefore be the next topic within this section.

Yet it seems a mistake when writers on 'the autonomy of ethics' stop short here. For the falsity of theological naturalism is compatible with theories on which mention of God must somewhere figure in the premises of moral reasoning: and the claim that there can be a consistent morality without religion, implicitly made, as I shall allege, by Hobbes, Spinoza and Shaftesbury, involves a further important step in the secularisation of moral theory — and a step, I believe, with which the theologian can sympathise.

Secularism in moral theory is yet different again. In its extremist form it alleges that talk of God, his will or his moral attributes is meaningless: discussion of secularism in this form will be reserved for the chapters following.

The most prominent form of secular moral theory deriving from the period under review has been utilitarianism. Theological and non-theologcial varieties of utilitarianism will be discussed in Section 2, together with the issues of the relation of utilitarianism to theistic ethics and of both to belief in human rights. In all its forms utilitarianism is secular at least in respect of urging the furtherance of human happiness: though this is to say little, as it is compatible with either theological naturalism as in Paley, atheism, as in Bentham, or indeed with intuitionism, (as in the writings of G. E. Moore). But, with appropriate amendments, it is also compatible with what I call 'anthropological naturalism' and with a certain relation of morality so understood to the doctrine of creation. Along these lines there will gradually emerge my own view of moral theory and its relation to theology.

Political theory I propose to treat as a branch of moral theory. I shall assume that questions like "Why ought I to obey the state?"

---

[2] According to Bourke (Vol. I, p. 224) this was the view of Püfendorf.

and "What are the duties of the Sovereign?" are fundamentally moral questions, and therefore that the secularisation of moral and of political theory go hand in hand. Thus the refutation of theological naturalism in ethics implies that positive law need not be derived from divine law, while the practical theorems that Hobbes derives from his account of human nature are at once moral and political as are the arguments put forward by Spinoza, Bayle and Locke for toleration. There certainly are traces of secularisation also in the work of specifically political theorists like Grotius[3] : but these cannot be separately discussed here.

B. The Refutation of Theological Naturalism.

Theological naturalism is the philosophical theory that ethical terms can be defined in terms of the will, purposes or commands of God. Though this theory was a minority view in the Middle Ages it later enjoyed wide support among Calvinists, and was also detected by Leibniz in Descartes:[4] while an analogous form of naturalism, that 'good' means 'commanded by the civil ruler' has sometimes been ascribed to Hobbes[5].

Proponents of the irreducibility of ethical terms are liable to employ two arguments, the argument from trivialisation — (if 'good' means '*X*' then the questions 'Are *X* things good' would be tautologous, which it never is) — and the argument from derivation — (ethical conclusions cannot validly be derived from non-ethical premises alone whether definitions or reports of fact; an ethical premiss is always needed). As A. N. Prior has shown, both these arguments were employed in the Early Modern period, the latter being implicitly used by Cudworth, the former explicitly by Price.

Cudworth's most satisfactory argument is against any account of goodness in terms of what is commanded. He points out that there is no obligation to do what is commanded just because it is commanded, unless whoever gives the command has legitimate authority and therefore the right to command[6]. In other words the

---
[3] Thus Bonhoeffer, Letter to a Friend, July 16th, 1944; Fontana, pp. 119-120.
[4] Thus N. Rescher, 'The Philosophy of Leibniz', p. 29.
[5] E.g. by A. N. Prior, 'Logic and the Basis of Ethics', Oxford, 1949, p. 13.
[6] 'British Moralists', Vol. I, pp. 108-9: this passage is extensively quoted by Prior at pp. 17f.

conclusion that an action is obligatory can only be derived from the premiss that someone has commanded it in conjunction with an ethical premiss to the effect that there is an obligation to obey that person. Cudworth also comes close to employing the argument from trivialisation: he points out that, if he is wrong, the proposition 'It is right to do what God commands' will be tautologous; and he assumes that his opponents cannot seriously believe this, or terms like 'good' will be 'names without signification'. He also remarks that, as God cannot make something just merely by willing it, the nature of justice must be independent of God's will.

The argument from derivation is also found in a number of moral philosophers through the rest of the early modern period. It underlies Hume's remarks in Treatise III:I:I about the underivability of 'ought' from 'is', and is likewise implicit in Kant's conviction that the fundamental principle of morality must be synthetic and *a priori*[7]. Meanwhile the argument from trivialisation had been employed in Price's 'Review of Morals'. Price declares that the implication of the truth of theories that "moral good and evil are only words for *advantageous* and *disadvantageous, willed* and *forbidden*" is that

> "it would be palpably absurd in any case to ask, whether it is *right* to obey a command, or *wrong* to disobey it; and the propositions, *obeying a command is right* or *producing happiness is right*, would be most trifling, as expressing no more than that obeying a command, is obeying a command, or producing happiness is producing happiness".[8]

Now both these arguments, it seems to me, are plausible until and unless a formula is actually found for defining an ethical term. If, however, such a definition can be produced, the argument from trivialisation collapses, for if 'right' means 'X' then the statement 'X things are right' and the question 'Are X things right?' will indeed be tautological. Moreover the argument from derivation only looks valid because the definitions offered for ethical terms are usually implausible, and it is therefore implausible that they supply the sense in which the ethical term in question is used in the

---

[7] Cf. 'Fundamental Principles of the Metaphysic of Morals', Translated by K. Abbott, Bobbs-Merrill, Indianapolis, 1949.
[8] 'A Review of the Principle Questions in Morals', Third Edition (1787), edited by D. Daiches Raphael, Oxford, 1948, pp. 16 f.

conclusion supposedly derived from them. In fact it is clearly invalid: for, from a definition of 'right' and a proposition to the effect that some type of act satisfies the requirements of the definition, it can validly be concluded that acts of that type are right.

Nevertheless a plausible definition of 'right' is hard to give: and until one is given, the argument from trivialisation is effective. And this is the case over theological naturalism: it is most implausible that "Is God's will right?" is a tautologous question. Thus Cudworth's argument successfully concludes that if God, the Bible or the Church command something, it is not *ipso facto* right or obligatory. At the same time this position is fully consistent with holding e.g. that we ought to do whatever God commands *because he is our benefactor*, granted that benefactors are owed special consideration. Cudworth's reasoning was in no way antitheological: it was indeed intended to show, among other things, that God was reasonable and just not *by definition*, but actually *in fact*. Cudworth did in fact establish the falsity of the former, a gain both for the secularisation of moral theory and for theology. But to find even an implicit denial that morality needs theologcial premisses, we need to look elsewhere.

C. The Adequacy of Non-Theological Premisses.

Hobbes in 'Leviathan' derives principles of obligation from men's wanting self-preservation above all else and from his insights into the most effective and rational means to this end. He assumes that pre-social men could exercise rationality; while his view about men's strongest desire tallies with (but is not derivable from) the form that human vitality is likely to take, granted Hobbesian mechanism and necessitarianism. The form of Hobbes' derivations is a valid one: for if M is a means to end E, and someone desires E above all else, then with respect to the end which is the object of their strongest desire they indeed *ought* to bring about M.

This, then, is how Hobbes' 'laws of nature' are derived: but as some[9] have urged instead that they are obligatory because they are

---

[9] Thus A. E. Taylor, 'The Ethical Doctrine of Hobbes', 'Philosophy', Oct., 1938: and Howard Warrender, 'The Political Philosophy of Hobbes', O.U.P., 1957. Their view is effectively rejected by J. W. N. Watkins in 'Hobbes System of Ideas', ch.V. In the present connection I am much indebted to Watkins.

commanded by God[10], it is worth consulting the passage where Hobbes himself seems to say this.

"These dictates of reason, men used to call by the name of laws, but improperly: for they are but conclusions, or theorems concerning what conduceth to the conservation and defence of themselves; whereas law, properly, is the word of him, that by right hath command over others. But yet if we consider the same theorems, as delivered in the word of God, that by right commandeth all things; then are they properly called laws."[11]

Here it is possible to construe the second sentence as implying that the dictates of reason can be derived from theology. Yet Hobbes could not have taken this view, since he holds that all we can know of God is that he exists[12], not what he is like. What Hobbes means is that the dictates of reason are derivable from nature, and nature is caused to exist by God. Therefore (if God has a will) the dictates of reason *must* also be laws of God. Thus the only theological reasoning which could support a Hobbesian law of nature is parasitic upon non-theological reasoning: the social and political agreements we ought to make are only commanded by God (if at all) because human life and the conditions of human life require them. (The possibilities of relating religion and morality on this kind of model will be discussed in Section 3.)

Hobbes, then, shows that a set of practical principles are derivable from statements about nature, and that they would still be so derivable even if nature were not created by God. He also presents his principles in such a way that men would act on them without religious motivation: short of a clash between fear of divine everlasting punishment and fear of death, motives inculcated specifically by religion are unlikely either to encourage us to act on Hobbes' principles or deflect us from them — unless we believe we have other obligations. But these Hobbes would contend we cannot have: our ends are fixed by our human physiology.

It was similarly held by Spinoza that we have no choice of

---

[10] Watkins (pp.85-7) finds this doctrine in Taylor at p. 418, and in Warrender at pp. 98-9.

[11] 'Leviathan', Part I, chapter 16: Oakeshott edition, pp. 104-5.

[12] 'Leviathan', Part I, chapter 12: Oakeshott edition, p. 68.

ultimate ends, (though Spinoza represents the ends we necessarily have as individuality and "freedom"[13]). And Spinoza similarly derives what we ought to do from our ends and from what rationally conduces to their attainment. Nor are theological reasons or motives needed to support the principles he derives. A further similarity between the ethical theory of the two men is their denial that terms like 'good' and 'bad' either stand for objective properties or are ever (severally) used in the same sense when uttered by different speakers[14]: for their sense varies (Hobbes) with the ends of the speaker or (Spinoza) the needs of the man spoken about.

If, however, it is not assumed that our ends are fixed for us, then we may be free to agree about ends and thus to have public standards of goodness, rightness, virtue and obligation. And in actual fact teleological theories of morality (theories on which either acts or rules are morally right because of their conduciveness to states of affairs desirable or valuable either intrinsically or for reasons other than moral ones) have usually included ends other than self-regarding ones, unlike the theories of Hobbes and Spinoza. Morality is hardly morality unless the welfare of others is respected. Yet even if this is conceded, the teleological moral theorist is no more obliged to derive his principles from theological considerations than were Hobbes and Spinoza.

A parallel criticism of Hobbes can be made from the Kantian viewpoint, on which teleological moral theories are false. Hobbes' principles are not moral ones, for they are only binding on those who want to save their skin. But properly moral principles are universally binding, regardless of what people want. (If the Kantian case is put *like this*, the teleological moral theorist can agree, in that desirable states of affairs are not always wanted.) The common criticism of Hobbes is then that his principles are neither disinterested nor display that respect on the part of agents for others which is essential to morality. Let Hobbes' reply, that on this understanding no-one can be obliged to be moral, men being so made as to preclude it, be set on one side as false, and the criticism be accepted. It still does not follow that moral principles need

---

[13] See S. Hampshire, 'Spinoza and the Idea of Freedom', in 'Studies in the Philosophy of Thought and Action', edited by P. F. Strawson, O.U.P., 1968: pp. 48-70.

[14] 'Leviathan', Part I, chapter 6, Oakeshott edition, pp. 32-3: 'Ethics', Preface to Part IV, Elwes translation, Vol. II, pp. 187-190.

either theological justifications or theological motives. For if the followers of Kant are right, and the moral "ought" is not conditional on the desirability of various states of affairs which obligatory actions bring about, then fundamental moral principles will be *sui generis* and underivable; and, further, anyone who acts on them from ulterior motives such as theological ones will not be fully moral.

It is not at all surprising, therefore, that the full logical independence of morality from religion was affirmed not long after Hobbes and Spinoza had shown the way. Thus Shaftesbury, in his 'Inquiry Concerning Virtue or Merit' assumes the separability of morality and religion, but implicitly vindicates his assumption in the course of testing whether religion fosters morality or not. For to do this he has to give an independent account of morality, which he does in terms of actions conducive to the public interest performed by those to whom the notion of 'public interest' is understood.[15] Shaftesbury's work was soon translated into French by Diderot and also into German, thus exercising a considerable influence both in Britain and on the Continent.[16] But for present purposes his importance lies in his giving an account of morality recognisable as morality, uncommitted either to egoism or necessitarianism, and yet independent of supports or sanctions supplied by theology.

That such an account is possible the thologian can, I believe, agree, (except in so far as duties to God may be derivable from facts about God in conjunction with other premisses). Once theological naturalism is rejected, theological premisses in moral reasoning are only likely to be relevant in conjunction with premisses like "We ought to pay special consideration to benefactors." But it makes sense to seek moral reasons for *this* principle: and such independent moral reasons may well constitute a check on the rightness of what alleged revelations of divine will enjoin. If, for example, respect for human welfare can clash with scriptural commands, then we have standards which allow us to decide what is right without resort to scripture. This is not to deny, of course, that theological premisses may sometimes be relevant to moral reasoning. It is just that they are not always needed.

---

[15] Shaftesbury's 'Characteristics', edited J. M. Robertson, (2 Vols., London, 1900) Vol. I, pp. 237-338, and particularly pp. 252-258.
[16] Thus Bourke, Vol. I, pp. 205 and 211.

And if that is so, it is crucially important that it should be recognised to be so. Unless the reasons for alleged obligations are understood and explained, action will be unspontaneous and reluctant. And if there are moral reasons independent of scriptural and ecclesiastical authority, men need to understand them if they are to make responsible choices for themselves, and rationally to reconsider old institutions and devise new ones in the light of changing circumstances. Once again, then, it is secularisation which conduces to human maturity: and, if so, the theologian is committed to sympathising with secularisation at least in this particular form.

Section 2: Theology and Utilitarianism

A. How Secular is Utilitarianism?

According to Plamenatz,[17] utilitarianism is the doctrine whose "adherents assert or assume the truth of the following propositions:

(i) Pleasure is alone good or desirable for its own sake; or else men call only those things good that are pleasant or a means to what is pleasant.

(ii) The equal pleasures of any two or more men are equally good.

(iii) No action is right unless it appears to the agent to be the action most likely, under the sircumstances, to produce the greatest happiness; or else men do not call any action right unless it is one of a type that usually produces the greatest happiness possible in the circumstances.

(iv) Men's obligations to the government of the country in which they live, and that government's duties to them, have nothing to do with the way in which the government first acquired power or now maintains it, except to the extent to which these origins and methods affect its ability to carry out these duties."

Plamenatz allows that these propositions are imprecise, but claims that some imprecision is necessary if the common beliefs of

---

[17] 'The English Utilitarians', (2nd edition, Oxford, 1958); p. 2.

Eighteenth and Nineteenth Century utilitarians are to be set out. And he goes on to show how the above propositions were accepted (among Eighteenth Century utilitarians) by Hume, Bentham and Godwin, and how according to Paley they are accepted by God.

A number of thinkers inclined to utilitarianism were also either necessitarians or actualists — Hume, Helvetius, Priestley and Godwin among them, and some of them proposed what, if the argument of Chapter 3 is correct, were secularist conceptual changes. Thus Hume urges that voluntariness is not necessary for a quality to be a virtue;[18]—Priestley that 'praiseworthy' means "influenced by such principles as will make a man happy in himself, and useful to others"[19]; and Godwin that the notions of desert and punishment strictly lack application. [20] But although the utilitarians were mostly inclined to an anti-theological doctrine of man in this connection, such views were inessential to their utilitarianism. On the subject of punishment, for example, a utilitarian only needs to hold that the moral justification of penalties can only be in terms of their promotion of happiness or their prevention of unhappiness: he need not take a view on the question of responsibility. (But this is enough to show, as proposition (iii) above suggests, that utilitarianism is essentially a teleological theory of morality (as defined in Section 1C above.)

It could also appear, in the light of proposition (iii), that utilitarians are committed to social reform. If the acts of public officials are only morally right in the circumstances mentioned, many Eighteenth Century institutions were morally in need of reform. Among English utilitarians, Priestley, Bentham and Godwin took this view:[21] according to Plamenatz they were spurred to radicalism partly as a result of Helvetius' rediscovery that men and society can be moulded by changes in the social environment which are within human control.[22] But not all utilitarians agreed that the rules of current society did not in fact maximise happiness: and Hume, Burke and Paley deployed utilitarian arguments for retaining the

---

[18] 'An Inquiry Concerning the Principles of Morals', Appendix IV, Selby-Bigge pp. 312-323. See also R. Attfield, 'Talents, Abilities and Virtues', 'Philosophy', July, 1971, pp. 255-8.

[19] 'Of the Doctrine of Necessity' in 'A Free Discussion', at pp. 150f.

[20] Plamenatz, p. 92.

[21] Priestley, 'Essay on the First Principles of Government', (London, 1768): Bentham, 'Introduction to the Principles of Morals and Legislation', (London, 1789): Godwin, 'Political Justice', (London, 1793).

[22] Op. cit., pp. 49f.

status quo. Utilitarianism was nevertheless potentially a force for reform, wherever the facts showed that new institutions would do more good. To this extent it was also a secular doctrine, since the institutions eventually to be criticised on such grounds included ones in which ecclesiastical power was vested.[23] But this is not to imply any incompatibility with the morality of the prophets or of the teaching of Jesus: the Bible often criticises social conventions on similar grounds. Indeed Priestley was both a Unitarian and a political radical.

Proposition (iv), however, is essential to a doctrine on which the justification of obligations lies in the good which habitual compliance with them would do. For this justification can clash with justifications of political obligation which appeal to the origins of Sovereignty, whether through Divine appointment or social contract. This was seen clearly by Hume,[24] and all later utilitarians followed him on this subject. In that this proposition disputes the view that the obligation to obey the Sovereign is unqualified because he rules by divine right, its promulgation is an instance of secularisation: but, as we have just seen, it was also used to subvert the secular contract theory. Once again there is no necessary conflict with theology, as at least the Protestant supporters of the Revolution of 1688-9 would perhaps have been willing to agree. It should at the same time be observed that at any rate this tenet of utilitarianism is compatible with the belief that citizens have rights the exercise of which the government is obliged to protect: for such protection might be part of the good which the Sovereign brings about and which justifies the subjects' loyalty. (More will be said of rights in Section 3B.)

In order to interpret proposition (iii) it is necessary to understand the diverse approaches of Hume and Bentham. Hume[25] regarded moral philosophy as a branch of the science of human nature. As a moral sense theorist he seems to have held that in calling something good we are expressing (which is not the same thing as stating) our approval of it: and he then seems to regard it as an inductive issue what things we do approve or call virtuous. A

---

[23] I do not wish to imply that non-teleological theories could not be secular, even in this self-same respect.

[24] 'An Enquiry Concerning the Principles of Morals', Section III, Selby-Bigge pp. 183-204. 'Of the Original Contract', edited by T. H. Green and T. H. Grose, London, 1889, Vol. II, pp. 443-459.

[25] See 'Treatise' III. and the second 'Inquiry'.

little research satisfies him that we call qualities virtuous which are either agreeable or useful, either to the man whose quality the quality is or to others. Now as what is agreeable is immediately pleasureable and as 'useful' is used of what conduces, ultimately, to pleasure or the diminishment of pain, Hume's finding is without doubt utilitarian, so long as it is understood that he is offering neither a definition nor a criterion of virtue or rightness, but purporting to describe the circumstances in which we express our sentiments by using moral terms. This does not, however, prevent Hume from explaining how it is that the moral and political institutions which we praise are in fact useful: indeed showing this is integral to his project. It should be added that the interpretation of Hume (and of his consistency) is highly controversial: I have attempted here to portray a consensus view. (Nor have I made Hume consistent: indeed if Hume is saying in some places that our moral judgements do not express propositions and in others that morally good qualities are either agreeable to someone or useful to someone, he will clearly be committed to inconsistency.)

Bentham, on the other hand, was uninterested in epistemology, but desired a clear moral vocabulary in which to discuss practical principles and issues. Finding the inherited moral vocabulary of little use, Bentham supplied a definition of rightness which is well set out as the first disjunct of Plamenatz' proposition (iii) above: and he goes on to say that

> "When thus interpreted, the words *ought*, and *right* and *wrong* and others of that stamp, have a meaning: when otherwise, they have none."

Thus Bentham is an ethical naturalist. (But his definitions satisfy few today.)

It is possible, however, to neglect the differences of approach of the two men and assess what *implicitly* they both supply, a criterion of rightness. Let it be assumed, for the present, that propositions (i) and (ii) give a satisfactory account of what it is to bring about good: the criterion can then be taken as declaring that either acts or rules are right which, as far as can be predicted, produce most good. (It is not of course rules that do good but habitual compliance with them: this rider should be read into the criterion.) The next difficulty concerns whether acts or rules should be assessed: here Hume and Bentham differ, but a compromise formula would be one on which actions should be assessed by the rightness of the rules they fall under where there are rules well-justified on utilitarian grounds, and only where there are no such rules should they be considered on their own merits. Acts of legislation will often fall into the latter class. This formula leaves many problems unsolved (e.g. cases where rules clash): nevertheless it makes the criterion clear except for marginal cases (granted again that problems about what is good are left on one side).

Now *if* we are allowed to hold, as the utilitarians did, that the justification of justice lies in its promotion of human welfare, or *if*, failing that, we are allowed to regard just distribution as an instance of the good which right actions are being said to promote, then it is hard to envisage either how utilitarianism clashes (here) with Biblical morality, or indeed how anything could be called a morality which is incompatible with the criterion in question. If moral rightness is unconnected with the promotion of *good* (just distributions included), it is hard to see how anyone can coherently use the phrase 'moral rightness'. The connection seems to be a necessary one. As to the morality of the Bible, Jesus appears on several occasions to have questioned established institutions on precisely such a teleological basis.[26] It is, incidentally, the same basis as that in which Bacon and Descartes found the justification of the pursuit of natural philosophy.[27]

The difficulties enter, however, when we begin to ask what will count as good. It has frequently been contended[28] that it may often be just to do what does not maximise happiness: thus, however broadly we contrue 'happiness', *unless* the bringing about of justice is included in what counts as good, the above criterion fails as an account of morality. Such problems will be considered in Section 3B below. Meanwhile it is necessary to point out that, despite appearances, they are not solved by proposition (ii).

Proposition (ii) may, *prima facie*, be taken to imply that pleasures ought to be distributed equally, and thus to be a principle of distributive justice. But this it does not say. Let it be assumed that different men's pleasures can in some way be compared, even if there are no units of measurement. The principle does not declare that extra pleasures should be withheld from all until all have received equal pleasures. Rather it offers

---

[26] Cf. e.g. Mk. 2 verse 27: Lk. 14, verse 5.
[27] See Chapter 1.
[28] E.g. by Price, 'Review', Raphael's edition, p. 160.

help to an agent who wants to know whether one man's pleasures count for more than another's; and he is told that they do not. This has several implications. One is that where he can produce more pleasure by benefiting others rather than himself, he should do the former. Another is that, if equal pleasure would result from benefiting a minority or a majority, neither act is more right than the other. This is because, on the proposition under consideration, if intense or long-standing enjoyment for a few is equal in extent to lesser enjoyment for each of a larger number, an equal amount of good is done by bringing about either.

What proposition (ii) does, however, preclude is preferring in all matters one's own benefit to that of others. While not urging self-denial or self-effacement, it is thus a principle of altruism. Human pleasure ought to be increased, whether it is mine or another's. The present proposition, then, far from being a politically radical claim, is very largely a reflection of that altruistic element without which (as was observed in Section 1C above) morality is not morality. In Hume, the proposition corresponds with the observation that we approve what is agreeable or useful to persons other than ourselves, an observation itself backed by the denial that all human motivation is the resultant of self-interest.[29] Nevertheless it implies more: for, were it acted upon, those already blessed with a happy life would often be further advantaged instead of those in need. Thus in conjunction with (i) and (iii) it may be a principle of injustice, and one hard to accommodate with morality at all. If so, agreement between utilitarians and Christian or Jewish moralists would reach a limit here.

The above remarks about Bentham and Hume will again serve to explain the disjunctive form of proposition (i). The common element here is that the utilitarianism of both men is a form of ethical hedonism. Now it is here, I shall claim, that utilitarianism embraces secularism. Before I justify this claim, it is only fair to note how some theists like Locke and Paley were nevertheless ethical hedonists.

Locke defines moral good and evil as the sources of divinely inflicted pleasure and pain, and Paley implicitly follows suit. Locke reaches this position by a more general definition of 'good' and 'evil':—

---

[29] See the second 'Inquiry', Appendix II, Selby-Bigge, pp. 295-302.

> "Things are good and evil only in reference to pleasure and pain. That we call good, which is apt to cause or increase pleasure, or diminish pain in us; or else to procure or preserve us the possession of any other good or absence of any other evil. And, on the contrary, we name that evil which is apt to produce or increase any pain, or diminish any pleasure in us; or else to procure us any evil, or deprive us of any good."[30]

The circularity of this Locke's fullest definition is elsewhere avoided:

> "Good and evil . . . are nothing but pleasure and pain, or that which occasions or produces pleasures or pain to us."[31]

Moral good and evil are then qualities of voluntary actions which, by complying or failing to comply with divine law, bring upon us appropriate pleasures and pains. Compliance with such laws, however, constitutes virtue, as God's laws require virtuous and beneficial actions. Thus being virtuous is the means to our own happiness. Locke is thus (at least in some passages) a theological naturalist, and at the same time an ethical hedonist: he believes that we ought to do what will promote our own pleasure.

Paley's God is more explicitly utilitarian: "Such . . . is the divine character, that what promotes the general happiness is required by the will of God . . ."[32] Paley relates obligation to the will of God by defining the former as "what I have a violent motive to do resulting from the command of another."[33] And since the motive consists in the hope of reward and the fear of suffering, Paley is also implicitly an ethical hedonist as well as a theological naturalist: he holds that I ought to do what will give me pleasure or prevent my suffering pain.

The refutation of Locke's and Paley's theological naturalism would however mean that, if morality is to have any altruistic content, their ethical egoistic hedonism must be rejected with it. But is hedonism in *any* form recognisable as a moral criterion? Not surely on the standards of the New Testament, on which the mature manhood to which people are called amounts to much more than just their enjoyment of pleasure. According to the New Testament people are benefited not only by being given enjoyment but also by becoming free.[34] Now being free will at least

---

[30] 'Essay', II.XX.2. Quoted by A. N. Prior, op. cit., p. 96.
[31] Ibid., II. XXVIII.5; quoted ibid.
[32] 'Principles', p. 55: quoted by Plamenatz, op.cit., p. 53.
[33] William Paley, 'The Principles of Moral and Political Philosophy' (1785), Book II, ch. II: 'British Moralists', Vol. II, p. 258.
[34] Romans 8, verse 21.

involve the exercise of one's capacities for rationality and discrimination, and also (normally) being allowed within society some scope for choice and the expression of one's own individuality. Utilitarians may point out that the exercise of one's faculties is pleasurable, and that freedom from constraint facilitates the promotion of pleasure. But even if they are right, it is implausible that the sole reason why the exercise of discrimination is good is its pleasurability or that the sole reason why freedom from contraint is good is its social utility. For the latter is also good as a necessary condition of the development of the individual concerned, and the former is good because it is contitutive of human welfare or human flourishing.

Accordingly a great many states of affairs are desirable not because of their contribution to pleasure or their diminishment of pain: nor, if we replace the word 'pleasure' with 'happiness' or 'pain' with 'unhappiness' does this cease to be true. Nor does the current criticism of utilitarianism (and other forms of ethical hedonism) hang simply on its incompatibility with Christianity. Rather it is that utilitarianism construes human welfare too narrowly. (This was eventually half-recognised by John Stuart Mill.) It can be agreed that what promotes human welfare is to that extent good, but it is false that human welfare consists only in pleasure. Were someone to maintain that the welfare of sentient beings and its just distribution were alone good, and alone what ultimately made right actions right, I should not know how to disagree. But (waiving problems about justice) morality is mischaracterised if it is held that the rightness of right actions hangs solely on the promotion of pleasurable sensations and activities. In other words proposition (i) is false.

Utilitarianism is, further, incompatible with the theistic doctrine of man. If man is made in the image of God and is human partly in virtue of a capacity for self-determination, no-one will flourish as a human unless that capacity is exercised. Yet classical utilitarianism (alongside hedonists like Locke and Paley, good theists as they were) denies that the exercise of this capacity is intrinsically good: rather it is only held to be good insofar as it is pleasurable or leads to pleasure. Often, of course, it neither is pleasurable nor leads to pleasure: yet the very exercise of the capacity in question shows that those powers in virtue of which their possessor is called a *man* are being, in some small measure, exercised. Thus on classical utilitarianism it is only right to educate people if the choices they are thus enabled to make are immediately pleasurable or issue in pleasure: whereas on the theistic doctrine of man to bring about something good. And each view of man has its moral implications. On the latter view respect ought to be paid to people's freedom and their need to exercise their own powers as individuals, because these things are intrinsically good: on a consistent interpretation of classical utilitarianism, such respect is only in place where someone's happiness is in prospect.

It will be clear that I have assumed in the above that facts about human flourishing are relevant to moral obligations. To this assumption I return in Section 2C. But meanwhile at least two difficulties have emerged for utilitarianism, concerned with justice and liberty. On both counts, utilitarianism is hard put to it to explain *rights*, (as was observed by Price)[35], and to the subject of rights I now turn.

B. Rights, Utilitarianism and Theism.

If utilitarianism cannot supply a satisfactory account of some of our obligations, it is likely to be similarly defective in accounting for people's moral rights to be treated in various ways and not to be treated in others. Thus there are moral reasons for helping the weak within society rather than the strong; and, as it is for their own sake as persons in need of help that they should be helped, they have a moral *right* to be helped. And that the weak have such moral rights is a matter of justice, but not plausibly a matter of utility in the traditional sense. Similarly if utilitarianism fails to justify the promotion of individual liberty as something good *as such*, it equally fails to account for the moral right to liberty, except where the exercise of that right would overall contribute to people's pleasure.

Similar problems for utilitarianism were noticed by Richard Price. While seeing that utility is one ground of rights and the sole ground of some rights,[36] he also claims that there are many rights which the public interest cannot justify as we know them.[37] The rights of individuals to life and liberty are among the objects of his concern: and it is certainly implausible that hedonistic utilitarianism can accord these rights the place morality normally does accord them.

Now one respect in which utilitarianism differs from many theories of morality is that it is prepared to offer reasons for the rightness of right acts, and supplies criteria on which the rightness of allegedly right acts can be questioned. As, in addition, its

---

[35] 'Review', Raphael's edition, p. 160.
[36] Op. cit., Raphael's edition, p. 164.
[37] pp. 159-161.

account of what makes right acts right allows their rightness to be tested fairly readily, it would be fair to term it secular in these respects alone, quite apart from others: for traditional customs and institutions are much more likely to be questioned on this basis than, say, on a criterion of rightness by which acts enjoined by a consensus of scriptural passages are right. In part what lends it this secular character is the fact that it is a teleological theory: acts or rules are held on such theories to be right because they contribute to what is good (i.e. desirable or valuable) by standards *other* than moral ones, and thus moral disputes are to be resolved by reflection on facts discoverable by some discipline other than ethics. (This is not to be confused with reductionist or naturalist theories of moral rightness: for an account of the criteria for the correct application of a term need not supply an analysis of that term.) But now it emerges that traditional utilitarianism is defective. Do problems about moral rights therefore set limits to all attempts to supply reasons for moral judgements, and undermine all theories which are secular in respect of being teleological (in the above sense)?

This would at any rate seem to be the view of Kant. For Kant regards it as an irreducible and non-derivative principle of morality that we should 'treat humanity... in every case as an end. . ., never as (a) means only'.[38] The rightness of such action is not to be justified by its contribution to any non-moral good. And this principle is clearly a suitable basis for a theory of moral rights: for if it is right so to treat humanity simply *as* humanity, then humanity has a right so to be treated.

Nevertheless the problem is partially alleviated if, instead of Plamenatz' proposition (i) above, teleologists count *human welfare* as what is (non-morally) good for its own sake. This at any rate at once allows us to make sense of a claim that an act is right because it increases liberty, even if no claim is made about any increase in enjoyment. For liberty will always be needed if people are to flourish as people.

But the problem is only partially alleviated: for it has not yet been shown how teleology can accommodate distributive justice, and the rights to which distributive justice gives rise. This can only be done if acts which are right because just can be presented as contributive to a *condition of society* in which what different individuals need if they are to flourish is supplied; and if they are right for that reason. This project involves the teleologist in forgoing treating the maximising of the fostering of human welfare as sufficient as a criterion of rightness unless the welfare of minorities is somehow given priority: for it may be unjust to foster the welfare

---

[38] 'Fundamental Principles', ('Grundlegung'), Abbott translation, p. 46.

of a majority and neglect that of a minority; and, if unjust, then wrong. Nevertheless, if it is the supplying of what individuals need if they are to flourish that is the concern of justice, the notion of human welfare would continue to occupy a prominent place in a suitably sophisticated teleological theory. I shall not venture here to offer such a theory but find hope that it can be accomplished in a recent paper of R. E. Ewin, called 'Justice and Injustice'.[39] Such a theory would at all events be likely to satisfy Price's concern over the right to life: for, except in rare cases made possible by the advent of respirators, nothing could be more deleterious to human welfare, than a person's being avoidably left to die.

Perhaps, then, a teleological theory of morality could be devised which would safeguard moral rights. Such a theory, while being secular in that it would allow of the criticism of social and political traditions, would nevertheless reflect what theists believe about man. For, once again, if man is made in the image of God and is human partly in virtue of a capacity for self-determination, no-one will flourish as a human unless that capacity is exercised. Life, health and liberty will then be needed by an individual if he is to exercise that capacity and if, a *fortiori*, he is to flourish. But morality is hardly morality unless agents count other people's welfare as a moral reason which supports actions that further it. Thus there are moral reasons why people's needs for life, health and liberty should where possible be supplied, and these reasons apply equally to all people alike. Therefore, on the theistic view of man, individual men have moral rights; rights to liberty, and to be supplied, where possible, with the means to stay alive and to be healthy. All this can equally be derived from what Price says of the needs of souls in his sermon, 'The Nature and Dignity of the Human Soul', although the only implications Price draws from these needs are (other people's) obligations, not the rights of the individual concerned.

Thus over rights as well as over obligations theism clashes with the utilitarianism of Plamenatz' four principles, though perhaps not with all forms of teleological theories of morality. This means, however, that the teachings of theism can be of help to those who find in utilitarianism too impoverished a description of morality. Historically arguments both of a utilitarian and a theistic kind were put forward side by side in the struggle for religious toleration and freedom of speech.

---

[39] 'Mind', Vol. LXXIX, No. 314, April, 1970, pp. 200-216. Ewin manages to relate the rewarding of merit to the contributions of the meritorious to the supply of *needs*. An amended teleological theory is presented in my 'Toward a Defence of Teleology', 'Ethics', Vol. 85, 1975, pp. 123-135.

Oddly, the very untheological ethic of Kant urges us to treat other humans and ourselves as intrinsically valuable in virtue of our humanity. This doctrine is incompatible with an ethic which seeks the majority happiness alone: yet, strangely, like the theistic view of man it is probably compatible with a teleological theory of morality in which the rightness of actions is related to their fostering of human welfare including the exercise of individuals' characteristically human capacities. To agree *here* with Kant in no way precludes commitment to a theory of morality which is secular because teleological.

C. God, Human Flourishing and Morality.

It is now time to draw some threads together. In Section 1 of this Chapter it is contended not only that theological naturalism is misconceived, but also that it is possible to give a non-theological account of morality. This would involve a criterion of what is moral which both excluded reference to God and is such that moral judgements could be derived from it in conjunction with statements of fact themselves exclusive of reference to God. Shaftesbury was one of the first to characterise morality in a suitable way, but many others, Bentham and Kant among them, were to follow suit (difference as their criteria of morality were).

One of the strands in the current Section has been the centrality of the notion of human welfare in any plausible criterion of moral rightness. While the hedonism of the utilitarians cannot account for our ordinary moral beliefs, it was contended that a broader form of teleological theory may be more adequate. If, further, God is benevolent and beneficent, his justice might well consist in his desire for the welfare of his individual creatures and therefore of their society: he would accordingly favour the social rules which are necessary for society to cohere and individuals to flourish within it.

If these threads are now woven together, it is possible to supply an account both of morality and of its relation to religion which, while preserving the better-grounded insights of secular theories of morality, nevertheless exhibits how morality may issue from the will of God. Curiously enough, this account will embody some of the elements in the systems of Locke and Paley (i.e. teleology, naturalism and belief in the relevance of God's will) though without their more objectionable beliefs (e.g. ethical hedonism and theological naturalism).

I begin, however, with a point mildly reminiscent of the views of Hobbes on the relation of God and morality. If God is the Creator of humans, he will know in what our welfare lies. But we cannot at once infer from this Hobbes' view that moral laws are thereby also God's laws. For this we also need premisses concerning God's benevolence and concerning the relation of human welfare and morality. But if it is additionally allowed that God is benevolent (and the grounds for this proposition are considered in a later chapter), then *eo ipso* God will desire our flourishing as people.

But how can one argue from facts about human flourishing (which will, in the light of the above, also happen to be facts about what God desires) to what morally *ought* to be done? There are grave difficulties in arguing from facts to propositions expressed in sentences including the word 'ought'. These difficulties, however, are diminished if 'ought' is so qualified as to disclose what range of reasons will count for present purposes: and I take such qualification to be achieved by inserting the term 'morally' in front of 'ought'. Not anything can count as a moral reason: and I could make no sense of the suggestion, were it seriously to be made, that contributions to human welfare are irrelevant when an act's or a rule's moral status are at stake. However *precisely* the relation should be expressed, there does seem to be an internal relation between the notions of morality and of human welfare: and it would further seem at least to be such that we can validly infer from the proposition 'Acts of type x conduce to human welfare' the further proposition, 'Those who can do so ought, morally speaking, to do acts of type x'. The conclusion of this inference need not be an expression of an overriding obligation, for there could also in particular cases be moral reasons for conflicting courses of action. I have not attempted to produce a criterion of rightness applicable in all situations. Rather the above conclusion conveys that *there are moral reasons* for the doing of acts of type x on the part of those able so to act.

The above theory is clearly a form of naturalism, for it involves the view that 'moral rightness' is capable of analysis. What *sort* of naturalism it is is harder to say: for several disciplines, sociology and psychology among them, are competent to discuss human welfare. Accordingly it is best termed 'anthropological naturalism' a label which clearly distinguishes it from the theological naturalism of Locke and Paley. It is also, obviously, a teleological theory, but one incompatible with ethical hedonism.

It might be objected that even if the above theory is allowed, there is little firm content to morality, for different cultures interpret the notion of human welfare differently. It would take me beyond my present terms of reference to attempt an adequate reply here. Suffice it to say that there is a core to the notion of human welfare (a core including the exercise of the capacity for self-determination) and that this core is implicit in what it is to be *human*;[40] a notion which must itself have a clear and invariable sense if it is possible to employ 'human' to mark off people from other animals. This core can be used as a test of the adequacy of the specifications which the ideas of different cultures supply concerning what human flourishing consists in.

If then God desires what constitutes the rationale of moral rules (and, by similar reasoning, moral virtues), he will favour the observation of these rules and the instantiation of these virtues. Thus, though we need no theological premisses in at least most moral reasoning, morality will still reflect the will of God. (I say 'most' since I have not discussed the alleged obligation to worship God, and its grounds). Further, granted God's benevolence, God is likely to make his will known through human moral reflection. This is in no way to argue for divine interventions in autonomous human thought: all that would be needed is that man is so created as to reflect on morality in a way which echoes God's will.

This means not only that the religious man will expectantly seek out moral revelations, which can then be ascribed to God. It also means that quite untheological moral thought may well express God's will, and that therefore moral theories fully in keeping with theism may be found in such secular thinkers as Bentham and Kant. And as we have seen, Bentham's stress on the rational criticism of traditional institutions against the criterion of (what he took to be) human needs, and Kant's stress on the value of the individual appear to embody emphases essential to theistic morality.

Thus secular moral theories, like secular science, were to a large extent the historical and logical outcome of theistic religion. The main qualification which this statement needs to receive is that theories such as utilitarianism sometimes stressed some elements in morality (impartiality, the promotion of happiness) at the expense of others (concern for the development of personality and the needs of minorities), and that theism was one of the sources from which correctives were available. Yet, as in the case of science, new life was breathed into moral theory as the constraints of ecclesiastical authority and religious dogma receded: and it was mainly secularising theorists who were able to appraise and criticise the new social conditions which came into being in Britain in the late eighteenth and early nineteenth centuries. Nevertheless

---

[40] See my 'On Being Human', 'Inquiry', 17, 1974, pp. 175-192, and 'Against Incomparabilism', 'Philosophy', 30, 1975, pp. 230-234.

their moral critique, like the later one of Marx, was in many respects a continuation of the prophetic tradition of Judaism and of primitive Christianity.[41]

---

[41] For an assessment of the morality of theistic attitudes to nature, see Chapter 1, Section 4C.

CHAPTER 5

THE GROUNDS OF THEISM I

Section 1: The Need for Natural Theology

A. Epistemology and Revelation.

If religious belief is to be criticised or defended, appeal must be made beyond purported revelations from God. Not will historical reasoning alone suffice for either purpose. Such reasoning must therefore take the form of natural theology, that is reflection about God on the basis of perfectly general considerations, accessible, at least in theory, to all, whether the recipients of an alleged religious revelation or not. Indeed this philosophical conclusion is properly one which theists need, and can afford, to welcome. The foregoing contentions will be justified in the course of the first Section of this Chapter, arising, as they did, from thinkers who recognised the autonomous character of philosophy alongside that of science and morals.

For the rest, the present Chapter will discuss criticisms of two arguments within natural theology, the ontological argument and the cosmological argument. In Chapter Six I go on to consider the teleological argument and its critics, and also the questions of God's goodness and of theodicy. If it can be shown to be probable that there is a benevolent God, part of the basis for the claim that there is a God of such a character as to be likely to reveal himself will already have been laid down. But to go beyond this basis would take me too far afield.[1] The present Chapter is concerned in part with the philosophical appraisal of more fundamental theistic tenets and of objections to them, and the present Section with the need of theist and atheist alike to have arguments respectively for and against them.

John Locke tells us[2] that revelation is a "way of discovering truths to men", namely that where "any proposition is not made

---

[1] I have argued for the more ambitious claim in a paper in 'Religious Studies', Vol. 9, No. 1, pp. 1-9, entitled 'The God of Religion and The God of Philosophy'.

[2] Essay, IV: XVIII: 2.

out by the deductions of reason, but upon the credit of the proposer, as coming from God, in some extraordinary way of communication." Revelation is thus propositional, and one of the sources of knowledge. Some modern theologians tell us that the Biblical notion of revelation is not propositional, and concerns not divinely transmitted information but divine action for the salvation of men. Insofar, however, as religious *beliefs* are sometimes said to rest on purported divine activity, there will still be propositions believed in as a result of the occurrence of divine revelation: 'belief *in* . . .' is, after all, only possible where there is also 'belief *that*. . .' Locke's definition will therefore serve, not only as explaining what was meant by revelation in his day but also as picking out an essential element of the meaning of 'revelation' wherever that word is used among theistic traditions. The chief qualification needed is that propositions "made out as coming from God" will only be *purportedly* revelatory, whereas a proposition "discovered to men" by God himself will actually *be* revelatory.

Both during, before and after the period under consideration religious doctrines would often be upheld on the strength of revelation. But during this period, as seldom before, the danger of circularity in such reasoning was often pointed out.[3] How do we know that something is revealed? It will neither do to reply "Because our religion tells us so" nor to reply "Because it has been revealed". Considerations somehow independent of revelation will thus be required. And what brought to the fore problems such as these in the Seventeenth and Eighteenth Centuries was the renewed interest in epistemology.

Interest in epistemology in its turn was prompted by a variety of factors: the rivalry of dogmatic religious faiths, the problems of natural philosophy, and also, at the outset, the quest of a number of Renaissance neoplatonists to describe the relations between the human mind and the universe. The problems of natural science were, directly or indirectly, part of the spur to enter upon philosophy for three of the epistemologists I shall mention, Spinoza, Locke and Kant: but this does not seem to hold good of the other, Edward Lord Herbert of Cherbury, who was also the earliest. It would be tidy if all the great secularising thinkers of the period could be viewed as in some way influenced by the new scientific movement of the Seventeenth Century, but Lord Herbert would seem to be an exception.[4] Nevertheless, they held in

---

[3] Among others by Locke at Essay IV: XIX: 10.
[4] See e.g. Meyrick H. Carré's introduction to his translation of 'De Veritate' (1624), Bristol, 1937.

common [5] the conviction that religious truth-claims needed, in the last resort, to be grounded — and appraised — in much the same way as other claims to knowledge. As remarked in Chapter 4, Section 1, Lord Herbert found truth-claims to rest ultimately on 'notitiae communes' or common notions, notions which commanded the assent either of all men or perhaps of all who were healthy of mind. It was natural that revealed truth should accordingly be tested on criteria which Lord Herbert would have claimed to issue from such 'notions' or propositions. Lord Herbert's epistemology is intended to furnish the basis for all knowledge, and it is mistaken to regard him as only able to appeal to the five *religious* common notions of Chapter IX. He also sets out in earlier Chapters to distinguish illusions from perceptions of reality and, in general, truth from falsity, and it is on such a basis that he is able to supply criteria for recognising revelations in Chapter X.

The more radical epistemology of Spinoza will come up for discussion in Section IB. The relevance of Locke's epistemology to revelation will be more immediately obvious: first, if all our knowledge is traceable either to ideas of sensation or to ideas of reflection, our knowledge that a particular proposition is revealed must be traceable to one or both of these sources, (even if its content cannot be); second, Locke's discussion of the degree of probability to be accorded to propositions grounded on testimony, and in particular on indirect testimony, offered scope for scepticism among later thinkers, often of an unduly far-reaching kind, about the historical claims of Christianity.[6] (It should however be granted to these thinkers that much more is required of testimony if it is to attest an event's being supernaturally caused than if it is merely to attest its occurrence.) Third, Locke's distinction between propositions according to reason, above reason and contrary to reason[7] readily led not only to the rejection of what is contrary to reason (as in Locke) but also (as in his disciple Toland)[8] to that of doctrines reason does not actually support. Even if Locke can give reasons for regarding the doctrine of immortality as a revealed truth, Toland can reply that if, despite this argument, it remains 'above reason' it is unreasonable to believe it.

---

[5] Though with some reservations on the part of Locke.

[5] For Locke, see Essay, IV: XVI: 10. For later thinkers see 'Deism: An Anthology', edited by Peter Gay, Van Nostrand. New York, 1968, p. 117 (a passage of Matthew Tindal's 'Christianity as Old as Creation'; also Rousseau, 'Emile', translated by Barbara Foxley, Everyman, London, pp. 261, 269f; Lessing, 'On The Proof of the Spirit and of Power', in 'Lessing's Theological Writings', selected and translated by Henry Chadwick, London, 1956, pp. 51-56, *passim*.

[7] Essay IV: XVII: 5-7.

[8] In 'Christianity Not Mysterious', Gay, p. 59.

Many of the arguments of the English Deists, developing as they do out of the epistemologies of Cherbury and of Locke, were taken over both by Rousseau, Reimarus and Lessing, and Lessing also borrowed from Spinoza.[9] A new epistemological note, however, was struck by Immanuel Kant, who contended in his 'Critique of Pure Reason' that the existence and nature of God could not be known by speculative reason at all, but only to the extent that they are postulates of practical reason.[10] One implication of these findings is spelt out in his 'Religion Within the Limits of Reason Alone'.[11] For purported revelations can be tested by the said postulates of practical reason, and indeed beliefs which exceed these postulates will, properly speaking, be beyond human comprehension. Kant's conclusions, however, cannot be assessed in isolation from some sort of discussion of his critique of speculative reason, an undertaking reserved for the two Sections following.

What can be said of the achievement of the epistemologists so far discussed is that their common claim that grounds are needed for truth-claims based on revelation is itself well-grounded. For there must be held to be some grounds for the proposition that a tenet has been revealed, if this proposition is sincerely asserted. To claim to know some proposition is necessarily to claim that there are good grounds which could be offered in its support, unless, that is, the claim is based on memory or perception. Knowledge that . . . cannot be groundless: such is the concept of knowledge. Thus at the very least we need criteria for recognising revelations or particular revealed truths, perhaps ones of the kind Cherbury propounds,[12] or at least of the more general kind proposed by Tindal.[13] We may also need the careful sifting of historical evidence:[14] and there may also be limits to what historical reasoning can establish (see Section 1B). Indeed at least this much can be said for Kant's reasoning: if a proposition, whether purportedly revealed or not, concerns God, then it can only be securely grounded on whatever form of reasoning *can* inform us about God. Further, granted what God must be like if he is our Creator, it is at least unlikely that even first-hand reports of unusual historical

---

[9] See Chadwick's introduction to 'Lessing's Theological Writings'.
[10] Translated by Norman Kemp Smith, Macmillan, London, 1968.
[11] Translated by Theodore M. Green and Hoyt H. Hudson, Harper, New York, 1934: at pp. 134-144.
[12] Carré translation, p. 308.
[13] Gay, pp. 116f.
[14] For more relevant principles, see Michael Goulder, 'Jesus the Man of Universal Destiny' in 'The Myth of God Incarnate', ed. John Hick, S.C.M. Press, London, 1977, p. 50.

events would suffice to do that alone. But this is to anticipate. The above claim of the epistemologists is, perhaps, best substantiated by the Savoyard priest in Rousseau's 'Emile'. As he retorts to an imaginary defender of 'Inspiration', "He who denies the right of reason, must convince me without recourse to her aid".[15] No-one is rationally obliged to listen to an appeal based on an alleged revelation alone, however allegedly self-authenticating. Herein the secularism of many of the thinkers discussed above was entirely justified, as theists can readily agree. The question which now arises, however, is that of what grounds will suffice for sustaining revealed religion, something which Cherbury and Locke at least wished to do.[16]

B. Is There a Revealer?

It has already been shown that the claim that a doctrine is a revealed one presupposes the claim that one has criteria for recognising revelations. Various possible criteria suggest themselves, such as the piety of the "proposer", or the morality of what he proposes: but I shall here discuss neither their relative merits nor their adequacy. For the more radical question arises whether, with respect to any proposition p, any historical event or action would suffice to show that the truth of p is revealed by God.

It is now time to introduce the epistemology of Spinoza, whose quest for the foundations of human knowledge was inspired by the similar quest of Descartes. (Spinoza thus took part like Locke and Kant in a movement one of the origins of which was reflection on the problems and method of natural philosophy.) According to Spinoza the foundations of knowledge lie in necessary truth, and all necessary truth is deducible from the divine nature.[17] Human perfection lies in contemplation of this eternal nature, and the Divine law consists in love of God adopted "solely because (a man) has knowledge of God, or is convinced that the knowledge and love of God is the highest good".[18] Spinoza's reasoning from his logic to his metaphysics cannot be assessed here; but the salient point is that according to Spinoza truths about God will be both timeless and necessary.

Accordingly he goes on to say, of the Divine law, "That it is universal or common to all men, for we have deduced it from universal human nature: (and) That it does not depend on the truth of

---

[15] Everyman translation, p. 265.
[16] For Cherbury, see Gay, p. 44: for Locke, see Essay IV: XVIII: 7, and 'The Reasonableness of Christianity', in 'Works', London, 1823, reprinted by Scientia Verlag Aalen, Germany, 1963, (Ten Volumes) Volume VII.
[17] See Chapter 1, Section 4A above.
[18] 'Tractatus Theologico-Politicus', chapter IV: Elwes translation, Vol. I., p. 60

any historical narrative whatsoever, for inasmuch as this natural Divine law is comprehended solely by the consideration of human nature, it is plain that we can conceive it as existing as well in Adam as in any other man . . . The truth of a historical narrative, however assured, cannot give us the knowledge nor consequently the love of God, for love of God springs from knowledge of Him, and knowledge of Him should be derived from general ideas, themselves certain and known, so that the truth of a historical narrative is very far from being a necessary requisite of our attaining our highest good."

Now many of Spinoza's claims here are open to objection, but at least one point commands respect, namely the proposition that necessary truths can only be derived from necessary truths. (Spinoza in consistency should have regarded even historical truths, if true, as necessary: but, being as aware as anyone that historical propositions lack this status, he chooses to regard them as not properly truths at all. Those, however, who allow that there are contingent truths do not have this difficulty, and Spinoza's point can then be rewritten, albeit in alien terms, in the form, "Necessary truths cannot be derived from contingent truths of history.") The point was in fact rewritten by Lessing in the form "Accidental truths of history can never become the proof of necessary truths of reason."[19]

One of the possible objections to Spinoza and Lessing (and more particularly to Lessing as, unlike Spinoza, he was a theist) is that not all propositions about God are necessary. This objection, which will be defended in the next two sections,[20] seems to offer scope for contingent truths, historical truths among them, to be of use as evidence in religion after all. And so it does, so long as we know of the existence and essential nature of God on other grounds: for certain events could be (timelessly) brought about by God, and accordingly could be evidence for his bringing them about, at least if we have reason to believe something else about him antecedently. But the proposition that a God able to create exists would have to be true for such events to count as evidence; and it is most unlikely to be rendered even probable by any historical events itself (for the conclusion would be disproportionate to the premises.) Thus even if God's existence is not logically necessary, historical events are not equal to affording it rational support: and, if so, are much less adequate for supplying evidence for whatever *is* necessarily true of God.

---

[19] In 'On the Proof of Spirit and of Power', Chadwick, p. 53.
[20] See also the definition of the doctrine of Creation (Chapter 1, Section 1D, note 19).

It can neither be true nor false that God reveals any proposition *unless God exists*. If then the historical facts concerned cannot be used as evidence for this, they cannot alone count as evidence that God reveals anything at all. Of course it will not do *just* to show it to be probable that God exists: for 'God reveals that p' entails 'God is of such a character as to be able and willing to reveal that p, if p is true'. And it was because of the lack of grounds for supposing that God was likely to reveal some of the propositions men allege him to reveal that both Rousseau's Savoyard Priest and later Kant doubted the revelatory character of much alleged revelation.[21]

The propositions entailed by particular claims about revelation may however come to appear probable if the existence of a *benevolent* God can itself be argued for.[22] The major enterprise, therefore, of upholders of revelation concerns arguing for the existential presupposition of all revelation, i.e. that God exists: a proposition which cannot be defended by an appeal to revelation without begging the question. Moreover theistic believers in revelation need to have grounds for believing that there is a God able to create, with all that that implies. Now even if these propositions lack the status of logical necessity, Lessing was correct to point out that the contingent propositions of history cannot support them unaided. How can even the life and death of Jesus begin to show that there is a necessarily timeless, omnipotent and omniscient God?

Nothing but natural theology can begin to show this. And indeed the resurgence of natural theology within the period under consideration reflects an underlying awareness of this truth. Men like Descartes, Boyle, Clarke and Leibniz were not content to appeal to their own basic religious convictions or to authoritative scriptures: instead they set out to give reasons with which to persuade non-theists, to reassure themselves, and to defend their own theism against charges of groundlessness. The reasoned defence of his religious beliefs by Clarke was in fact found by at least one man to be the only basis of sane belief among the conflicting claims of purported revelations. The man I have in mind is Rousseau's paragon of a religious teacher, the Savoyard Priest, who found in natural theology and in morality a calm basis for sifting his way through the clamour of dogma.

At the same time if nothing but natural theology can begin to show that God exists, the assaults on natural theology in the name of human reason need to be treated all the more seriously. It will

---

[21] See, respectively, 'Émile', book IV, and 'Religion within the Limits of Reason Alone'.

[22] As pointed out in Chapter 2, Section 6C, God might be able and willing to reveal his will without doing so through miracles.

not do to allege that faith has no truck with reason, even if the 'belief *that*...' which may emerge from reasoning is not the whole of the 'belief *in*...' or the commitment of faith. Reasoning remains essential if it is seriously to be held that there is a God to believe in. If, then, philosophical theology shows that there are no grounds for this existential claim, the basis of religion, revealed religion included, is undermined.

Section 2: *The Ontological Argument*

A. The Significance of the Argument.

Any attempt to enquire into the credentials of revelation, such as those discussed in Section 1 above, is an exercise of autonomous reason free from religious preconceptions, at least insofar as revelation is not taken for granted but scrutinised instead: and every such attempt is therefore an instance of secularisation. Some such enquiries conclude that the claims of churchmen to knowledge of various sorts are based on inappropriate grounds or no grounds at all: and this is the spirit of secularism. It has been observed that sometimes, as when men of religion take their stand on revelation alone, this secularism is justified, and also that when secularism involves an undue scepticism about historical testimony it is not justified. Beyond this point I am unable within the limits of the present work to take the assessment of such secularism further, as the criteria needed for such an assessment (e.g. criteria for the recognition of revelations) would require separate discussion. It can, however, be concluded that in at least one respect the attempt to explore the grounds of revelation merits theological praise and encouragement: for unless such grounds can be found religious belief stands (or falls) unsupported, and no non-believer is rationally obliged to take it seriously.

But if the exploration of the grounds of belief belongs to secularisation, so does the exposure of bogus purported grounds for belief. Nor should this activity receive theological censure, wherever theologians care about truth. In the rest of this Chapter and in the next, Seventeenth and Eighteenth Century criticisms of arguments in natural theology will be considered. Space will not permit discussion of the propounders of the arguments rather than of the criticisms: yet to discuss the critics rather than the propounders of the arguments is justified insofar as the critics took secularisation a good deal further than those they argued against. It should at the same time be remembered that to criticise arguments in natural theology is to do natural theology: and also that some of the critics (I am thinking of Gassendi and of Kant) were themselves religious believers, who saw their reasonings as beneficial to true religion and not deleterious to it.

I begin with the ontological argument not because it is customarily treated of first, nor because I believe it successful, but because of its significance, and because of problems about the notion of God which its discussion will reveal. A philosophical discussion of arguments for the existence of God should properly begin with an examination of the notion of God which the arguments argue to be instantiated. I shall claim, however, that the ontological argument is concerned with a crucially different notion of God from that of the cosmological argument. The former notion, moreover, is set out in the initial premiss of any plausible form of ontological argument for the existence of God, and only when the implications of that premiss have been explored can the important difference between the two notions concerned be remarked. Only at the end of this Section, therefore, will the concept of God itself come up for detailed consideration.

Meanwhile, before the criticisms of the argument of Gassendi, Hume and Kant are considered, the pivotal significance ascribed to the argument should first be noted. For Kant maintains[23] that the cosmological and teleological arguments turn out to depend on the ontological argument. If he is right, then the failure of the ontological argument would mean that there are no theoretical grounds on which theism rests; and that God's existence cannot be asserted, since an utterance is only intelligible as an assertion when there is at least the possibility of grounds for the proposition put forward. Should the critics of the argument, then, show it to fail, theism will lack grounds, unless, as argued in later Sections, Kant was wrong in this matter.

But the significance of the argument is not limited to this. For in an article in 'Mind', 1948,[24] J. N. Findlay has argued as follows. The conclusion of the ontological argument is that the existence of God is a necessary truth, and this conclusion is derived from the notion of God. But no existential proposition is a necessary truth. Therefore the notion of God is such that the existence of God is impossible. And further no other notion of God is adequate to the needs of worship. The ontological argument thus commits us to atheism.

---

[23] 'Critique of Pure Reason', pp. 510 and 524.
[24] Entitled 'Can God's Existence be Disproved?'

154 FINDLAY'S ARGUMENT RESTORED

I shall in due course dispute Findlay's claim that no other notion of God than that of the ontological argument is adequate to religious belief and attitudes: but even if I am right, the rest of Findlay's reasoning would still show, if successful, that those who accept the success of the argument are committed to agnosticism. One of Findlay's premisses, however, is false: for not all existential propositions are contingent. The proposition that realities exist is a counter-instance. There are, however, a number of ways of restoring Findlay's argument. For the ontological argument either assumes or purports to show that God is a necessarily existent being, and therefore one which necessarily exists. Now at least on some views (as discussed in Sub-Section B) there is an extensional (as opposed to an intensional) use of 'exist' present in the first though not in the second occurrence of 'exist' in the following question such that it is both intelligible and non-tautological: "Does there exist a necessarily existent being?" If this question *is* intelligible and non-tautological, grounds will be needed for asserting the existence of a necessarily existent being, (the sense of the terms here employed remaining intact from the above question.) But at least plausibly we could never have such grounds. Therefore on these same views acceptance of God's necessary existence, to which all wielders of the ontological argument are committed, commits one at best either to groundless affirmations in religion or to permanent agnosticism, since one can never claim grounds for the belief that there is such a God. If then these views are correct, the success of the ontological argument would be fatal to rational religious belief, in that such religious belief is possible only if the conclusion of the argument is false. And if so, the service of its critics to religion is great indeed; and all the more so if other independent arguments exist which argue to the instantiation of the concept of a God whose existence is not conceptually necessary.

B. The Objections of Gassendi and Kant.

Hume's and Kant's central criticisms of metaphysics do not apply to the ontological argument. Hume holds that there are no synthetic *a priori* propositions,[25] whereas Kant holds that although there are some such propositions we cannot know them to be true when they surpass possible experience.[26] But the conclusion and the premisses of ontological arguments for the existence of God are necessary truths because analytic, and are thus not (*pace* Kant) synthetic at all. Objections to the

---
[25] 'An Enquiry Concerning Human Understanding', Section IV, Part I, and Section XII, Part III.
[26] 'Critique of Pure Reason', p. 194.

argument usually attempt to show, therefore, that there is something amiss with the claim that God's existence is necessary.

It is indeed a peculiarity of the ontological argument that objections of other sorts are liable to prove futile. For if there is nothing wrong with the inclusion of 'existence' in the notion of God, then anyone is entitled to introduce the term 'God' in such a sense that part of the meaning of 'God' is 'existent'; and they can then validly conclude that God's existence is logically necessary. They would, it must be allowed, need to specify what *sort* of thing it was whose essence included existence: otherwise no sense could even so be made of their conclusions, as we should not be able to tell what sort of individual was being said necessarily to exist. But at least a start would be made by their stipulating that they were talking of an omnipotent, bodiless person: and any remaining difficulties about identifiability could further be overcome in some such was as by pointing out that this person would be related to any given spatio-temporal object by his causing or at least permitting its existence. If, then, 'existence' can be allowed to figure in the definition of something like this, some form of ontological argument seems bound to succeed in establishing its conclusion.

This means that we can neglect the difficulties experienced by Descartes, Spinoza and Leibniz in formulating such an argument. For we already know whereabouts critics would have to aim their criticisms, and can go on to see if they succeed. Would a being, whose essence included having all desirable qualities, necessarily exist? Or, in other words, could 'existence' be included in the definition of such a being, or indeed of any sort of being?

Hume's Cleanthes replies to these questions with what amounts to a flat denial.

> "Nothing that is distinctly conceivable implies a contradiction. Whatever we can conceive as existent we can also conceive as non-existent. There is no Being, therefore, whose non-existence implies a contradiction."[27]

But the second sentence here not only begs the question: it is also false. We can conceive of existents as existing, but not as being non-existent, insofar as they are existents: whereas according to Hume existents *qua* existents might not exist.

The question is also begged in at least two places in Kant's

---

[27] 'Dialogues Concerning Natural Religion', Part IX, in 'Historical Selections in the Philosophy of Religion', edited Ninian Smart, London, 1962, p. 230: also in 'The Philosophical Works of David Hume', edited anon., (4 Vols), Boston 1854; Vol. II.

Section entitled 'The Impossibility of an Ontological Proof of the Existence of God'.[28] The first passage runs thus:

> "If, in an identical proposition, I reject the predicate while retaining the subject, contradiction results; and I therefore say that the former belongs necessarily to the latter. But if we reject subject and predicate alike, there is no contradiction; for nothing is then left that can be contradicted. To posit a triangle, and yet to reject its three angles, is self-contradictory; but there is no contradiction in rejecting the triangle together with its three angles. The same holds true of the concept of an absolutely necessary being. If its existence is rejected, we reject the thing itself with all its predicates; and no question of contradiction can then arise."

Now this is tantamount to the claim that we can without contradiction say of some necessarily existent being that it does not exist, and that therefore there is nothing for its defining characteristic of existence to hold good of. But on the argument under consideration any necessarily existent being is bound to exist, and therefore the claim which Kant regards as innocuous would in fact be a self-contradiction. In other words Kant must give reason to show that existence cannot enter into a thing's concept: otherwise it will not do to claim that things defined as existing do not exist: indeed it is plausible to hold that they must exist.

A little later Kant attempts to do this by the remark that "every reasonable person must admit that all existential propositions are synthetic." But this is just as question-begging and false as the affirmation of Hume discussed above. All that proponents of the argument, like Descartes and Leibniz, would need to do, is deny this claim, perhaps with the aid of examples about realities, historical persons and the like.

The discussion is therefore furthered when Kant attempts to supply a reason why 'existence' cannot figure in a definition. Kant's objection is on much the same lines as the Objection of Gassendi to Descartes, which should be noted first. Gassendi claims [29] that existence "is a perfection neither in God nor in anything else; it is rather that in the absence of which there is no perfection". And he continues,

> "This must be so if, indeed, that which does not exist has neither perfection nor imperfection, and that which exists and

---

[28] 'Critique of Pure Reason', Transcendental Dialectic, Book II, Chapter III, Section 4, Kemp Smith translation, pp. 500-507. The two passages are at pp. 502 and 504.

[29] Haldane and Ross, 'The Philosophical Works of Descartes', Vol. II., p. 186.

has various perfections, does not have its existence as a particular perfection and as one of the number of its perfections, but as that by means of which the thing itself equally with its perfection is in existence, and without which neither can it be said to possess perfections, nor can perfections be said to be possessed by it. Hence neither is existence held to exist in a thing in the way that perfections do, nor if the thing lacks existence is it said to be imperfect (or deprived of a perfection), so much as to be nothing".

Kant, for his part, put the point more explicitly: 'being' is not a "real predicate", and the concept of being cannot be added to the concept of a thing so as to enlarge or modify it. A hundred real thalers are not qualitatively different from a hundred possible thalers.[30]

Gassendi implies that nothing can be predicated of that the existence of which we do not presuppose: and this doctrine is plausible, since apparently if there is not believed to be something in existence to be characterised by a speaker's predicates, he cannot predicate them at all, since in his belief there is nothing to predicate them of. But this is false: it makes perfect sense to predicate "having four legs" of unicorns. Existence is therefore not that in the absence of which predication is impossible.

Some further reason is therefore needed to sustain the doctrine that existence is not a real (or logical) predicate and the related and crucial doctrine that 'existence' cannot enter into classifications or definitions. Kant points out that when we say that a thing *is*, we do not modify the notion of the thing:[31] but then, nor do we modify the notion of my house by predicating of it "being looked at". Kant needs, of course, to show not only that 'existence' is in certain respects unlike ordinary predicates but also that it is unlike them *in that it cannot enter into definitions and characterisations:* but we have already seen that he cannot succeed here, as it does enter into notions like 'existent' 'historical person' and 'reality'.[32] And it would seem to follow that the ontological argument is successful: for necessarily existent beings must exist.

But this would be a mistaken conclusion. Certainly existential propositions can be intensional, and merely spell out for us the meaning of the subject term, as in 'Necessarily existent beings (necessarily) exist'. But, as Shaffer reminds us, existential propo-

---

[30] Op. cit., pp. 504 f.
[31] Op.cit., p. 505.
[32] Other arguments to sustain the doctrine have been convincingly refuted by Jerome Shaffer in 'Existence, Predication and the Ontological Argument', 'Mind' Vol. LXXI, N.S. No. 283, July 1962.

sitions can also be used to assert that a certain concept has application. This is the extensional use of existential propositions. Shaffer produces the following list of expressions which are typically used in assertions about the extension or lack of extension of particular concepts: '... exist', '... are nonexistent', 'There are...' 'There are no...', '... are plentiful', '... are scarce', '... are extinct', '... are mythological', '... are found in Africa'. This extensional use of 'exists' is not the only use: *pace* Gassendi, Hume and Kant, there *is* an intensional use, and on such occasions of use, 'exists' is indeed a predicate since it enters into definitions. But whatever is included in the intension of a term, it is never inappropriate, I wish, with Shaffer, to claim, to go on to ask if the corresponding concept *applies* to anything, or if there are any things of that sort.

Thus it is part of the meaning of the term 'event' that events occur or happen: the notion of a non-occurrent event is incoherent. Therefore events necessarily occur. Nevertheless it makes perfectly good sense to ask if the notion of event applies to anything, and with respect to any period of time we can always enquire whether there have been any events in it, or whether any events have occurred in it. And here the word 'occurred' is used in asking an extensional question.

Similarly although all thoughts (in the sense of thinkings) are necessarily thought, it makes good sense to ask if any have been thought: and correspondingly although existents necessarily exist, it makes perfectly good sense, I wish to hold, to ask if there are any. For whatever the nature of our conceptual net, it is always an open question whether it catches anything or not. Thus to say that God necessarily exists is to say that nothing is God unless it could not not exist: but it is an open question whether there is anything of this sort.

Kant seems to have wished to maintain that 'exists' is always used extensionally, and never used otherwise. Nevertheless the above principle to the effect that intensional propositions do not settle all questions about existence shows that Kant was after all right to claim that it makes sense to deny that there are any necessarily existent beings. For this must make sense if it makes sense to ask if there are any, in a sense such that the answer is not already settled by the intension of the phrase 'necessarily existent being.'

Shaffer allows that someone might wish to include 'having application' in the concept of something, and therefore show that that something necessarily has application. But this possibility is in no way prejudicial to his case. For an extensional question will still makes sense, of the form, "But *is* there anything of this sort (namely something answering to a concept which necessarily has application)? Accordingly whatever is built into the concept of a thing, further grounds are always needed to show that there is one. Thus, for all that the ontological argument shows that necessary beings necessarily exist, it is inconclusive on the issue of whether there are any.

C. The Concept of God.

The above refutation of the ontological argument applies to any argument which attempts to establish the existence of a necessarily existent being on conceptual grounds alone, and therefore applies even to the second of 'Anselm's Ontological Arguments' discussed by Norman Malcolm in a paper so entitled.[33] Malcolm, however, adduces some extra grounds from Spinoza, which are of current relevance. For in support of Proposition XI of the First Book of his Ethics, the proposition that God or substance (as understood in Spinoza's sense) necessarily exists, Spinoza argues from God's uncreatability and indestructibility, and concludes that the existence of such a being is necessary.

Now it must be granted to Spinoza and to Malcolm that the propositions that God has not come into existence and will not cease to exist are necessary truths. This is part of what is meant by God's eternity. Further, such a notion of God is needed both for the language of worship and for the doctrine of creation. It is needed for the language of worship because on any other notion the object of worship would be limited and dependent on what was external to himself. And it is needed for the language of creation, because to be able to create God must have the power to bring into existence whatever can without contradiction be brought into existence, and must at the same time be subject to no external power, or the question of his own creation by something external would arise. The existence of the Creator must therefore be independent of all other existences, and he must therefore be uncreatable and indestructible.

It does not follow from this, however, that it is self-contradictory to say "God does not exist" in any sense of that sentence, or therefore that God exists necessarily. All that follows is that *if* God exists, at no time can he not exist. Certainly it will be a necessary truth that if God exists something exists without beginning and without end in time: for the divine life is necessarily timeless. But it in no way follows that there exists (let alone necessarily exists) a necessarily timeless being, nor indeed that 'existence' is included in the notion of God. We can certainly say, with Spinoza, that there is

---

[33] In 'Philosophical Review', Vol. LXIX, No. 1, January 1960.

no explanation beyond God of God's existence: what we cannot say, however, is that therefore God exists necessarily.

All this has a bearing on two matters which are of interest in their own right. First, Kant is correct in a number of observations about the Leibnizian form of the cosmological argument: and second, religious belief does not need the notion of a necessarily existent being at all.

Kant alleges that the second part of that form of the cosmological argument which he criticises requires the ontological argument.[34] According to Kant, the proof which Leibniz calls *'a contingentia mundi'* runs as follows. "If anything exists, an absolutely necessary being exists." There are two things to notice here: one is that Leibniz' argument is intended to show the existence of a necessarily existent being (even though I alleged in Section 2A above that this is not the notion with which the cosmological argument is concerned). The other is that this is only the first part of the argument, for we have yet to learn what the necessary being is like. According to Kant the proof proceeds as follows:

> "The necessary being can be determined in one way only, that is by one out of each pair of opposed predicates. It must therefore be *completely* determined through its own concept. Now there is only one possible concept which determines a thing completely *a priori*, namely, the concept of the *ens realissimum*. The concept of the *ens realissimum* is therefore the only concept through which a necessary being can be thought. In other words, a supreme being necessarily exists."

Kant now correctly observes that the second stage of the argument rests on the premiss "All absolutely necessary beings are *entia realissima*." His next move is to require that this judgement must be convertible into "Some *entia realissima* are absolutely necessary beings." Since such conversions are valid if the "all" ... proposition concerned has existential import, this is, as Peter Remnant has pointed out,[35] an unexceptional move.

Remarking that what holds good of one *ens realissimum* equally holds good of any other, Kant now quite fairly concludes that to be committed to the second stage in the argument is to be committed to the view that all *entia realissima* are absolutely necessary beings, or that all beings without limitations and with all desirable qualities are necessarily existent beings. Remnant ably summarises Kant's verdict: "Not only is the latter principle the con-

---

[34] 'Critique of Pure Reason' pp. 508-514.
[35] 'Kant and the Cosmological Argument', 'Australian Journal of Philosophy', 1959, pp. 152-5.

clusion of the ontological argument, but the ontological argument constitutes the only even plausible attempt so far to establish the truth of this proposition." This verdict is surely true, and the latter half of it is lent further support by the above remarks on Spinoza and Malcolm. Spinoza attempted to show that a being eternally possessed of infinite attributes necessarily exists; but in one of his proofs of Proposition XI of Ethics, Book I (that discussed above) argues for this conclusion invalidly from such a being's uncreatability and indestructibility. This particular proof failed because the notion of existence is not part of the meaning of 'eternity'. Thus Kant is correct to hold that a genuinely ontological argument, i.e. one in one of the premisses of which existence is included in the essence of the subject under discussion, is needed if such conclusions as that all perfect beings are necessary beings are to be drawn. On the other hand if existence is stipulated to be one of the characteristics of such a perfect being, such an ontological argument could itself be valid, though innocuous: unless, that is, someone wanted to conclude from it alone that there actually were such beings, in the extensional use of "there actually were."

Leibniz, however, had not wanted to do this: for he relied on the first stage of the argument as the proof of a necessary being. (That stage will be considered in the next Section.) I take it, then, that Kant was correct in holding that the cosmological argument he was considering required the ontological argument; but that in the circumstances concerned this requirement is not fatal to it, as the ontological argument would not be needed to establish as if from scratch any extensional existential proposition. Nevertheless much else is undoubtedly wrong with the argument Kant was considering, including, as I shall maintain, its attempt to establish the existence of a necessary being (in the first stage). Now if I am right in claiming that the cosmological argument is not concerned with this concept at all, then the criticism that it required the ontological argument will after all miscarry, even though it was quite appropriate as a criticism of Leibniz' form of the argument.

I now turn to the notion of God required by religious belief. Need the God in whom believers believe be a necessary being as well as an eternal being?[36] The above discussion of Spinoza has shown that the proposition 'x is an eternal being' does not in any way imply the proposition 'x is a necessary being'. Findlay,[37] however, holds that a God whose non-existence is conceivable is a limited God. But if such a God is also uncreatable and indestruc-

---

[36] Priestley, at pp. 397f of 'A Free Discussion' (1778) objects to Clarke's view that the doctrine of creation requires a God whose existence is logically necessary.
[37] Op. cit.

tible and necessarily timeless, it is hard to see how he is limited.

It might be supposed, by way of reply, that the question "What brings it about that he exists rather than not exists?" could arise, whereas no corresponding question could arise in the case of a necessarily existent being. For, it might be contended, even if we suppose that matter is without temporal beginning or end, it still makes sense to ask what brings about its existence.[38] Why then should what is askable of unending matter not also be askable of a timeless God, so long as his non-existence is conceivable?

The answer is that, first, God's timelessness is necessary, unlike that of matter, and secondly that God cannot be created or destroyed (see above). If God exists, therefore, nothing could either bring about his existence or make it to cease: and therefore, if God exists, no question concerning the reason why he exists can arise. But this is not to settle the question whether God exists or not: it leaves open the question of whether there *is* a necessarily timeless God or not. Accordingly religious belief does not need the notion of a necessarily existent being.

What is more, religious belief needs to be rid of such a notion, at least if it is to be rationally defensible. It will be argued in the next Section that there are grounds for belief in a necessarily timeless being, in the form of the cosmological argument. But such grounds do not begin to show, *pace* Leibniz, that there exists a being whose non-existence is unthinkable. God's necessary timelessness is a postulate required by the argument, but God's necessary existence is not so required. This being so, it is hard to see what possible grounds there could be for ascribing necessary existence to the being whose existence is there argued for. The only argument adequate to such a conclusion would be an ontological argument supplementary to the conclusion of the cosmological argument. But such an argument would have to show that necessary existence was already implicit in the notion of a necessarily timeless being: and this has been shown to be false. Moreover the cosmological argument contains a synthetic premiss, and therefore supports only a synthetic conclusion. The conclusion it supports is not, therefore, one the denial of which involves a contradiction. Thus the non-existence of the timeless being to whose existence it argues is conceivable. (This argument is not quite conclusive, as necessary existence of an intensional kind might still somehow be included in the notion of a necessarily timeless being: but, as shown above, it is not.)

To claim, then, that there exists a necessarily existent being is to claim what there could be no reason to believe. But this idea not

---

[38] See chapter 2, Section 3B.

only stretches credulity. For to see that there could be no reason to believe a proposition (other than a self-evident one) is to cease to be able to regard it as true, and by then belief itself is barely possible.

In general the notion of God argued to be instantiated by any argument for the existence of God must be related to the grounds of that argument, if that argument is to be valid. Thus the cosmological argument does not establish the existence of an intelligent creator, nor the teleological argument the existence of a creator of matter. Whether these arguments supplement each other in the respects concerned remains to be seen. Meanwhile it will have become clear why it is not possible to discuss any single notion of God prior to discussion of the arguments themselves.

What has been maintained, however, is that the ontological argument does not establish the instantiation of any notion of God, and that its purported conclusion is disproportionate to the other arguments, and redundant for and positively harmful to theistic belief. Men like Gassendi and Kant who sensed its invalidity thus merit both philosophical and theological gratitude, even if technically they failed to establish their point.

Section 3: The Cosmological Argument

A. Creation and the Deity of the Argument.

In the course of the present Section objections to the form of the cosmological argument put forward by Hume's Demea and by Leibniz will be considered, and the argument itself will be presented so as to secure it, as far as possible, against the criticisms of Hume and Kant. But first it will be of help to observe the relation of the argument to the doctrine of creation, and assess some particular criticisms of its conclusion in that light.

First, the success of the cosmological argument would be insufficient to etablish the doctrine of creation (as set out in Chapter 1, Section 1D above). For that doctrine maintains that God creates purposively, whereas the cosmological argument in no way suggests that the being whose existence must be postulated to explain that of material objects can have purposes.[39]

Second, at least one element of the doctrine of creation follows from a principle of the argument. For if material objects exist and

---

[39] This was part of Kant's point (Section 2C above) when he objected to the claim that a necessary being must be a perfect one.

their existence is only to be explained by the existence of a necessarily timeless, placeless and omnipotent being, then it will be this same being that brings about their existence. Further the argument lends support to a claim represented above as integral to the doctrine, the claim that it is not a necessary truth that God creates material objects. For even if creation could be demonstrated, the claim that God creates does not for that reason express a necessary truth. Further, the argument does not require the postulation of the existence of a timeless being whose essence it is to create material objects, as opposed to one whose essence it is to be able to create material objects. There being, accordingly, no grounds for holding that God is necessarily creative, it is reasonable to hold, what the argument does support, that God in fact creates, but not that he cannot help it or needs must.

Third, the argument in no way requires us to deny what theists would claim when they assert that God would have existed even if there had been no material objects. God's existence must be independent of material objects if (as at least the doctrine holds) he can choose either to create or not to create, and if, as the argument suggests, the proposition that he creates is synthetic. Now certainly were there no material objects and no change, there would be no grounds for belief in God's existence (quite apart from the obvious fact that there would be no people to believe that God exists.) But this does not show that there would then be no God. Indeed the argument requires us to hold that there would be. For the argument requires us to hold that, as there *are* material objects, their existence is only to be explained by the existence of a necessarily timeless, placeless and omnipotent being: and the existence of such a being is in no way causally dependent on that of the material objects which, in fact, happen to exist. Nor does this conclusion commit those who accept it to the view that God's existence is logically necessary: we have already seen that neither uncreatability nor indestructibility (nor their conjunction) implies that.

One modern objection both to the doctrine and to the argument may however now be raised. Nothing, it may be said, can be said in our language to exist independently of other things unless it can be identified independently. For an individual's existence is necessarily the existence of an individual of some sort, and to be able to be said to exist is therefore to be capable at least in principle of being identified as a member of that sort. Further, for a member of any sort to be able to exist independently, i.e. in complete isolation and alone in an otherwise empty universe, members of that sort must be identifiable independently of other things. Now if

God exists, he is an individual: [40] abstractions and qualities are unable to create. But it is in principle impossible to identify him independently of material objects. Accordingly no argument can succeed in showing that he exists, since the proposition that he exists is unintelligible.

In face of all this it must be agreed that God is necessarily of some sort or other.[41] Indeed he is necessarily of a sort members of which are necessarily timeless, placeless and omnipotent. This is, in fact, part of the answer to Hobbes' difficulties about religious language (mentioned in Chapter 1, Section 2B above). For the sense of predicates ascribed to God will in the light of this observation partly hang on their being ascribed to something necessarily timeless, placeless and omnipotent: such is the essence of that which they are predicated of. And this is at least part of the information we need in order to make sense of them. Thus creating in the case of God will necessarily be timeless, and thus unlike the creating of a human sculptor (among other ways) in that temporal limitations are in his case absent. In the case of God, creating will be the timeless bringing about of what can exist in time.

It must be further granted that God cannot be identified independently of his creatures.[42] He can, however, be picked out through them as that which can bring any one of them we care to pick out into existence, or at any rate as that which can bring into existence the matter of which any one of them we care to pick out is composed. But this is a perfectly adequate means of identification, at least in the present case: nor, of course, does it beg the question of God's existence. There could be difficulties in other sorts of cases of such indirect identification, as there might be doubt about *which* individual had been picked out. But in the case of God such doubts cannot arise. To be God is to be omnipotent, and there cannot be more than one omnipotent being, (though there could, of course, be less than one). Thus the claim that nothing can be said in our language to exist independently of other things unless it can be identified independently of them is a claim which miscarries. Rather it should be said that "nothing is a substance unless it is either (theoretically) independently identifiable or it is or could be the cause or effect of something which is so independently identifiable". And God will therefore be a possible substance.

Of course in a world in which there were no creatures, God

---

[40] See R. Attfield, 'The Individuality of God', 'Sophia', Vol. X, No. 1, April, 1971, pp. 20-27.

[41] See R. Attfield, ibid.

[42] Thus Michael Durrant in 'The Logical Status of 'God'', Macmillan, London, 1973, pp. 27, 33f, 55, 56.

would not be identifiable at all. In that case there would of course be no language in which to say that he exists. But given the language we now use, if we imagine there *never* being any material objects, can we make sense of the proposition that in such a universe God exists? For God is identified as that necessarily timeless being that is able to bring material objects into existence, and apparently therefore could not then be identified. Nevertheless, as there are material objects, we can identify as their possible cause a God who, being necessarily timeless and omnipotent, exists independently of such material objects:[43] and this is to pick out a God who, were he not to bring or to have brought their existence about, could still have existed just the same, and could even so be picked out as the originator of any material objects which there might have been. So it does make sense to say that a God who is picked out through his creatures could have existed even if they had not.

Now these considerations lead on directly to one of the objections of both Hume and Kant to the cosmological argument, and one which, since it concerns any argument in which causal entities are postulated, can be considered before the arguments of Demea and Leibniz are set out. This is the argument that postulated causes must be proportionate to the effects they are postulated to explain, since there are no grounds for postulating more than is strictly necessary. It is found most explicitly in Hume's 'Enquiry', Section XI,[44] but also occurs in Kant's section on "The Impossibility of the Physico-Theological Proof":[45] as it is a general consideration, Kant would no doubt approve its application to the cosmological argument also.

More will be said in answer to this objection in Chapter 6, Section 1, on the subject of the teleological argument. What can now be said is that the principle not only allows but also requires us, when postulating causes, to postulate what is sufficient for bringing about the effect for which an explanation is sought. If then a causal explanation is sought of there being matter at whatever times and places matter is to be found, the postulation of nothing less than a timeless and placeless cause will do. For no material objects and no person with a material body could be responsible for the existence of matter at all times and places, nor could their qualities or relations. Only therefore an immaterial being could bring the existence of matter about, and one at that with control over all times and places and hence timeless and

---

[43] See further R. Attfield, 'The Lord is God: There is No Other', 'Religious Studies', 13, 1977, pp. 73-84.
[44] Selby-Bigge, pp. 136-7.
[45] 'Critique of Pure Reason', pp. 522 f.

placeless. Moreover such a being would have to be uncreatable and indestructible: for if the question of the explanation of the existence of matter arises, so also would that of the explanation of the contingent fact that any creatable and destructible being happened to exist. Only the existence of a necessarily uncreatable and indestructible being would suffice to answer and thus to stop a succession of such questions, if such a question is legitimate in the case of matter in the first place.

Here is may be objected that there is nothing wrong with an unending succession of questions about the explanation of temporal existences, each one being answerable, but each answer giving rise to a further question. Granted that the existence of an uncreatable and indestructible being would curtail further questions, why should any question about the existence of creatable beings at any stage be answered by this answer rather than by an answer about the existence of yet another creatable being (and so on)? Perhaps, then, the concept of an uncreatable and indestructible being is after all redundant. The answer to this objection is that there is nothing wrong with an infinite regress of such questions, but that the succession of answers generated gives rise to the further question, "What is the explanation of there being whatever creatable beings there are"? or, "Why does the set of creatable beings have members?" This question is as legitimate as the initial question, and cannot be answered by postulating the existence of a further creatable being. Only the postulation of the existence of an uncreatable being will suffice in answer to this question.

If, then, the initial question is askable, we have grounds for postulating a necessarily timeless being, and unless we have other grounds for additionally postulating e.g. a being of infinite duration and extent or of a succession of creatable beings, it is more economical not to do so. Yet so long as the postulation of a cause of matter is required, then the postulation of an uncreatable, indestrucible and necessarily timeless being is necessary if the very point of Hume and Kant is to be satisfied.

Nevertheless Hume and Kant do score at this point against that form of the cosmological argument put forward respectively by Hume's Demea and by Leibniz, for each of these latter believes the argument to establish the existence of a "necessary being". But not only does religious belief not need this notion and fare best without it: the cosmological argument does not begin to establish that it is instantiated, as Hume and Kant each point out. To be able to create, what is postulated must, indeed, be necessarily timeless, placeless and omnipotent, and indeed uncreatable and indestructible, as pointed out above. But its existence need not be conceptually necessary; and so the contrary claim goes unsupported by the argument. Hume claims that the knowledge that that which creates is a necessary being is impossible for us "while our faculties remain the same as at present",[46] while Kant also protests that such knowledge is beyond our understanding,[47] and that "absolute necessity is a necessity that is to be found in thought alone."[48] Without assenting to their grounds, I endorse their conclusion that the argument does not prove the existence of a being which could not not exist, and the denial of the existence of which would be self-contradictory.

But to accept this is not to accept that the argument establishes nothing. After all, when Aquinas argued by cosmologcial reasoning for God's existence, he did not have in mind the existence of something whose non-existence was inconceivable, — not even when he spoke of God as a "necessary being". For Aquinas a necessary being was a timeless or incorruptible being, one which, in Geach's phrase,[49] has "no inner seeds of its own destruction". This point I take to have been established by Kenny in 'The Five Ways'.[50] Aquinas was well aware that to establish that God's non-existence was inconceivable, the ontological argument would be required. Why then, did Demea and Leibniz suppose otherwise?

The reason is probably another of Hume's objections.[51] For if the existence of matter, being contingent, requires explanation, but is explained by something else which exists contingently, then that something else appears equally in need of explanation: indeed the chain of explanations can only apparently come to an end with the postulation of something whose non-existence is inconceivable. This, however, is a fallacy. Certainly if questions about the existence of what exists contingently are legitimate in the first place, we are obliged to go on asking them except where it is unintelligible to go on. But in the case of an uncreatable and indestructible being it is unintelligible to raise such questions. To put the matter another way, it is false that everything for the existence of which it makes no sense to ask a reason is a logically necessary being: for whatever both cannot come into being and cannot cease to be will constitute a counterinstance. Demea thought that to have

---

[46] 'Dialogues Concerning Natural Religion', IX, in 'Hume's Philosophical Works' (4 Vols.), edited anon., Boston, 1854; Vol. II, p. 490.

[47] 'Critique of Pure Reason', p. 513.

[48] P. 516. Priestley's objection to Clarke at "A Free Discussion", pp. 397-9, has a similar basis.

[49] 'God and the Soul', p. 77.

[50] Anthony Kenny, 'The Five Ways', London, 1969, pp. 46-8.

[51] 'Dialogues', IX, p. 491.

the reason for one's own existence within oneself was to exist as a matter of logical necessity:[52] but if by this he meant "to be of such a sort that the question of the reason of one's existence cannot arise is to exist as a matter of logical necessity" then his inference was wrong.

Like Hume, Kant at least considers the possibility of the intelligibility of questions concerning the source of God's existence.[53] At the same time Kant recognises that there is something amiss about such questions: but as he wishes to set up a paradox of pure reason at this point, he allows the question to be both intolerable and irresistible. Since, however, such questions are in fact unintelligible, the paradox does not arise.

Some light having now been thrown on the notion which the argument *may* possibly show to be instantiated and its relation to the doctrine of creation, it is appropriate to turn to the main argument and the other criticisms which Hume and Kant raised.

B. The Initial Premiss.

In the form of the cosmological argument ascribed by Kant to Leibniz the premiss to which a general principle of causality is conjoined is, 'Now I at least, exist.'[54] But what is needed in the initial premiss of a cosmological argument is the proposition that something happens to exist, i.e. that something exists the nonexistence of which is conceivable; for the existence of something whose essence it was to exist would not require explanation: whereas it has recently been argued by Hector-Neri Castañeda[55] that my statement "I don't exist now" is self-contradictory. I have no wish, nor need, to get to grips with his argument; for in case it is successful, it would be better to argue from some more obviously synthetic existential proposition and not from 'I exist'. Leibniz' premiss will therefore be disregarded.

The premiss with which Hume's Demea implicitly sets out [56] is that *something exists:* but he is also prepared to countenance the possibility that there is an infinite sequence of causes and effects, and to meet this possibility supplies a new premiss, along the lines of 'There has existed a particular succession of causes from eternity'.

---

[52] Hume 'Dialogues', IX, p. 489. Leibniz is represented as arguing similarly by Kant at 'Critique of Pure Reason', p. 508, footnote a.
[53] 'Critique of Pure Reason', p. 513.
[54] 'Critique of Pure Reason', p. 508.
[55] 'On the Phenomeno-Logic of the I', 'Akten des XIV. Internationalen Kongresses fur Philosophie', Herder, Vienna, 1968.
[56] 'The Philosophical Works of Hume', Vol. II, p. 489.

This new premiss appears, however, to entail the proposition that something exists and someone might claim that this proposition is itself one whose denial would be self-contradictory. Hume at least considers the possibility that the existence of matter is necessary,[57] though Kant appears to rule it out,[58] and rightly so. Indeed, as far as matter is concerned, the dictum ascribed to Samuel Clarke by Hume[59] holds good: "Any particle of matter may be conceived to be annihilated", — and indeed any particle of matter we care to think of need not have existed at all, for we can imagine the non-existence of any given material particle. It may however be alleged that the existence of material particles does not even so call for explanation, in that it is impossible that there should have been no such particles and in that we cannot conceive the non-existence of all of them. At least some, in other words, necessarily exist, though no given one need exist. Now it must obviously be granted that if there were no matter, there would be no language among humans in which to note the non-existence of matter. But it follows neither from this nor from any other truth that at least some matter necessarily exists. Necessarily if there is human language there is matter, and there *is* human language: but the proposition that there is human language is synthetic, and so also is the proposition that there is matter.

That there is matter, then, is a suitable premiss for cosmological reasoning. In order to affirm that there is matter, it is not necessary to show that it makes sense to talk of the set or totality of material objects: it is enough to secure the admission that there is at least one. Now it may be that modern science has no particular use for this notion of matter: but this would in no way cast doubt on the existence of matter, as what persists through perceptible change. For unless the metaphysical postulate that matter (in this sense) exists is true, the existence of three-dimensional tangible objects and the occurrence of change would be impossible.

But though the existence of matter is a true and a suitable premiss, and is also a premiss of the argument to which Hume's Cleanthes replies, it is not Demea's premiss, (although it does, of course, entail one of Demea's premisses, that there is something). Demea is prepared to allow that the antecedents of each particular existence are infinite in number. He also holds, however, that, if so, the existence of the entire set of them poses a cosmological problem. (When he talks of a succession of causes, I take him to

---

[57] Op. cit., pp. 491, 493.
[58] Op. cit. p. 517. See further Fred Sommers, 'Why is there Something and not Nothing', 'Analysis', 26.6, June 1966, pp. 177-181, and Herbert Guerry, 'Sommers' Ontological Proof', 'Analysis', 28.2, December, 1967, pp. 60-61.
[59] Op. Cot., p. 491.

TALK OF TOTALITIES 171

mean a series of events happening to things or of states of things, each related to its successor as cause to effect. Demea is perhaps then to be taken as speaking not so much of a set of individual substances as of a set of the states of substances.) For there might have existed a different set, or no set at all. (And, though he does not say so, this would, if true of an infinite set, be equally true of a finite set, something which could be relevant if the past is finite in extent.) Accordingly 'There exists an unexplained set of states, namely the set of states of all material objects' appears to be another suitable premiss, in that this set appears to call for explanation.

Two objections now arise, however, namely that talk of totalities and universes must be confused as it leads to antinomies and paradoxes, and that in any case even if it does make sense no explanation is needed for wholes, once an explanation has been supplied for each and every part. The relevance of the first objection would be a prohibition on talk of "the set of states of all material objects", as being senseless talk. (Demea does not in fact need to bring in *all* material objects as opposed to all material objects related either as cause or as effect to some one given object, e.g. the floor he was standing on: but to make sense of this expression we need to make sense of the expression "all material objects".)

Kant is probably committed to such a prohibition, except where "regulative principles" are concerned: for he holds that if the world can be thought of as a whole, it is either finite or infinite: but each of these propositions is false, something Kant believes he has demonstrated in his 'First Antinomy'.[60] Therefore the world cannot be thought of as a whole, as absurdities result if it is so conceived. But to uphold this reasoning Kant must prove the falsity both of the world's infinity and of its finitude. Yet we can see that he fails to do this simply by looking at the first paragraph of his disproof of its infinity.[61] Kant points out that if the world had no beginning in time, an infinite series of states of things would have cropped up by now, and then alleges that this is impossible, as infinite series cannot be completed. But infinite series of states can be infinite in a certain direction from a given determinate state: and an infinite length of time can just as easily precede the present moment as follow it. Thus if we trace time backwards from any given moment there is nothing absurd in claiming that it is infinite in extent. Only the irreversibility of the passage of time and time's consequent apparent direction renders this hard to accept: if we envisage time as a traveller which has reached the present, we have to picture it as having completed a journey from somewhere a

[60] 'Critique', p. 449. For the 'First Antimony', see pp. 396-398
[61] P. 397.

finite distance away. But the direction of the passage of time is irrelevant when we are considering the extent of time, for then we can reason forwards or backwards indifferently. Kant thus fails to show that thinking of the world as a whole leads to absurdities.

The objection could however be supported by the claim that there are no such things as material objects as such: i.e. that the notion of 'material object' gives us no principle for counting individuals, and that the corresponding expression is not a sortal expression. All these points I grant. Whatever is a material object is necessarily either a table or a chair or . . . a member of some kind or sort of material object.

The expression "material object" is thus parasitic on expressions which designate sorts of material object. But it does not follow that there is anything amiss with the expression "all material objects": for this expression can fairly be taken to mean "all the members of all the instantiated sorts of material objects". (No doubt some particles of matter would now be included several times over, but this does not matter if all we want to do is to pick out whatever particles are causally connected to some given object, e.g. a particular floor. To be included more than once is after all to be included.)

Similar objections and similar replies would also apply to talk of all the states of any one given material object (of whatever sort): the argument can, perhaps, be taken as read. My conclusion is that there is nothing unintelligible about the phrase Demea needs, i.e. "the set of states of all material objects." I turn therefore to Cleanthes' claim that once the existence of the parts of a given whole has been explained, the existence of that whole as a whole is in no need of further explanation; and that therefore there is no sense in which the set of states of all material objects is in fact unexplained.

Now if each of the states Demea is concerned with is causally explained by an earlier one (something Demea is happy to allow), Cleanthes' principle would show that the series as a whole has been explained already. But has it? R. G. Swinburne argues persuasively, in 'Philosophy' October 1969,[62] that the cause of a series of states, where there is such a cause, will be "the set of those causes of members of the series, which are not themselves members of the series". If, then, such a series as Demea mentions is infinite, no (scientific) causal explanation of it is possible, as every cause of a member of the series belongs to the series: and indeed if such a series is finite, no such (scientific) causal explanation of it is possible either, since if the world is of finite age there have occurred

---

[62] Vol. XLIV, No. 170, pp. 339-340.

no states outside the series. The series is not therefore explained by the explanations of its members, nor can it be explained scientifically at all. The latter proposition, however, does not show it to be inexplicable, whereas the former shows it to be so far unexplained. Swinburne's argument accordingly supports the view that Demea's premiss is a suitable one for cosmological reasoning after all.

C. The Need for an Explanation.

Cosmological reasoning begins when it is noticed that something happens to exist or occur but need not; and it continues with the claim that there must be an explanation. What principle of explanation is involved here, and can it be sustained?

Leibniz' principle, according to Kant, is "Everything contingent has a cause"; this is a variant of what Leibniz sometimes called "the Principle of Sufficient Reason".[63] The principle of Hume's Demea is "Whatever exists must have a cause or reason of its existence".[64] For various technical reasons, and also to be consistent with the rejection of determinism in Chapter 3, I put forward instead the following principle: "The existence of whatever exists but might cease to exist or might not have existed and the actuality of whatever is the case but might cease to be the case or might not have been the case has an explanation of some sort." This is compatible with a rejection of determinism because it is not held that all states of affairs have a *causal* explanation: some human actions will not be explicable solely by causes, but will still be explicable by the agent's reason. But in the light of what has been said above about the absurdity of asking why God happens to exist (Chapter 5, Section 2C) the principle needs modifying: the following clause should be appended: "except where it is necessarily uncreatable and indestructible." It is needed because otherwise questions about the explanation of God's existence would be in place.[65]

If this principle is accepted, an explanation must be sought for the existence of matter and, indeed, of the set of states of all material objects: alongside any other contingent facts which are scientifically inexplicable, such as the occurrence of change. Thus Demea did not rely for reaching his conclusion on the false principle that an infinite regress of causes and effects is impossible, a principle

---

[63] On which see Chapter 2, Section 4. The principle quoted is from Kant's 'Critique of Pure Reason', p. 508, footnote a.

[64] 'Philosophical Works', Vol. II, p. 489.

[65] The principle of explanations has been worded to forestall the difficulties raised in William L. Rowe's 'The Cosmological Argument', 'Noûs' V, 1971, pp. 49-61.

which Aquinas, by contrast, does seem to have needed.[66] The objection that an infinite series of causally related states of things is possible does not trouble Demea since he incorporates it in his own argument. Nor does his argument rest on the claim that since every event has an earlier cause there must be a first cause, prior to every event: an invalid argument which depends on a tacit shift in the sense of 'every'.

Now although the principle set out above cannot itself be demonstrated, it is a principle which has to be accepted, at least for ordinary practical purposes, by anyone who wishes to cope with life and get a grip on events around him. It is also accepted as a presupposition for their own purposes both by historians and by natural scientists. The explanations sought by historians will often be in terms of people's reasons and motives, not in terms of causes: but this practice is fully in accordance with the principle. And as for scientists, we have already seen that they assume that there is no difference in phenomena without there being an explanation (Chapter 1, Section 2C). Certainly it has already been allowed that cosmological explanation is non-scientific (Chapter 5, Section 3B above): but what needs to be shown is why a principle which is everywhere else appealed to without hesitation should be rejected in cosmological reasoning and in natural theology in general. And anyone who accepts the principle cannot consistently deny that, since the existence of matter can (and can only) be explained by the existence of a being necessarily timeless, uncreatable, indestructible, omnipotent and about whose own existence further questions are absurd (see above), we should in reason postulate the existence of such a being. Such a postulation is not rationally obligatory in that it cannot be shown independently of other cases that the principle applies to the case in point: yet unless good reason can be shown for not applying this widely accepted principle of explanations to the phenomenon of matter, it would be rational to assume that it does so apply.

Hence the extreme importance of the objections of Hume and Kant to talk of causation beyond all possible experience, and also to claims to have synthetic *a priori* knowledge. If they succeed, the principle enunciated above will not apply to the existence of matter or of change, or to the occurrence of the series of the states of whatever material objects there are. I shall postpone discussion of synthetic *a priori* propositions until after that of causes, and consider first Kant's view that we can have no knowledge of

---

[66] Thus Kenny, 'The Five Ways', pp. 23-7.

causing except of causing which is in time and in space,[67] and then Hume's view that to talk of the cause of the universe we should need (*per impossibile*) to be able to observe a constant concomitance between several universes and some other sort of thing which accompanied their birth.[68]

Kant affirms that "the principle of causality has no meaning and no criterion for its application save only in the sensible world". It may certainly be conceded to Kant that but for spatial and temporal events and changes we should have no notion of causation, and it may also be granted (along Humean lines) that normally we speak of causation only when there is evidence of spatial or temporal conjunction or connexion. It may also be granted that typically causes precede their effects, and that if God's creation is envisaged as preceding the observable events of our experience, paradoxes are likely to ensue.[69] But not all causes are chronologically prior to their effects — some are simultaneous — and, as to God's creation having a date, if it is to explain what it is postulated to explain, it must be timeless and not the earliest event. Kant's main complaint concerns rather the coherence of this postulation. We can only have knowledge of what it is in principle possible to experience. But that which brings about the conditions which make experience possible necessarily could not be experienced. Accordingly nothing could count for or against the claim that matter is created, and talk of explanations of its existence is empty and idle.

It is, however, reputable scientific practice to postulate unobservable entities by way of explaining what cannot otherwise be explained; thus talk of causing can reasonably be divorced from the ordinarily used criteria for recognising causes and their effects. Further, if there could be non-spatial and non-temporal causing, the criteria would be certain to be other than the ordinary criteria: and indeed in the case on hand the problem of criteria scarcely arises anyway, as we know what is to be explained and the problem of saying what causes it is largely the problem of how to describe that the existence of which has to be postulated, i.e. how to say what it would have to be like. The real issue, therefore, is whether there can be non-spatial and non-temporal causing.

Now clearly there cannot be non-temporal *changes* (i.e. in the character of what already exists): the idea of one thing *changing*

---

[67] 'Critique', p. 511, and *passim*. A similar point is implicit in Hume's 'Enquiry', Section XI, Selby-Bigge, p. 142.

[68] 'Enquiry', Section XI, Selby-Bigge, p. 148.

[69] Ibid., p. 416. A similar point was made in d'Holbach's 'Système de la Nature', (1770): see David C. Goodman, 'The Enlightenment: Deists and 'Rationalists' ', p. 51.

another is only conceivable if words like 'already' retain a sense, but this they only do if they are applied to temporal sequences. What is at stake in the present case is, however, different.[70] What is at stake is whether (timelessly) one being can bring other beings into existence, beings so made as to exist in time. What is created does not, in being created, change from what it was like beforehand: rather it comes into existence. Now even this requires there to be a timeless action: but there must be if the existence of matter is to be explained.

Perhaps the action of creation is the only timeless action. It is at any rate unlikely that there are timeless actions performed by other agents. And if so it is not surprising that causing is usually temporal and spatial, so much so that we find the idea of exceptional cases hard to accept. Nevertheless it would be misguided to contend that all cases of causing must resemble paradigm cases. Divine creation *could* not resemble everyday causing at all closely. What is more, the creation of the conditions which make experience possible, i.e. the creation of matter (in the above sense), is necessarily unamenable to experience. Kant's principle of there being no hope of arriving at a well-founded truth when the bounds of experience are crossed in effect legislates against the explicability of anything which cannot be explained by temporal processes. But there might have been no matter, or matter but no change, or again changing matter which underwent a different series of states from those we see: so why is there matter, why is there change and why are there these states and not others? We cannot, then, assume that all explanation is scientific in character. The notion of 'bringing into existence' has a possible application to matter, to its states and to change, but such explanations of the existence of matter, its states and of change would necessarily be non-scientific. Kant's objection, then, appears to beg the question, or rather to ban it prematurely.

At the same time Kant is right to protest at any easy assimilation of creation to ordinary cases of causing. For apart from differences already mentioned, the agent who creates is unlike ordinary causes in being necessarily unobservable. His (or its) character is mysterious except insofar as it can be known by inference from what can be experienced. We are not entitled to cast doubt on all unexperienceable causing: but neither are we entitled by the cosmological argument to claim to know how, much less why, the creative agency creates. Certainly we can tell that there must be a causally independent being (of whatever sort), timeless, uncreatable and indestructible, and able to bring into being what-

---

[70] See Geach, 'God and the Soul', pp. 82-4.

ever can without contradiction be said to be brought into being. But we must not be misled by our own language of 'ability' and 'bringing about' into supposing that on the strength of the cosmological argument we know this agent to be personal or purposive. Personal language is the most accessible model for conceiving of the causing of matter:[71] but the cosmological argument does not licence us to claim to have established its appropriateness to the exclusion of other kinds of language. The Kantian critique of the grounds of religion is the surest guarantee against facile anthropomorphism among theists.

The passage of Hume to be considered runs as follows:[72]

> "In a word, I much doubt whether it be possible for a cause to be known only by its effect (as you have all along supposed) or to be of so singular and particular a nature as to have no parallel and no similarity with any other cause or object, that has ever fallen under our observation. It is only when two *species* of objects are found to be constantly conjoined, that we can infer the one from the other; and were an effect presented, which was entirely singular, and could not be comprehended under any known *species*, I do not see, that we could form any conjecture or inference at all concerning its cause. If experience and observation and analogy be, indeed, the only guides which can reasonably follow in inferences of this nature; both the effect and cause must bear a similarity and resemblance to other effects and causes, which we know, and which we have found, in many instances, to be conjoined with each other."

The context of this passage shows that the alleged singular effect is the universe, and that Hume is therefore disputing the coherence of the claim that God causes or caused it.

There are, as Swinburne points out,[73] two objections (at least) in this passage. One is based on the claim that before we can say that something of a given kind caused something of another given kind, we must (at least) have observed several members of the former kind (and, of course, in conjunction with individuals of the latter kind). But this is just false: it would prevent us making causal remarks of any sort concerning the recurrent sightings of the footprints of the Abominable Snowman or of the surfacings of the

---

[71] I am here in debt of gratitude to an unpublished work 'Christ is of God' by D. G. Attfield, a work which may have influenced this section at more points than one.

[72] 'Enquiry', Section XI, Selby-Bigge, p. 148.

[73] 'The Argument from Design', by R. G. Swinburne, 'Philosophy', Vol. XLIII, No. 165, July 1968. Swinburne is in fact commenting on the parallel passage from the 'Dialogues'.

Loch Ness monster. When events are experienced of a somewhat different kind from any whose cause we have experienced, we are not thereby debarred from postulating causes of a suitably different kind such as to allow of the explanation of the observed effects. There must, certainly, be some analogy between the explanations of the two sorts of case, but this analogy is not lacking in the cosmological argument, where the fact of matter's happening to exist is explained by a cause suitable to itself in the same way as we explain the fact of particular children's happening to be born or particular events' happening to occur by causes suitable to themselves.

The more interesting objection is against all causal explanations of objects which are the only one of their kind, the Universe being taken to be such an object. Now much depends here on how we understand the expression "the Universe". For if we mean "whatever exists", then there are special difficulties about causal explanations; since there could be no external cause of the Universe so construed, and God would in any case be included in it if he exists. Indeed such difficulties may underlie Kant's protests about knowledge-claims about totalities regarded as wholes. If, on the other hand, we take "Universe" to be short for "created Universe", then all the major questions are begged from the outset. As far as I can see, however, no similar difficulties arise if "the Universe" is taken to mean "the set of material bodies distributed in empty space".[74]

But now we can see the falsity of Hume's principle. For, as Swinburne remarks, there is only one human race yet observed, yet anthropologists are forming and testing causal theories about its origin. So at least some unique things can be causally explained. It might here be objected that there are other races, but no other Universes: but it can quite properly be replied that nothing is in all respects unique, and that the existence of the Universe (in the above sense) resembles other explainable existences in being contingent. (Matter and change are, come to that, in certain respects unique, but their existence is also contingent.)

These objections accordingly miscarry, and so I turn finally to Hume's objection to synthetic *a priori* propositions, and Kant's opposition to the propriety of synthetic *a priori* assertions. Hume argues that books concerned neither with "abstract reasoning concerning quantity or number" nor containing "any experimental reasoning concerning matter of fact and existence" should be committed to the flames as containing "nothing but sophistry

---

[74] A formulation based on that of Swinburne, ibid., p. 208.

and illusion":[75] and although he excludes theology as containing the latter his other writings make it clear that he disputes the possibility of basing theology on reasoning from experience. Kant, as we have seen (Section 2B above) tolerates synthetic *a priori* propositions but protests at synthetic *a priori* truth-claims when they exceed experience.

Now as far as the arguments and as far as the implications of religious belief are concerned the proposition that God exists is synthetic, as we have seen. Whether it is *a priori* or not is, however, hard to decide. It is not a scientific hypothesis, not allowing of predictions which would be impossible without it, nor is it based on any particular experiences as opposed to others. If such are the requirements for being empirical, then it is not empirical. But neither is the proposition, 'There are material substances'. If whatever proposition is not empirical is *a priori* and these are the necessary conditions, either conjunctively or disjunctively, of empiricality in propositions, then Hume is wrong to deny that there are synthetic *a priori* propositions.

The problem then becomes whether they can be known. But at least some such propositions can be known. For if anything can be known, it can be known that there is language, itself an *a priori* but synthetic proposition on the above basis. But some things can be known, for I know that this book has an author. We do not have quite the same grounds for the synthetic but (on the above account) *a priori* proposition that God exists: but we do have grounds; i.e. the need for an explanation of the fact that matter happens to exist and the fact that nothing but a necessarily timeless being's existence can begin to explain it.

Sometimes, however, propositions are said to be *a priori* whose truth-value is in no way whatever dependent on what can be observed. But if nothing could be observed, there would be no grounds for belief in God. Accordingly God's existence is not *a priori* in this sense.

To summarise, I grant to Kant that no argument can show that the notion of a necessary being has extension, and therefore that the cosmological argument does not establish that it does. On this point Hume's Cleanthes is right and Hume's Demea is wrong. On the other hand there is (at least some) matter and there might not have been: there has occurred a particular set of states of material objects, but there might have been a different one: and there is change, but there might have been none at all. But the existence of whatever exists but might cease to exist or might not have existed, and the actuality of whatever is the case but might cease to be the

---

[75] 'Enquiry', Section XII, Part III, Selby-Bigge p. 165.

case or might not have been the case has an explanation of some sort, except where it is necessarily uncreatable and indestructible. Therefore change, matter and its series of states have explanations. Now explanations by agents' motives and agents' reasons only apply if there is an agent who performs some action, and the action in this case would have to be the bringing into being of what happens to exist and the bringing about of the actuality of what is actual: whereas a causal explanation in this case would involve there being something which causes such existence and actuality. Therefore there is something which brings about or causes this existence and these facts.

But to bring about either matter, its states, or change, the agency concerned would have to be timeless or he or it could not bring about the existence of whatever is subject to temporal predication. Further he or it would have to be uncreatable and indestructible, or the principle of explanation accepted above would require the fact of his (or its) happening to exist itself to be explained and the existence of something which really was uncreatable to be postulated.

On the other hand if he (or it) were known to be able to bring about change, or particular sequences of changes, but not known to be able to bring matter into existence, he (or it) would neither be known to be omnipotent nor even remotely to resemble the object of theistic worship. In this respect, quite apart from the question of necessary existence, I find Demea's argument unsuccessful with respect to the conclusion desired: except that when Demea says that there might have been no succession of causes and effects at all, he may be taken to imply that there could have been no matter, and therefore to be asking a cosmological question about the existence of matter itself as well as about the occurrence of its states. If, however, the agency postulated is able to bring into being whatever can conceivably be brought about, he (or it) will thereby be omnipotent, and, since these abilities are essential to him, he (or it) will be necessarily omnipotent.

To some degree Hume and to a great degree Kant were induced by the impressive spectacle of scientific achievement to require explanations to conform to the likeness of scientific ones, and not to transcend the bounds of experience. Their desire to limit assertions to the knowable and to what there can be serious grounds to believe was both philosophically and theologically praiseworthy, and had important implications for the claims which religious men in particular were wont to make. Their conclusions nevertheless issue in a secularism which, granted that there is no argument other than the cosmological argument for the existence of an omnipotent deity, would undermine the doctrine of creation and with it most theistic belief. This would be secularism because the existence of an omnipotent God could figure in no system or area of rational belief. This secularism, however, proves unwarranted on being carefully assessed.

Kant, it should be added, saw himself as "denying *knowledge* in order to make room for *faith*".[76] Belief in God, freedom and immortality was to be re-established on the basis of the postulates of practical reason; and a moral argument was to show that we cannot but believe in God if we take our ordinary moral beliefs seriously. Such an argument has no place in a work on secularisation, but it is fair to observe that Kant's moral argument is widely regarded as one of his weakest. Let us take it, then, that Kant cannot "make room for faith". To deny knowledge of God would still have been a service if the beliefs concerned had been, as Kant supposed, ill-grounded: men would have been enabled to lead more rational realistic lives. I have argued, however, that belief in the existence of a deity is rational, and that no premiss on which it is based is less than probable, even if we cannot here speak of knowledge; and indeed that were there no deity there would be no matter, no experience, no knowledge and indeed no philosophy.

---

[76] 'Critique of Pure Reason', p. 29.

CHAPTER 6

THE GROUNDS OF THEISM, II

Section 1: The Teleological Argument

A. Introductory.

Priestley, I shall argue, was mistaken in holding that the Cosmological Argument is "the only proper argument for the being of a God" (Chapter 3 Section 2C above). But the Teleological Argument is often considered to have been laid to rest by Hume. As it happens, some of Hume's general objections have already been discussed in Chapter 5, Section 3 as having a bearing on the cosmological argument: while a critical assessment of some premises proposed during the Seventeenth Century has already been given in Chapter 2, Section 2 and 3. This assessment will turn out to preclude the need for a detailed discussion of initial premises except where they concern order through time, but over arguments from these premises it will prove important to scrutinise Hume's objections in detail. The objections of Kant add little to and are largely dependent on those of Hume,[1] and thus need not be discussed independently.

The topic, however, is not a straightforward one. To what sort of deity does, or should, the argument argue? To what extent is this argument independent of the cosmological argument? And how far is the issue of divine purposiveness bound up with that of divine benevolence? The answers to the first two questions hang on the assessment of the argument itself, but the third can be tackled at once.

Insofar as the argument is intended to show not only that the world's order has a cause but also that it is designed, its conclusion implied not only that the causal agency is intelligent but also that it (or better, he) has desires of some sort: for to design is to act intentionally and therefore to have desire as well as belief (or knowledge). It does not, however, imply that the desire is of one particular sort rather than another, much less that what the causal agency desires is the good of his creatures, except in that a love of order is involved. Only if the world's order appeared designed to

---

[1] Cf. N. Kemp Smith, 'A Commentary to Kant's "Critique of Pure Reason" '; 2nd edition, London, 1923, p. 539, note 3.

promote the good of, perhaps, sentient creatures would the issue of the designer's benevolence arise. Equally if the world seems not maximally conducive to human flourishing, this in no way shows that its diachronic regularities are not the outcome of design. For the designer could love order but not men.

Only at one point need the issue of benevolence impinge directly on a teleological argument. It was pointed out in Chapter 2, Section 3C above that a teleological question arises even for an infinite world if the space-time trajectories of material particles somehow bespeak order. But we could only discern such order on some criterion, and the criterion there suggested was their beneficiality to men. Were they more beneficial than any possible alternative set, there would be evidence of design, and evidence, as there argued, independent of that of natural regularities. Such an argument, however, is very difficult to assess, and will be considered not here but alongside other arguments about theodicy in the next Section. Here it will be contended that there are other recognisable sorts of order in no way dependent for their recognition on a criterion of beneficiality, and that it makes good sense, therefore, without touching on the issue of God's goodness, to claim that the behaviour of material particles in accordance with natural laws is more orderly than it might have been.

It is suitable to observe at this stage that if this latter proposition can be sustained, another form of the cosmological argument is made possible. For, in accordance with the principle of explanation accepted in Chapter 5, Section 3, order which happens to exist but might not have has an explanation, even though in the nature of the present case no scientific explanation is possible. Now any teleological argument will depend on some parallel causal argument. In each case the causal argument will maintain that a certain sort of order has a cause, and the teleological argument goes on to maintain that, like the cause of a machine, that cause is purposive. It now becomes clear how some objections to the cosmological argument are also objections to the teleological argument: for perhaps we cannot maintain that there is a cause of any sort, let alone a purposive one. In what follows I shall concentrate on the respects in which teleological reasoning goes beyond cosmological reasoning, seeing that the conclusion of the new form of cosmological argument would add little or nothing to that of the forms discussed above.

B. Two Kinds of Order.

As was seen in Chapter 2, Section 3A above, Sir Isaac Newton argued for the existence of a Cosmic Designer from two sorts of order, from the laws of nature and also from the apparent contrivance of the organs of animals to fit their functions. In his article 'The Argument from Design',[2] R. G. Swinburne draws a corresponding distinction between kinds of regularity or order.

"There are in the world two kinds of regularity or order, and all empirical instances of order are such because they evince one or other or both kinds of order. These are the regularities of copresence or spatial order, and regularities of succession, or temporal order. Regularities of copresence are patterns of spatial order at some one instant of time . . . Regularities of succession are simple patterns of behaviour of objects, such as their behaviour in accordance with the laws of nature. . . "

Now as Swinburne points out, Hume's Cleanthes (often) and William Paley (usually) dwell on regularities of copresence, like that of the human eye. But to inferences of there being a designer of such regularities Hume's Philo has several trenchant objections. First, *if* the analogy with machines and their human designers requires us to postulate a designer for the eye's regularity, then we are obliged not to postulate a designer more imposing than would be needed to explain this regularity, and a designer at that as much like a human as possible, or the analogy will be implausibly weak. (Dialogue V). Such a designer, for instance, would only need control over a part of the Universe; whereas, as Swinburne argues, the main reason for postulating a *bodiless* designer is his operating at all times and places throughout the Universe:[3] thus there is no reason why such a designer should not have a body.

Second, such a postulation is not required anyway. The regularity of the eye may be explicable in ways closer to organic than mechanical order, in which case it will not need a designer (Dialogue VII): or it may be explicable as the outcome of the random collocations of material particles travelling through infinite time (Dialogue VIII). In any case how could animals survive unless their parts were adjusted to their functions? (Dialogue VIII). This latter question, while not singly adequate as an objection, foreshadows Darwin's theory of the evolution of species through natural selection, and also hints at the crucial weakness of teleological arguments based on regularities of copresence. This weakness is that, given long enough for the laws of nature to operate, virtually any such regularity is likely to arise, and that there may be perfectly natural processes which serve to

---

[2] 'Philosophy', July 1968, p. 200.
[3] For this argument see ibid., p. 209, and Chapter 6, Section 1C.

explain the occurrence of extremely complex and seemingly purposive order in nature.[4]

In short, such teleological arguments involve physical theology. The possibility of a natural explanation is prematurely despaired of, and resort is had to supernatural intervention. By pointing out other possibilities of explanation, Hume reveals that his opponents are forsaking scientific reasoning before seriously assessing its resources, and thus can be added to those who took part in the assault on physical theology himself. (See Chapter 2). Hume's arguments thus implicitly affirmed the right of biology to apply its techniques to an area often previously reserved for theologians, and at the same time undermined much bogus theology.

For the rest, I shall concentrate on regularities of succession. It should, however, be recalled all along that Hume was opposing arguments from regularities of both sorts, and that as his contemporaries did not argue only from regularities of succession, he was not in a position to concentrate on such arguments alone. Nevertheless since the explanation of regularities of copresence brings in regularities of succession (like evolution), it is not surprising that teleological questions have been raised about *this* sort of regularity, and ones not as easily shown to be redundant or futile.

The new premiss, then, is that material bodies either always, or almost always (see Chapter 2, Section 6C) behave in accordance with natural laws. Non-repeatable counter-instances to natural laws however ingeniously formulated would, if they occur, constitute counter-evidence, but we have seen that the evidence for such counter-instances is poor (Chapter 2, Section 6B and C). But sometimes, it may be pointed out, humans intervene in the otherwise unimpeded course of nature, and if the conclusions of Chapter 3 were correct, these interventions cannot always adequately be explained on the basis of natural laws and initial conditions alone. But human agency assists and does not detract from the teleological argument. On the one hand, as Swinburne points out,[5] sometimes humans are responsible for regularities of succession, as when a dancer's body goes through a pattern of movements, and this fact suggests the possibility that even those regularities of succession for which humans are not responsible may be explained by "the rational choice of a free agent":[6] while on the other hand, even if human actions make the world less tidy,

---

[4] A similar point is made in Diderot's 'Lettres sur les Aveugles'.
[5] 'The Argument from Design', pp. 200, 202, 204.
[6] Ibid., p. 203.

they scarcely throw into doubt the fact that, by and large, events comply with observable natural regularities.

Properly, however, the relevant premiss states that given initial conditions of one and the same sort, like events *happen* to arise, that events *happen* to obey natural laws, and that there *happen* to be few, if any, non-repeatable counter-instances to our formulations of natural laws. It is insufficient to point to order: it is at least necessary to point to there being more order than there might have been. Only this can form an adequate basis for that causal argument on which the teleological argument is based.

Now the objection to this argument is sometimes made, and ascribed to Hume at that, that *any* universe must be orderly, and that therefore there is nothing to explain. Hick[7] finds such an argument in Hume's 'Dialogues', Part VIII.[8] Such an objection has two possible bases. One is that the constituents of any universe must be classifiable, or they could not be thought of as things *of any sort,* and thus their set could not be conceived either. This however, has no effect on the argument under consideration. For, as argued in Chapter 2, Section 6A and Chapter 3, Section 1B, it is conceivable that events might not be explicable by natural laws, and yet that things should still be classifiable. That events *do* obey laws is a contingent fact, for there could have been more non-repeatable counter-instances. The premiss implies that our (classifiable) world is more orderly than other possible (classifiable) worlds.

The other basis for the objection is the fact that, were there no regularities of succession, there would be no human life, and therefore no humans to discuss the nature of the universe. I certainly grant that any universe discussible by humans as the one of which they are part will embody regularities of succession. But this is not to concede that any universe must embody regularities of succession. The objection, then, is groundless, and the striking degree of order displayed by the world around us remains in need of explanation, granted, at any rate, the principle of explanations of the previous Section.

The form of teleological argument under consideration will, as pointed out above, have two stages, in one of which all that is alleged is that the world's order has a cause, and in the other of which the more ambitious claim is made that it has a designer. It

---

[7] At 'Arguments for the Existence of God', (London, 1970), p. 10. See also his note 25, on p. 123.

[8] For a discussion of Kant's views on the subject, see J. A. Brunton, 'The Second Analogy and Levels of Argument', III(a) and (b), in 'Kantstudien', 62 Jahrgang, Heft 3, 1971. My disagreements with the Kant of Mr Brunton will shortly become obvious.

would therefore be well to review Hume's objections to there being a cause of this particular sort of order first, before the latter more analogical stage is discussed.

As we have already seen (Chapter 5, Section 3C) Hume has a double objection to explanations of the unique by the unique. He holds that before such causal explanations are legitimate, other such causes and other such effects must have been observed by us. The falsity of both principles was also there shown. Hick, however, finds in Hume's objection to explanations of the unique a separate point about the dubiety of the notion of probability as applied to such contexts,[9] a point which would be relevant only to the inference to a designer, or the second stage. There is accordingly no need to say more about Hume's double objection here.

One other objection, however, needs to be considered now. For, as we have seen above, Hume's Philo maintains (in Dialogue VIII) that given long enough, ordered systems are bound to arise, and therefore that no explanation of this order, or no more, at any rate, than a scientific explanation, is needed. But as Swinburne points out[10] Hume here relies for his explanation on the operation of natural laws, and thus only produces an explanation of regularities of copresence, not of regularities of succession. Could one, then, explain regularities of succession by other such regularities? The sustained applicability of natural laws, as observed over long periods, is a fact which militates strongly against the view that their observation by material particles e.g. in the present decade has itself somehow evolved: and in any case on the one hand natural laws, if there are any, necessarily apply to all times and places alike; whereas observation suggests that a great many of them exist, and that almost all events comply with one or another of them. Nevertheless sometimes one description of a regularity can be subsumed under another and, to that extent, explained by a more general regularity. Thus any given regularity of succession may be scientifically explained. What, however, cannot be scientifically explained is the fact that there are any, or that material particles obey them. Even if all regularities were to be comprehensively subsumed under one description triumphantly supplied by the advocates of unified science, the fact that that description held good of our world would still need explanation.

Granted, then, the principle of explanations accepted above (Chapter 5, Section 3) and the fact that in the present case there could only be an explanation in terms of motives if there were also

---

[9] 'Arguments for the Existence of God', pp. 13-14.
[10] Op. cit., pp. 210-11.

a causal explanation, the world's order would seem to have a cause, Hume and Diderot notwithstanding.

C. What Sort of Cause?

The conclusion of the second stage of the teleological argument is that the world's order is caused by "the rational choice of a free agent",[11] and that accordingly the existence of such an agent must be postulated. But why is this sort of explanation preferable to any other? Certainly order is sometimes produced by rational agents, and certainly if we have to go beyond scientific explanations to explain the world's order, an explanation by rational agency is a possibility. But are there no other possibilities? Hume points out that there are other sorts of things than rational agents which produce order. "A tree bestows order and organization on that tree which springs from it, without knowing the order; an animal in the same manner on its offspring."[12] (Hume is of course not thinking of *intelligent* activity on the part of animals.)

Yet, as Swinburne reminds us,[13] only regularities of copresence can be explained by vegetation or by generation. The tree and the animal only produce their offspring because of the operation of regularities of succession which are entirely outside their control, let alone devised or caused by them. Such agency cannot therefore be introduced to explain regularities of succession, not at any rate unless it is so redescribed as to be presented simply as a non-rational causal agency not itself subject to regularities of succession. But by then the analogy with vegetables and non-human animals and the way in which they produce order becomes slight, even though the possibility of such being the cause remains (*pace* Swinburne, pp. 203f).

More needs to be done, however, to show that the hypothesis that the world's order is caused by rational agency is both better supported than the alternatives and well enough supported to be accepted. Certainly one alternative suggested by Hume (Dialogue V) will not do, namely that there was a committee of rational agents that caused the world's order. As Swinburne says, "When postulating entities, postulate as few as possible".[14] Occam's principle applies despite Hume's view that the contrary is true when we have no other information. Further, as Swinburne goes on to say,

"If there were more than one deity responsible for the order of

---

[11] Swinburne, ibid., p. 203.

[12] Hume, 'Philosophical Works', Vol. II, p. 477 (Dialogue VII). The same passage is quoted by Swinburne; ibid., p. 210.

[13] Ibid., p. 210.

[14] Ibid., p. 210.

the Universe, we should expect to see characteristic marks of the handiwork of different deities in different parts of the Universe, just as we see different kinds of workmanship in the different houses of a city. We should expect to find an inverse square law of gravitation obeyed in one part of the universe, and in another part a law which was just short of being an inverse square law — without the difference being explicable in terms of a more general law. But it is enough to draw this absurd conclusion to see how ridiculous the Humean objection is."

That alternative, then, is less well supported by the evidence. But is the hypothesis of one rational agent itself well enough supported?

That hypothesis is both arrived at and supported by analogical reasoning, the relevant principles of which are the reasonable assumptions that qualitatively identical effects almost always[15] have qualitatively identical causes, and that similar effects are *likely* to have similar causes, but that effects which are different in kind are likelier to have different causes than similar ones. Such principles are the basis of one kind of inductive reasoning, which proves fruitful e.g. in science and history. Nevertheless they need not be confined to science and history, particularly when, as in the present case, we find an effect (i.e. the regularities of succession of our world) which resembles effects musicologists, historians and social scientists can study (e.g. the ordered course of a song, the execution of a five year plan or the ordered production-sequence of a factory), yet which itself is unamenable to historical explanation, not being a possible outcome of human action.

Analogical reasoning is obviously at its strongest when both causes and effects (both known and postulated) are exactly alike, as Hume pointed out (Dialogue V, and *passim*.) But the cause of natural regularities must obviously be more powerful than human agents are, and accordingly somewhat unlike human agents. Moreover when Cleanthes, the advocate of the teleological argument, shows signs of postulating by way of conclusion a *bodiless* agent, Hume's Philo protests both that the analogy will not stand being so stretched, and that such a postulation is in any case unnecessary.

I take the second point first. As conceded above, if the order to be explained consists in regularities of copresence Philo's protest is quite justified. An embodied rational agent could conceivably have made the ancestors of animal species much as we now find their descendants, and have left them to reproduce themselves; and such an agent would bear a closer analogy to humans than a bodi-

---

[15] For the possibility of exceptions see Ch. 1, Section 1D., p. 25.

less agent would. But if the order to be explained consists in regularities of succession, the cause must after all be bodiless. For such an agency must exercise control equally over all times and places alike; whereas to have a body is to exercise immediate control over one particular part of the universe only, and to be able to act on other places and have effects on other times only indirectly, and by moving that body. So only a bodiless agent could explain the set of the regularities of succession.[16]

A bodiless agent must be postulated because the effect to be explained is somewhat unlike the effects of human agency. The reasoning thus falls short of analogical reasoning of the strongest kind. But it does not follow from this that it is unacceptably weak. Instead it falls under the rubric that similar effects are likely to have similar causes. *Probably*, the cause of the regularities of succession around us is rational but bodiless.

The bodilessness of this agent actually derives support from a principle of Hume himself, the principle that postulated causes should be proportionate to know effects, and of a status sufficient to have explanatory force, though of no greater status. It is possible, though, to construe Hume as having a further point to make in the passage from 'Enquiry', Section XI, discussed in Chapter 5, Section 3A above.[17] His words are "When we infer any particular cause from an effect, we must proportion the one to the other, and can never be allowed to ascribe to the cause any qualities but what are exactly sufficient to produce the effect."[18] Hume *at least* here says that postulated causes must be adequate but no more than adequate to their (presumed) effects. But he may also be saying that if the cause of a phenomenon X is being postulated, it may only be characterised as "the cause of X", or, more reasonably, it may only be characterised, granted that only a's *could* cause X, as "the a which causes X." Now if Hume is saying this, he is prohibiting us from ascribing rationality to the cause of regularities of succession: for they could conceivably be caused by a non-rational agency. Swinburne here objects that all scientific progress would be abolished by this restriction, since science proceeds by the reasonable ascription to postulated causes of characteristics other than those sufficient to produce a known effect.

Hume's reply would probably be that what is reasonable in science is not necessarily reasonable in natural theology. Hypotheses in science which exceed the currently available evidence can be tested against new evidence in experiments:

---

[16] Thus Swinburne, ibid., p. 209.
[17] Thus Swinburne, ibid., p. 207.
[18] Selby-Bigge, p. 136.

hypotheses in natural theology which exceed what is strictly necessary cannot be tested at all, except on the information for the explanation of which they were found not to be strictly necessary in the first place. To reply thus would be to concede the principle but powerfully to resist the natural theologian all the same.

Now I should be prepared to grant a follower of Hume the difference, but not to accept the prohibition. For if, among a's that could cause X, a's that are also b's are much the likeliest to be the cause of X, then it is after all reasonable to claim that probably an ab caused X, even if an a which was non-b could conceivably have done so. The problematic word here is 'probably'. But before that is discussed, it is important to see what Hume's principle of proportionality *does* establish on the current subject.

What Hume's principle establishes is that first we ought not, on the strength of the teleological argument alone, to postulate an *omnipotent* rational agent. This point is brought out by Kant.[19] Whatever else a producer of order must be able to do, he need not be able to create matter *de nihilo*. So long, then, as there is no separate ground for holding that he can (and the teleological argument offers no such ground), we are obliged not to postulate on its basis alone an omnipotent agent. Not that we need define the agent postulated as necessarily of limited power: the argument does not require the producer of order to be *un*able to create matter. Nevertheless the teleological argument emerges, in this respect if no other, as inadequate for the requirements of the theist. To point this out was a shrewd secularising blow on the part of Hume and Kant: for it was thereby shown that those who eschewed such apparently *a priori* reasonings as the cosmological argument and rested their belief on the teleological argument alone had an inadequate basis for the cognitive claims about God they made; and many since the time of Newton had been of such a turn of mind.

Hume's principle also establishes, second, that the producer of order need not be timeless. Certainly he would not have come into existence and will not cease to exist, at least as long as matter exists to be ordered. But just as the question arises why there is matter at all, so, as far as the teleological argument goes, does the corresponding question in the case of the cosmic designer. It makes sense to ask whether his existence is timelessly brought about just as it makes sense to ask whether that of matter is timelessly brought about. For, as far as the argument goes, he may act at various times and places, unlike the creator of matter who (as pointed out in Chapter 2, Section 2) brings about the existence of whatever exists in space and time and must therefore be timeless. Once again the

---

[19] 'Critique of Pure Reason', p. 522.

argument does not show that *only* the minimum required *can* hold good of the producer of order: it does not show that he is *not* himself timeless. For it is *possible* that the producer of order timelessly brings it about that material particles obey natural laws at all times and all places. But we do not *know* that he is like this *on the strength of the argument*. As far as the argument goes all that we can postulate is a rational bodiless agent of infinite duration and extent, just as, where the argument alone is concerned, we can only postulate a very powerful agent who need not be omnipotent.

To admit this much is to admit another point of Hume's, namely that the existence of the designing mind would itself be in need of explanation (Dialogue IV). This I would accept, unless it can be shown that, despite the above, the producer of order, as postulated by the argument, is after all uncreatable and indestructible. But to show this, grounds independent of the teleological argument would be needed. What I do not grant is that this fact casts doubt on the argument's conclusion. Doubt would, perhaps, be cast on the explanatory force of the conclusion if the principles used in reaching it led to an infinite regress of questions about the cause of the producer of order, the cause of the cause of the producer of order, . . . and so on: for the explanatory force of an infinite regress is slight indeed. But we have already seen reason to suppose that the only explanation of contingent existences which are such that it makes sense to ask the reason for their existence is, once the sphere of scientific explanations has been transgressed, the existence of a necessarily uncreated being (Chapter 5, Section 3A). Accordingly in the present case also we may suppose that the explanation of any sequence of causes of regularities of succession would ultimately lie in the existence of a being the reason for whose existence it made no sense to ask.

The sequence of explanatory questions would thus reach a resting place, and accordingly the explanatory force of the postulated existence of the producer of order remains undiminished. The motive of Hume's point was almost certainly to cast doubt on the sense of seeking an explanation of the regularities of our world in the first place: but not even were an infinite regress of explanations to ensue would it follow that no (non-scientific) explanations could or should be sought. Nevertheless to have shown that the existence of the designing mind would need explanation is another implicit achievement of Hume's propounding his principle of proportionality for postulated causes: for certainly the teleological argument does not require us to postulate a *self-explanatory* being about whom no further questions can be asked.

Now it was pointed out above that the kind of analogical argument which the teleological argument instantiates is not of the strongest kind, and that its conclusion is no more than probable. Two questions arise from this, namely whether nothing more can be said in favour of the conclusion to render its probability more acceptable, and, more radically, whether the notion of probability can enter into this particular issue. The less radical question will be taken first.

The degree of support of the conclusion of the argument depends, as Swinburne points out,[20] not only on the similarities between the effects considered but also on "the degree to which (it) makes explanation of empirical matters more simple and coherent". Now if the conclusion of the argument is false, two sorts of explanation are required for "empirical matters", natural laws, and the free choices of rational agents (which, as I have argued in Chapter 3, and as Swinburne also argues, are not explicable solely in terms of natural laws and initial conditions): and, even if it is allowed that both the existence of minds and the existence of laws have causes, yet there is still no guarantee that those causes are of the same sort. But, as Swinburne remarks,[21] "It is a basic principle of explanation that we should postulate as few as possible kinds of explanation." Now if the laws of nature are themselves to be explained by rational agency, the duality of ultimate types of explanation disappears: for rational agency becomes the single ultimate kind of explanation. Nor can this simplification be achieved otherwise, for, as has already been pointed out, rational agency is not explicable by causal laws. Thus "if the amount of similarity between the order in the Universe not produced by human agents and that produced by human agents makes it at all plausible to do so, we ought to postulate that an agent is responsible for the former as for the latter (sic)". (I take the last phrase to be short for "as agents are for the latter".)

Swinburne does not regard this consideration as decisive: the whole question still depends on the question of "the amount of similarity". The important point, however, is that granted Swinburne's "basic principle of explanation" as above, less similarity is required, since the very economy of the conclusion of the argument now turns out to lend it added support. Nor can Occam's razor be adduced at this stage against the postulation of a cosmic designer, for once my principle of explanations (Chapter 5, Section 3C) has been accepted, there will certainly have to be allowed to be a cause of the world's order of some sort or other.

---

[20] Ibid., pp. 205-6.
[21] Ibid., p. 206.

These considerations, I submit, strengthen the conclusion that the existence of a bodiless rational agent who causes the regularities of succession in the universe is probable.

But does this conclusion make sense? Hick[22] argues that there is no possible basis for probability statements about the universe as a whole. The "domain" of the probability statement in question would be the entire universe, so no proposition which applied only to the codomain of that proposition, i.e. what lies outside the universe, would suffice as evidence for it. Propositions, however, about parts of the universe cannot be evidence either. But all propositions of probability are relative, somehow or other, to evidence. Since, then, there could be no evidence or counter-evidence for such propositions, they are senseless. Hick believes this reasoning to destroy the validity of all probabilistic theistic arguments, and also to be the point Hume was really making in the passage in Dialogue II and its twin at Enquiry p. 136 (Selby-Bigge).

Hick is correct in holding that the statement that the natural regularities of succession around us are caused by a bodiless cosmic designer has the whole universe (or at any rate all times and places) as its scope (though it does not, of course, concern the free choices of rational agents). But at the same time the universe could have been otherwise, a fact which justifies us in asking why it is ordered as it is. Moreover once it is allowed that this order has a cause of some sort or other, several logical possibilities arise. The cause could be non-rational, or rational, and it could be a rational individual or a rational committee. Even the latter possibility *is* a possibility, despite the fact that to postulate it as true would involve an uneconomical hypothesis. The question, then, of which of these possibilities is to be preferred as the cause of regularities of succession will depend on which of them bears the closest analogy to causes of order which are observed.

Now were there no possibility of drawing analogies between the universe and its parts, this final stage of reasoning could be successfully resisted. For it such analogising made no sense, neither would it make sense to say that any of the possible causes of order was more probable than any other of them. Hume, as we have seen, does (sometimes) take the view that the universe cannot be compared with anything within it, (though not always, as when (Dialogue VII) he compares it with a vegetable). Hick, however,[23] sees the futility of such a prohibition: if something is unique in one respect, it need not be (and, it should be added, will not be) unique in every respect (for nothing is unique in every respect). Thus the

---

[22] At 'Arguments for the Existence of God', pp. 28f.
[23] Op. cit., p. 13.

universe resembles the nitrogen cycle, the Gregorian calendar, or a folk-song in point of embodying regularities of succession.
There are several conclusions to be drawn. One is that a postulable cause of order which is preferable both in point of analogical support and also, consequently, of explanatory force, may properly be regarded as more probable than other postulable causes, and that it is mistaken to hold that no probability statements can be intelligibly made about the natural regularities of the universe as a whole. Another is that once it is accepted that regularities of succession have some cause or other, the most probable cause becomes outright probable. And a third point is that the conclusion of the argument is better supported even than the analogy of cosmic and humanly produced order, taken together with considerations of economy of explanation, may have seemed to make it. For what is at stake in the second stage of the argument is not whether to postulate a cause of order, but what sort of cause that cause is most likely to be. Were there no case for postulating a cause of some sort or other *in any case*, the support afforded by considerations of analogy and economy could well seem defective. If similar effects are (merely) likely to have similar causes, then if someone forgets that effects necessarily have causes they may well infer that it is possible that a given effect, despite being similar to another which has a cause, has no cause at all itself: and this inference could be *legitimately* inferred if they altered the premiss to one reading, 'Similar *phenomena* are likely to have similar causes.' Indeed a number of Enlightenment philosophers saw the matter in this light. But granted the principle of explanations (as in Chapter 5, Section 3C) and therefore the *first* stage of the argument, considerations of analogy and economy are quite adequate for the second stage.

D. Two Arguments, Two Deities?

We have seen that, granted the principle of explanations of Chapter 5, Section 3C, the cosmological argument renders it probable that there is an uncreatable, indestructible and necessarily omnipotent being (of some sort or other), and the teleological argument establishes the probability of there being a rational bodiless agent who is able to produce the regularities of succession around us but who may well not be omnipotent or timeless. The conclusions of the two arguments are thus distinct, and this fact reflects partial mutual independence. On the other hand the teleological argument rests both on the (said) principle of explanations and on a form of cosmological reasoning as its first stage: and, further, the explanatory force of its conclusion would at least be seriously diminished but for the fact that cosmological reasoning shows that the series of entities postulated in answer to questions about the cause of the producer of order, and its cause, and its cause, etc., is itself explained in all probability by the existence of an uncreatable being. Yet not even here does the teleological argument appeal to the *omnipotence* of the God of the cosmological argument, (an indispensable feature of the deity of that argument if his existence is to explain the existence of matter as well as its states and its changes). Thus the teleological argument establishes both less and more than the cosmological argument, and does so to some extent independently of it, i.e. without appeal to its full conclusion, and partially along independent lines.

But both arguments allude to there being a necessarily uncreatable being of some sort: and in the case of the cosmological argument economy required that only a being of these qualities be postulated, and not a sequence of intermediary beings as well (Chapter 5, Section 3A). Further, the producer of the world's order could, for all we know, be uncreatable, and thus of such a sort that questions about the reason of his existence were absurd: it is just that the teleological argument alone does not license this conclusion. The same considerations of economy, then, require us to eschew theistic binitarianism and identify the cosmological and teleological deities.

The reasoning involved is as follows. We have reason to postulate the existence of an uncreatable and omnipotent being of otherwise unkown nature. We also have reason to postulate the existence of another bodiless being, this time a rational being which, so as to produce order by free choice, must be deemed to have knowledge and wants, and thus to be *capable* of thought and desires, and thus to be personal. This second being may only be of infinite duration, and not timeless: but if he is not timeless, we are obliged to postulate two beings in all. Economy then requires us to ascribe to one and the same being the qualities of each, since all these qualities are compatible. There will therefore be an uncreatable, indestructible and necessarily omnipotent and bodiless being who is a rational and personal agent able intentionally and intelligently to produce the world's order. (The expression from "able" to "order" is needed in that previously omnipotence was so understood as not to include the ability to cause whatever could be caused in an *intentional and intelligent manner*. The omnipotent cause of all matter and change might not have been personal, even though talk of omnipotence *usually* presupposes a personal agent.)

Thus the two arguments lead to a single, personal deity. This notion has many problems, such as those of timeless knowledge and timeless action, which cannot be discussed further. But it also has many advantages. First, the assertion can be abandoned that the cosmological deity may bring things into being in an impersonal way, an assertion only made because of the limitations of the cosmological argument. Action-terms can now properly be ascribed to him without undue linguistic strain. Second, Hobbes' problems about talk of God (see Chapter 1, Section 2B) are further allayed, as also are Palmer's (see Introduction): for we know more of the level at which predicates ascribed to God are to apply, namely that of an uncreatable and omnipotent *personal agent*. Third, the doctrine of creation, assumed by religious believers, and also by early modern scientists as an incentive to observe, experiment and detect God's mathematics in nature, itself receives a large measure of vindication. Thus a minimal basis for theistic religious belief turns out to be capable of defence, and at the same time those who trust in the worthwhileness of persevering with scientific method receive further rational encouragement; for the ordering of an intelligent Creator turns out after all to be open to discovery.

It remains to acknowledge the integrity of Hume's secularising critique of the theistic arguments. Just as he foreshadowed Kant's contention that the cosmological argument fails to show that there is a necessarily existent being, so in the case of the teleological argument he established that, taken alone, the argument does not establish the existence of the deity of theism. The existence of such a deity can only be supplied with a rational defence if both the arguments are taken together; though if, as above contended, such a defence is available, Hume's secularism[24] will, of course, have been shown to be largely unjustified. But his secularism on another subject, that of divine benevolence, has yet to be examined.

---

[24] Like the secularism of Hume and Kant over the cosmological argument (see Chapter 5, Section 3 above) Hume's secularism here consists in his implication that belief in divine creation can have no place in any set or area of rational beliefs. And I take it that Hume *does* imply this, despite his occasional pretence, e.g. in the 'Enquiry', to the contrary.

Section 2: The Goodness of God

A. General Arguments For and Against.

An intelligent deity could be benevolent, malevolent or indifferently disposed towerds the welfare of his intelligent creatures. But Hume, as we shall see, produces reasons for thinking that he is at best indifferent (Dialogue XI) on the basis of certain empirical evidence. It is therefore important to investigate whether there is a basis for the theistic belief in God's goodness. As Hume's Philo there remarks, this belief can only be adhered to in the light of apparent counter-evidence if grounds can be adduced in its favour.

Since God's desire for the welfare of his intelligent creatures is at stake ('welfare' being construed broadly as in Chapter 4, Section 2), 'evil' will be understood as harm to such creatures or their failure to flourish in some respect or other, together with whatever contributes to such failures to flourish or is deleterious of their welfare. Thus I shall not take into consideration the "evil" alleged by Kant[25] to be present in the (so-called) injustice of the wicked not always being made to suffer before they die for their wickedness: for it is far from certain that such suffering would contribute to rather than detract from the welfare of most people. Although writers like Butler had sometimes implied that the wicked usually are punished in this life,[26] and a secularising protest was therefore in place, Kant's difficulty is not the one I am concerned with. Wickedness and suffering, however, are both included under the terms of this definition of 'evil'.

Some writers and thinkers[27] have supposed that God's goodness may be established *a priori* (in the strongest sense of that expression), or alternatively by cosmological reasoning: but the three preceding sections show there to be no basis for this supposition. Even if God is defined as being benevolent, a new argument would be needed to establish the extensional existence of such a benevolent God, and no *a priori* or cosmological argument could establish this. Yet grounds are needed; and are readily to be found, somewhat along the lines of Butler's reasoning, in the Creator's provision for intelligent life, for the development of mature characters in many self-determining human agents, and for the existence of cooperative human societies to the benefit of most,

---

[25] 'On The Failure of All Philosophical Essays in Theodicy', from 'Essays and Treatises', (1791), translated W. Richardson: in 'Philosophy of Religion', edited Julius R. Weinberg and Keith E. Yandel, New York, 1971, pp. 91-101: at p. 95.

[26] 'Analogy', *passim*.

[27] Thus Leibniz, 'Theodicy', *passim:* Hume's Demea, Dialogue X, 'Philosophical Works', II, pp. 502f.

if not all participants. The grounds, then, of belief in God's goodness must be contingent and empirical, just as Butler and Hume's Cleanthes supposed.[28] The sort of grounds proposed by Demea, in terms of the evils of this world being matched by outbalancing benefits over the course of eternity, may or may not establish the possibility of God's benevolence, but certainly do *not* establish God's benevolence itself.

Such being the belief at issue and such being the nature of what could count as favourable evidence, it is not surprising that in an age when the foundations of theistic belief were subjected to scrutiny various thinkers saw fit to consider unfavourable evidence. Thus Descartes put forward[29] (and attempted to explain theistically) the evil of human error, a matter later raised by Hume:[30] whereas Pierre Bayle anticipated Hume and Kant in adducing human wickedness and suffering in his 'Reply to the Questions of a Provincial'[31] (a reply directed at Leibniz). Similar objections to Leibniz were eloquently articulated later by Voltaire in 'Candide'.

The objections were, however, best summarised by Hume's Philo in Dialogue X:[32]

"Why is there any misery at all in the world? Not by chance surely. From some cause then. Is it from the intention of the Deity? But he is almighty. Nothing can shake the solidity of this reasoning so short, so clear, so decisive; except we assert that these subjects exceed all human capacity . . ."

The latter assertion is in fact made by Kant,[33] but is only supportable if Hume's pattern of reasoning is entirely inappropriate to its subject, which is not apparent. Hume's argument, however, needs supplementing. God might lack the knowledge, the skill or the awareness of his own power needed to prevent misery and other evils, at least as far as the passage quoted goes. But the deity postulated by the teleological argument is sufficiently intelligent not to lack the necessary knowledge, skill and awareness. Thus if we describe God's intelligence, skill and awareness (taken together) as his 'wisdom', Hume may be taken as asserting that it is inconsistent to maintain that God exists, is omnipotent, is wise (in the above sense) and is benevolent *and* that evil exists. If there exists

---

[28] Butler, 'Analogy': Cleanthes, Dialogue X, p. 503.
[29] Meditation IV: Haldane and Ross, Vol. I.
[30] In his first Enquiry, Section XII, Part I; Selby-Bigge, p. 153.
[31] Chapter 144: Vol. III, p. 812: the reference is owed to Leibniz, 'Theodicy', p. 183.
[32] p. 505.
[33] Op. cit., pp. 96-101.

such a God, the occurrence of evils is, Hume implies, impossible. Belief in God's goodness in face of such objections requires further justification, to supplement the evidence cited above: and this is the task of theodicy.

Theodicy, then, is usually concerned with the *consistency* of admitting the existence of evil and yet at the same time asserting that God is omnipotent, wise and good. Thus construed, even a successful theodicy would not establish or support the belief that God is good or benevolent. To point this out was an achievement of Hume in Dialogue XI; and that is why some amount of favourable evidence has to be produced, (and preferably at the outset, as above). This done, the belief stands unless objections like that of Dialogue X prove conclusive, or unless some particular sort of evil can be shown to occur which a benevolent God would not allow, or unless some other theory explains the phenomena better. The key question is therefore whether Hume establishes his objections as conclusive.

B. Theodicy, Self-Determination and Rationality.

Some evils (in the above sense) are the outcome of human choice or else such as humans could prevent, or could have prevented: and some again are of neither sort. Traditionally these two kinds of evils have been distinguished as moral and physical evils respectively: thus Kant in the essay already mentioned.[34] I shall retain this terminology, with the single warning that it should not be confused with a rather different distinction employed in Chapter 4, that of the morally good (or bad) and the non-morally good (or bad). Roughly that distinction rested on whether the reason for desirability was moral or not, while this one rests on the *origins* of what harms intelligent creatures. On the terminology here adopted, nuclear fall-out is a moral evil, whereas earthquakes are physical evils. The present Sub-section is concerned exclusively with moral evil, and therefore the problem of physical evil will remain unsolved at the end of it.

In the case of moral evil it is possible to reconcile God's existence, omnipotence, wisdom and goodness with the fact of evil by means of what Plantinga[35] has called 'The Free Will Defence'. This line of argument goes back at least to Leibniz.[36] It is not so

---

[34] Op. cit., p. 92.
[35] 'The Free Will Defence', reprinted in 'The Philosophy of Religion', edited Basil Mitchell, Oxford, 1971, pp. 105-120. Hume (p. 519) calls 'physical' evils 'natural evils'.
[36] 'Theodicy', pp. 192, 378.

much that a world which contains free creatures is more *valuable* than one that does not (Plantinga's term, p. 106), since it would be hard to say what is meant by 'valuable' here. The defence rather concerns, or should concern, what is involved in God's *benevolence*. As above, I take God's benevolence to be a desire for the welfare of his intelligent creatures. But (as contended in Chapter 4, Section 2) the welfare at any rate of humans involves the development of the capacity of self-determination, what can (as a shorthand expression) be termed the exercise of free-will. Therefore benevolence involves permitting the exercise of free-will. But to be free is to be free to do both good and harm. Whether good or harm is done is thus the responsibility of the creatures concerned: it is not the responsibility of God. For God cannot make free creatures who are so made that they are unable to do other than what is right, for bringing about such free action is logically impossible. To be able to do nothing but what one does do is not to be free at all. Some creatures actually do wrong: but if God is benevolent he must allow them to do so.

This argument will not quite do as it stands. For example a creature able to do only what is right may yet have some freedom, i.e. a choice between two equally good actions. But such creatures could not develop mature human characters: this requires choices between alternatives some of which are less than ideal. The logical impossibility, then, is of God creating creatures with the kind of freedom which can lead to the development of a mature character and which also are free to do only what is right. Since benevolence involves desire for human welfare, mature development included, a benevolent God must therefore allow the possibility that wrong choices be made.

Another reply resembles one made in another connection by Hume's Philo.[37] Even if God must, if benevolent, allow wrong choices to be made (this reply goes), why should he not prevent harm accruing from those choices to those creatures which are the objects of his benevolence? There are two counter-replies. One is that, since such interventions would be observable, men would learn that apparently wrong actions never had evil consequences. The scope for choice would thus be unduly narrowed, as there would (once again) be no genuine choice between good and evil. All serious opportunities for choice would have been taken away. The other counter-reply is that were God to intervene thus in the operation of natural laws, no-one could foresee the consequences of their actions (except that they would not be evil). Thus it would be impossible to reason or plan for the future, study the natural

---

[37] pp. 511f.

world, or control it: and the development of the capacity for self-determination would be enormously retarded. Thus Philo's reply miscarries.

There are a number of other possible reples to this argument. Some rest on the belief that free will and causal determinism are *not* logically incompatible: therefore God can after all make free creatures do what is right.[38] This incompatibility has however been argued for above (Chapter 3, Section 1). There are yet others again, e.g. those of J. L. Mackie.[39] But these are stated, restated and as ably rebutted by Alvin Plantinga,[40] all with a dexterity I cannot hope to emulate (and with a fullness of text which it would be inappropriate to copy).

I take it, then, that 'The Free Will Defence' is successful as far as moral evil is concerned, and that the true strength of Hume's objections lies in the question of physical evil. But for the sake of completeness a few remarks are due on the topic of error.

Now no-one is likely to claim that a benevolent God would make his intelligent creatures omniscient: such creatures would never have to exercise themselves in distinguishing truth and falsity, could not develop by learning, and, there again, would find it hard enough to forgive each other for their misdeeds, let alone to forget. The problem of Descartes (and his successors) was rather our mistakes of *judgement*: and Descartes blames such mistakes on man's will.[41] This certainly appears strange, as few men choose to believe what is false or voluntarily enter into error. On the other hand many mistakes are to some extent our own fault. We could have looked around more for evidence, or have developed better habits of inference and discrimination. Certainly some of our false beliefs are rationally based, the evidence having been inadequate: but to ask a benevolent God to remedy this is to ask him to make us omniscient. And the other mistakes are moral[42] evils, (when they are evils at all) in that human effort could have prevented them. But once again the exercise of such effort is indispensable for mature human development: a benevolent God would not therefore remove all opportunity for it, and therefore has to allow mistakes of judgement to occur. Descartes was not altogether wrong.

Thus what 'The Free Will Defence' establishes over wrong

---

[38] Robert Young discusses these matters in Ch. 14 of 'Freedom, Responsibility and God'.
[39] 'Evil and Omnipotence', Mind, LXIV, (1955), Section 4.
[40] Op. cit., Section I and II.
[41] Op. cit.
[42] In the current sense. They are rarely, if ever, immoral.

actions is established by a corresponding 'Rationality Defence' over mistaken beliefs.

C. Human Welfare and Natural Regularities.

The current problem is whether "the existence of *physical evil*... is inconsistent with the existence of an omniscient, omnipotent and all-good Deity".[43] Plantinga's solution here is to point out that there is no inconsistency so long as there could be a free non-human spirit such as Satan who causes physical evil. So long as this possibility is not nonsense, its unlikelihood does not matter. It could be added on Plantinga's behalf that such a spirit could be identified and individuated as the cause of (apparent) physical evil. Presumably Plantinga also holds that a benevolent, wise and omnipotent deity might desire that such a spirit should have opportunities for choice. I find Plantinga's logic flawless: a (creaturely) Satan could exist, and accordingly the appearance of inconsistency is illusory.

On the other hand, should there be grounds for holding that there is no such spirit, the apparent inconsistency would remain, unless it can be dispelled in some other way: that is, it would remain if, to the set of allegedly inconsistent propositions, there were added the proposition that there is no free non-human malevolent spirit able to cause what appears to be physical evil. Now economy of hypotheses requires us to be sceptical about such an evil apirit unless the postulation of his existence is necessary, i.e. is well-supported by the evidence and better supported than any alternative hypothesis. This being so, there is more than one reason for doubts about the Devil.

For one thing, as Hume points out against Manichaeanism,[44] the "uniformity and steadiness of general laws" throughout time and space is evidence against there both being a good and an evil spirit. It might be replied that physical evils comply with natural laws, and that what Satan is responsible for is not infringements of natural laws but certain individual natural laws which are overall harmful. But it is not at all evident that there are any natural laws of this nature. (See Section 2D).

Another difficulty is as follows. If a malevolent deity has to be postulated to make theism cohere with observable facts, theism itself (its new supplementary hypothesis included) loses a considerable part of its support. The conclusion of the teleological argument was partly accepted because of its economy: for the

---
[43] Thus Plantinga, Section III, p. 118.
[44] Dialogue XI, p. 519.

hypothesis of a single rational bodiless agent able to control events at all times and places simplified the number of sorts of explanation at the same time as requiring only one new entity to be postulated. If it is now declared that natural regularities are only susceptible of explanation by rational agency if there are two (or more?) rational agents, the theory that the cause of order is nonrational will become at least almost as likely. Indeed it would be preferable to either theory to opt for the view which Hume gives to Philo (Dialogue XI) that there is a rational cause of order *indifferent* to the welfare of men.

There being, therefore, no necessity to postulate non-human spirits whose acts make all apparent physical evil really moral evil and on whose freedom and development God looks with benevolence, it is better to assume that there are none, and set about a non-demonological theodicy. (It is, indeed, dubious whether any doctrine ascribing power to Satan is compatible with the doctrine of Creation: a point made by the Dutch Cartesian and Calvinist, Balthasar Bekker:[45] and indeed it would be sad if Bekker's great contribution to secularisation, the denial that "witches" can have concourse with the Devil, had itself to be denied on the strength of autonomous human reasoning in natural theology).

The first step to an alternative theodicy over physical evil is to inquire what sort of differences the objector would expect to find between a world created by a benevolent Creator and our own world. *Ex hypothesi* a benevolent deity desires the welfare of his intelligent creatures: but how better should this welfare be promoted? Some objectors[46] simply assume that a benevolent deity would intervene in the operation of his own natural laws so as to bring about happier states of affairs: Hume, on the other hand, *argues* for the point.

In the course of Dialogue XI, Philo sets out four sorts of physical evils which supposedly both cause most of our misfortunes and are unnecessary and such as could be avoided, granted a deity with the power and the will. Of these four sorts the second is the most radical: for Hume alleges that God need not "conduct the world by general laws" without exception, but could exterminate evil by "particular volitions".[47] Hume also suggests that such interventions could pass unnoticed, natural causes being so hard to understand in any case: but here at least he is mistaken, in that non-

---

[45] In 'De Betoverde Wereld' (1690): English translation, 'The World Turn'd Upside Down', London, 1700, page b.8.

[46] E.g. J. J. MacIntosh 'Belief-In', 'Mind', LXXIX, No. 315, July 1970, pp. 395-407. I have replied in 'Belief in God', 'Sophia', Vol. XI, No. 2, July 1972, pp. 1-4.

[47] 'Philosophical Works', Vol. II, pp. 511f.

repeatable counter-instances to natural laws would become so numerous that would-be scientific observation, at least on a twentieth-century scale, would be more than likely to remark terrestrial instances. But this is not the core of Hume's case. He accepts that in a world lacking general laws (of nature) "no man could employ his reason in the conduct of life", but insists that a few particularly well-placed interventions, such as "some small touches given to Caligula's brain in his infancy" would do a great deal of good, and that there is no reason known to us why a benevolent Providence would refrain from them. The possibility of there being unkown reasons may render God's goodness and physical evil consistent, but cannot establish that God is good.

Once again, even if Hume is right, belief in God's goodness is not undermined: and, as was observed above, there is in any case much favourable evidence which actually supports this belief. Yet unless there *are* unknown reasons, Hume's objection makes that belief seem hard to support: for he has apparently managed to portray a somewhat better possible world (better from the point of view of overall human welfare), and a truly benevolent, omnipotent and wise deity would surely create that world which best complied with his own (benevolent) desires. So it is important to ask whether a benevolent deity would intervene as Hume says he would be likely to.

Now a parallel objection was considered above, concerning the possibility of divine interventions to remove the evil consequences of wrong human choices. One of the replies there given was that no-one would in such a world be able to predict the consequences of his own or others' actions with any assurance. A parallel reply is appropriate here. In a world where God intervened with the operation of natural laws to remove gross evils, the ordinary course of nature could not be understood, as there would be no regularities of unrestrictedly general application to observe. But what cannot be understood and predicted cannot in general be controlled. Even if interventions were few, both human science and human effort would be stultified: science for the reasons given, and human effort because whatever was done would be prone mysteriously to be undone or miscarry — for the products of the most blameless effort often have seriously evil consequences, which an omniscient God would prevent by "particular volitions". This reasoning does not hang on the divine interventions being observed, but rather on the fact that no unalterably regular natural sequences of events would exist to be observed under such a dispensation, and so men would find nature mysterious and have little hope of taming it.

The evils of such a dispensation would therefore be so great that there is reason to suppose that a benevolent Creator would create nothing but a world in which the operation of natural laws was unimpeded except by the free choices of his intelligent creatures. Only thus could such creatures develop into mature understanding of the world around them and secure for each other the benefits necessary for their welfare.

To say this, however, is not to produce a theodicy over physical evil. For nothing has yet been said about *which* natural laws a benevolent deity would be likely to bring into operation. Possibly, as far as anything yet said goes, such a deity would have made a *better* regular world than ours (from the point of view of human welfare). Indeed Hume supplied some suggestions in this direction,[48] and these must now be considered.

D. Which Regularities?

In reply to the evidence which favours belief in God's benevolence, the objector now contends that some of the natural laws in operation in our world conduce less than other possible ones to human welfare and more than other possible ones to human misery: and that this proposition is not consistent with the proposition that there is an omnipotent, wise and benevolent Creator by whom our world is created. As seen above, the inconsistency claim is itself dubious, for baneful natural laws could be the work of a Devil. My present concern, however, is not to challenge the inconsistency claim (thus avoiding a demonological theodicy), but to enquire whether the objector's contention about natural laws can itself be sustained. For unless grounds can be adduced to support it, belief in God's goodness can rest undisturbed, on the basis of the favourable evidence.

The onus, therefore, is on the objector, who must describe at least one natural law as a possible alternative to one of those in operation in our world, which would conduce more to the welfare of intelligent creatures (or be more 'optimific'; a term well-suited to the present context). Hume's suggestions in Dialogue XI about avoidable evil are more or less in place as possible grounds for such an objector, (except his second, which concerns "particular volitions" and has already been discussed).

The first suggestion is as follows: pain is unnecessary for the survival of species, as a diminution of pleasure would suffice instead as a spur to "vigilance in the great work of self-preservation". To this I shall not object that pleasure is not a sensation, as I believe, with Urmson, that some pleasures are

---

[48] pp. 510-511, 513-517.

sensations.[49] My objection is rather that a spur to action must be something to which we must attend, and that whereas sensations are necessarily attended to, their diminution or absence is not necessarily something we are aware of, and is in fact something we only occasionally become aware of. But a spur is needed which to have is to attend to. Moreover we do already, as things are, undergo decreases in pleasurable sensations when e.g. hungry or tired: but it is not such decreases which draw our attention to our needs, but sensations, notably pangs and pains. Accordingly some such sensation as pain is necessary if we are to be apprised of the need to preserve ourselves.[50]

After Hume's suggestion about "particular volitions", which is the second of his four points, there follows his third suggestion: misery would be the less if species were equipped with extra powers, whereas, the world being as it is, the distribution of faculties is so frugal that only the minimum endowments necessary have been allocated to the several species. Like the suggestion about pain, we can update this suggestion as implying that evolution might have been more optimific, and thus take it to be of current relevance.

It is hard to see, however, just what Hume would wish to see added, except in the case of humans. The faculties which species actually have *do* allow them to survive, (or they would not survive): and whereas extra powers in any given species might make it more populous, it would if so expand only at the expense of other species, the balance of nature as it now is being upset. In the case of humans, however, Hume does spell out what a more optimific law of nature would be like: people would overall be endowed with "a greater propensity to industry and labor" and "an equal diligence with that which many individuals are able to attain by habit and reflection".[51] But, as I have argued elsewhere,[52] such characteristics are necessarily dependent on effort, and are at least in part the outcome of habits of choosing. God cannot then create people both free to form habits of their own and equipped at the outset

---

[49] J. O. Urmson, 'Aristotle on Pleasure', in 'Aristotle', edited J. M. E. Moravscik, Macmillan, London, 1968.

[50] Roland Puccetti, in 'Is Pain Necessary?', Philosophy, 1975, speculates on some of the evolutionary advantages of conscious pain-perception. But while accepting lingering and non-aversive pain as a by-product of the same capacity, he considers it a problem for the theologian. Yet a neural cut-off mechanism for eliminating such pain would probably have had selective disadvantages, and such capacities must be shared, if at all, by all members of the species. God could conceivably have created persons who did not inherit capacities as members of species do: but they would not, to say the least, have been humans.

[51] p. 514.

[52] 'Talents, Abilities and Virtues', 'Philosophy', July, 1971.

with such qualities. Hume in fact often ascribed to heredity and natural endowment much that seems to us nowadays to depend more on habits formed early in life, on the encouragement (itself typically a free human activity) of other people, and on the agent's own responses to such encouragement.

Hume's fourth and final suggestion is that many natural phenomena, though indispenable (e.g. for cosmic stability), yet fall short of their purpose. This argument looks like an unallowable appeal to final causes: it looks as if Hume would need *a priori* to know the purpose of each phenomenon before he could carry out his assessment. But his examples, (the damage done to life, including human life, by wind, rain and heat) suggests that the only allowable criterion in the present issue can after all properly be introduced, i.e. the extent of the optimificity of these phenomena, or, more properly, of the natural laws with which they comply.

It is not at all evident, however, that any alternative laws, governing e.g. either gas pressures, condensation or heat radiation, would, across the entire domain of their application, be more optimific than the ones we have. This is not a closed issue, but it can be said with some confidence that in a world governed by any such alternative laws human life would almost certainly be unrecognisably different. For if, as argued above, a benevolent deity would only create a regular world, the alternative regularities must apply to all times and places alike, with innumerable differences from the familiar world of our experience, many of them inconvenient or harmful.

To take another such case, it might be suggested that the evil of cancer could be prevented on more optimific biological laws. Such laws would however be those concerning cellular multiplication and decay, and would accordingly have to apply to the behaviour e.g. of those bacteria on which human life depends. Even here, then, it is far from clear that the natural laws of our own world are not maximally optimific, despite the terrible extent of the suffering which occurs in accordance with them.

Hume's third suggestion could, however, give rise to another difficulty in the present connection. Is not animal suffering unnecessary? Could not a benevolent deity have devised better evolutionary laws? A somewhat narrow-minded reply would be the observation that only the welfare of *intelligent* creatures is at stake, and that accordingly animal suffering except that in a few mammalian species is beside the point. But because we can sympathise with the desires and the feelings of animals, this technically correct reply is unsatisfactory: for such suffering is at all events a matter of deep regret and pity. Without redefining 'evil' so as to include all animal suffering, can such a pitiful phenomenon be reconciled with the benevolence of a deity who might be expected to sympathise with animal suffering somewhat as many humans do? The necessity of pain for survival will only be part of such an answer: yet if human and animal life is to be at all like what it now is, it would appear that there must be a system of food chains among animal species, which must obtain their own food by preying on each other and on vegetable species, and maintain a balance of animal populations. Only under some such conditions could human life and that of other mammals evolve and survive.

Perhaps, however, someone may one day with ingenuity describe alternative natural laws whose overall observation in the universe would be likely to be more optimific than those in force in our world. I can see no *a priori* reason why this could not be achieved: for there could be different natural laws. On the other hand, the onus is, as pointed out above, on the objector: so all that is needed for a theodicy over the issue of physical evil to be successful is for any actual suggestions of alternative more optimific natural laws to be undermined or cast into doubt. As far as I am aware, no such suggestions so far produced pass scrutiny: objectors have failed to show that the natural laws of our world are incompatible with, or even constitute evidence unfavourable to divine goodness; and so the belief that God is good can stand as probable on the basis of the favourable evidence mentioned at the outset. For the actual natural laws seem more optimific than any envisageable alternatives.

A similar discussion about physical evil to the present one on the subject of natural laws is possible over the space-time trajectories of material particles (on which see Chapter 2, Section 3B). If the set of the past spatial and temporal positions enter into the explanation of a particle's present position alongside natural laws, it is possible to inquire whether a different set of space-time trajectories might not have been more optimific, i.e. to ask if the world would not have been a better place were matter at each successive time distributed differently in space. As in the case of natural laws it is proper to point out that the world as it is has made human life and some degree of the development of human individuals possible; but again it is theoretically open to an objector to suggest an alternative space-time trajectory for any particle or mutually influenced set of particles. In practice, however, it is so difficult to say what the set of consequences would be in the present had the past been different in any such way, that such objections are unlikely to be upheld. At the same time it cannot be asserted with any confidence that the space-time trajectories of particles in our world *are* more optimific than any alternative set. But this is because of lack of information, and does not cast doubt on God's goodness while evidence of the optimificity of actual distributions of matter in space remains.

It remains to remark that the evidence for God's benevolence is also evidence, along the lines of Chapter 4, Section 2C, for God's loving or favouring concern by humans for one another's good, and that the above discussion may thus serve to support belief in God's moral attributes. And *if* God's love of righteousness can be taken to imply that he is likely to reveal himself, and in such a way that he can be recognised, these propositions too receive support.[53] But there is neither the space nor the need to discuss this latter issue here.

Once again, Hume's secularism appears to have been premature: yet granted the somewhat naive optimism of some of his contemporaries, his resolve to search out the evidence and counter-evidence for belief in God's goodness to the limits of the powers of human reasoning was entirely justified. It has also prompted at least a few theists in the course of time to forgo assertions about God's goodness, based on faith alone, and to accord to reason that place in theology which the secular attitude of Hume had claimed for it. Not that Hume always pressed such claims (witness Dialogue XII): yet even the compromise position purportedly arrived at there[54] differs from orthodox theism precisely because of the *reasoned* critique Hume saw fit to apply to the latter. Such reasoning can neither reasonably be declared out of order, despite the sublimity of its subject, nor, once it has been embarked on, be forgotten, passed over or suppressed. Indeed theists can welcome autonomous reasoning alike in science, morals and natural theology.

---

[53] See R. Attfield 'The God of Religion and the God of Philosophy', Vol. 9, No. 1, March 1973, pp. 1-9.

[54] Op. cit., p. 528.

CONCLUSION

Secularisation, I have argued, should not be opposed by believers in God. On the contrary, Jewish and Christian theism is compatible with many of the more central tenets of secularisation, and indeed positively implies them. Moreover historically it encouraged their acceptance. Most obviously this applies to the fundamental tenets of science: that the material universe is regular and accessible to human investigation, that in like circumstances like phenomena occur, that it is possible for users of the empirical method advocated by Bacon, Galileo and the early Royal Society to learn truths about nature, and that there is even a duty upon some to carry out such an investigation for the benefit of human beings and other sentient creatures. Yet the same connection also holds good over both ethics and natural theology: certain of the strands in utilitarianism and also in theories of human rights have close logical ties with theism, nor did the connection escape notice in the period I have considered; while both the right of philosophers to scrutinise basic tenets of theism by autonomous methods of their own and the need for grounds if theistic belief is rationally to be held turn out both to be implicit in theism and to have been seen to be so.

The link is perhaps most obvious over science, despite instances of ecclesiastical suppression and scientific self-censorship. Lynn White is consistent in attacking technology and the doctrine of creation together (granted that technology is nowadays based on the application of science): and certainly to reject the rational and empirical approach of science would logically imply the rejection of theism at the same time. It does not, of course, follow that theism favours applications of science which blight the lives of coming generations or despoliate the living environment of those now alive: indeed the very duty to understand nature which theism implies receives its rationale from the benefits which flow when in the light of such knowledge as people can muster resources are either responsibly used or responsibly conserved. Rather than justifying any and every exploitation of nature, theism embodies criteria which enable use and misuse to be distinguished. Accordingly those concerned over the various problems facing mankind, ecological ones included, would do well not to eradicate the theistic roots of our scientific and technological view of the world; indeed it would be better in place to tend and cultivate them.

Bacon quite properly opposed the view that any creature was sacred or any recess in nature prohibited to science: and as a believer in creation he was consistent in taking this view. But it did not commit him or his followers to the view that nature is wax in human hands, to be moulded to suit the convenience of any class, state or generation. Rather it commits them to the responsibility of man for his own future, to opposition to fatalism and to support for tackling problems in the light of understanding both of nature and of human needs.

This theistic concern for the satisfaction of human needs issued, in due course, in secular ethical theories such as utilitarianism. As we have seen, a succession of philosophers remarked the mistakenness of the view that ethical terms need to be religiously defined: there must, they pointed out, be moral standards quite independent of religion if morality is to comprise a defensible system rather than a set of arbitrary injunctions, or indeed if theistic ethics are to be taken seriously. Once again theism requires the autonomy of an area of human reflection. As over science, there turned out to be pitfalls in the application of such a method, as when utilitarianism seriously misconstrued the nature of human needs: yet once again the remedy was not the abandonment of a secular approach, but better analysis and its more consistent application. (I have supplied above some outlines of a possibly more satisfactory theory). And despite such pitfalls, secular ethical theorists have often inherited the mantle of the biblical prophets and urged social change sooner and more effectively than those prophets' institutional heirs, the moral theologians of the church.

It is, however, over natural theology where theists have been most reluctant to accept the competence of an autonomous secular approach. Mistakenly is has been held that faith is unamenable to reason, and that natural theology is in any case condemned to bankruptcy. Yet, as shown in Chapter 5 above, many theists in the period studied saw the need of religion for grounds independent of itself, and set out both grounds and objections alike with commendable candour. I also argued there that they were entirely correct in this approach: theism demands the autonomy of epistemology and logic just as much as of science and ethics, even if it is imperilled itself thereby. Indeed the tending of the theistic roots of our scientific view of the world, which was commended above, is only as defensible as theism itself: hence the investigation carried out in Chapters 5 and 6 into the secular critique of theism by such philosophers as Hume and Kant.

On the part of philosophers like Hume and Diderot, and to some extent Kant, this critique certainly amounted to a form of secularism: but secularism must be treated on its merits. As I hope to have shown, it has often been entirely justified. A good example is the attack on physical theology related in Chapter 2: bringing in God to explain the unexplained was both bad physics and bad theology, and deducing the nature of nature from the nature of God was as bad, if not worse. This form of secularism has continued to be needed in face of geological theories involving supernaturally induced catastrophes and biological ones involving supernatural origins of species. Over the nature of man Priestley's opposition to dualism as a basis for belief in the freedom of the will was both secularist and well-justified: while (on the definitions I have used) the same is true of the attack by Cudworth, Price and others on the theological naturalism in ethics. Indeed when both Hume and Kant objected to the claim that a *necessary* being is shown to exist by the theistic arguments, they were perfectly right, as they also were in pointing out that the teleological argument is insufficient to uphold alone the doctrine of creation. Where religious claims are false, no-one can complain at secularism.

Discovering which ones are false, however, depends on assessing the arguments: and in the above assessment it emerged that secularism has quite often been ill-grounded. Thus the application of Spinoza's rationalism to scientific method and to the possibility of miracles would have undermined that belief in contingency which is the stimulus for scientific observation: whereas necessitarianism (see Chapter 3) not only clashes with theistic ethics; it undermines every ethical system and is itself rationally untenable. Likewise, and despite what is usually said, Hume's and Kant's criticisms of the teleological argument were fatal only to some of its contemporary forms; their adverse verdicts on the cosmological argument were misconceived; and neither they nor others have shown the world's evils to be incompatible with God's goodness.

Indeed the assessment of these matters in Chapters 5 and 6 issued in more constructive findings. Thus the cosmologcial argument does support, as a probability, the existence of an omnipotent, uncreatable and indestructible agent with the ability to create spatial and temporal creatures: the teleological argument does suggest the probability that the contingent regularities of nature are due to an intelligent designer: and, taken in conjunction, these arguments uphold the rationality of belief in the theistic doctrine of creation. Moreover (see Chapter 6) there are positive grounds for belief in the concern of this Creator for his intelligent creatures, and hence his readiness to make accessible to them what conduces to their good (not excluding the disciplines of science, ethics and philosophy). There is, of course, much more room for argument about all this: yet the best way to show that natural theology has a constructive contribution to make has proved to be to do some in practice, and thus to prepare a counter-critique of its secularist critics, and bring out thereby the extent and the limits of their achievement.

Nevertheless to reason in this way is to pay the secularists the compliment of endorsing their own presupposition, that human reason is to be used unfettered as to methods, subjects or conclusions. Theistic believers can, I have contended, applaud this presupposition, reflecting as it does an element of that maturity to which, at least according to the Old and New Testaments, those created in the image of God are called.

Yet the unfettered use of human reason cannot be regarded as an ally of all religious beliefs. Besides the examples of well-directed secularist attacks set out above, and the vulnerability just mentioned of nineteenth century theories of divine interventions in the geological and biological spheres, psychology and sociology have disclosed that religion serves many functions other than the glory of God and the benefit of his creatures. Further the application of secular moral standards has been seen in many places to undermine whatever justification there was for religious control over society, and has also led to attacks on doctrines such as those of Hell, penal substitution and sacrificial atonement. Meanwhile, as the authors of 'The Myth of God Incarnate' have recently disclosed, it is particularly difficult to defend or even to state intelligibly the doctrines of the Incarnation and of the Trinity, or to find criteria for recognising revelations on which the particularist claims of either Judaism or Christianity stand up. Indeed the propositions about God upheld above probably raise extra problems for those doctrines. The exploration of such problems would be a further legitimate exercise in secularisation, but it cannot be tackled here.

Religious believers in more and more countries must, in fact, come to terms with living in pluralist societies which they can no longer hope to dominate: while modern societies are obliged, without being able to rely on religious solutions or certainties, to tackle such vast worldwide problems as those of poverty, overpopulation, pollution, and the depletion of natural resources. Yet, as we have seen, the theist is still entitled to claim, despite secular criticism, that the material universe is created, that people are intended to exercise dominion over it in a responsible way which allows for the welfare of present and future generations as a whole, that either severally or collectively they are able to do so, and that morally they should and must. These well-grounded claims remain a crucial stimulus to the secular, technological and political imagination which is now needed as much as any revelation ever was.

At the same time there also remains a need for the painstaking sifting and analysis of arguments, whether political, technological or, in the case of this book, philosophical, historical and theological. Arguments in all these subjects need careful scrutiny; those in this book are no exception.

BIBLIOGRAPHY

AARON, R.
'John Locke', O.U.P., 1937.

AQUINAS, T.
'Summa Theologica', translated 'Fathers of the English Dominican Province', (22 Vols.), London, 1911-1924.

ATTFIELD, D.
'Christ is of God'. (Unpublished manuscript).

ATTFIELD, R.
(1) 'Science and Creation', 'Journal of Religion', January, 1978.
(2) 'Clarke, Collins and Compounds', 'Journal of The History of Philosophy', XV, 1977, pp. 45-54.
(3) 'Talents, Abilities and Virtues', 'Philosophy', July, 1971, pp. 255-257.
(4) 'Toward a Defence of Teleology', 'Ethics', 85, 1975, pp. 123-135.
(5) 'On Being Human', 'Inquiry', 1974, pp. 175-192.
(6) 'Against Incomparabilism', 'Philosophy', 30, 1975, pp.230-234.
(7) 'The God of Religion and The God of Philosophy', in 'Religious Studies', 1973, Vol. 9, No. 1, pp. 1-9.
(8) 'The Individuality of God', 'Sophia', X, 1971, pp. 20-27.
(9) 'The Lord is God: There is No Other', 'Religious Studies', 13, 1977, pp. 73-84.
(10) 'Believing in God', 'Sophia', XI, No. 2, July 1972, pp. 1-4.

AYERS, M.
'The Refutation of Determinism', London, 1968.

BACON, F.
(1) 'The New Organon', edited Fulton H. Anderson, Indianapolis, 1960.
(2) 'Novum Organum', edited Thomas Fowler, Oxford, 1878.
(3) 'Works', edited by Ellis, Spedding and Heath, (7 Vols.), Longmans, London, 1887-92.

BIBLIOGRAPHY

BARROW I.
'Mathematical Lectures Read in the Publick Schools', translated John Kirby, London, 1734.

BEKKER, B.
'De Betoverde Wereld' (1690), translated anon. as 'The World Turn'd Upside Down', London, 1700.

BENTHAM, J.
'Introduction to the Principles of Morals and Legislation', London, 1789.

BERKELEY, G.
(1) 'Essay Towards a New Theory of Vision', Dublin, 1709.
(2) 'Principles of Human Knowledge', (1710), edited G. Warnock, Fontana, London, 1962.
(3) 'Alciphron' in 'Works' edited Luce and Jessop, London, 1949.

BONHOEFFER, D.
'Letters and Papers from Prison', Fontana, London, 1959.

BOURKE, V.
'History of Ethics' (2 Vols.), Doubleday, New York, 1968.

BOYLE, R.
'The Works of the Hon. Robert Boyle', edited by T. Birch, 6 Vols., London, 1772.

BROOKE, J.H.
'Natural Theology in Britain from Boyle to Paley' in 'New Interactions between Theology and Natural Science', Milton Keynes, 1974.

BRUNTON, J.
'The Second Analogy and Levels of Argument', in 'Kantstudien', 62 Jahrgang, Heft 3, 1971.

BUTLER, J.
'Works', edited W. E. Gladstone (2 Vols.), Oxford, 1896.

CARRÉ, M.
(1) 'Pierre Gassendi and the New Philosophy' in 'Philosophy', January, 1958.
(2) 'Platonism and the Rise of Science', 'Philosophy', 1955.

CASTAÑEDA, H-N.
'On the Phenomeno-Logic of the I',
'Akten des XIV. Internationalen Kongresses für Philosophie', Herder, Vienna, 1968.

CLARKE, S.
(1) As Leibniz, G., (3) below.

(2) As Collins, A., (1) below.
(3) 'A Discourse Concerning the Being and Attributes of God, Etc.', London, 1719.

COLLINS, A.
(1) 'Letter to Dodwell, Etc.', London, 1731.
(2) 'Dissertation on Liberty and Necessity', London, 1729.

COMMONER, B.
'The Closing Circle', Jonathan Cape Ltd., London, 1973.

COX, H.
'The Secular City', S.C.M., London, 1965.

CUDWORTH, R.
(1) 'The True Intellectual System of the Universe', edited J. L. Mosheim, London, 1845.
(2) (Sundry unpublished MSS. See footnote 37, Chapter 3.)
(3) 'A Treatise of Freewill', in Raphael, D., (1) below.

DESCARTES, R.
(1) 'The Philosophical Works', translated by Elizabeth S. Haldane and G. R. T. Ross, 2 Vols., C.U.P., Cambridge, 1967.
(2) 'Oeuvres', edited C. Adam and P. Tannery, Paris, 1897-1913.

D'HOLBACH, Paul Dietrich, Baron
'Système de la Nature', Paris, 1770.

DURRANT, M.
'The Logical Status of 'God' ', Macmillan, London, 1973.

EWIN, R.
'Justice and Injustice', 'Mind', 1970.

FARRINGTON, B.
'The Philosophy of Francis Bacon', Liverpool University Press, Liverpool, 1964.

FINDLAY, J.
'Can God's Existence be Disproved', 'Mind', 1948.

FLEW, A.
'God and Philosophy', Hutchinson, London, 1966.

FOSTER, M.B.
'The Christian Doctrine of Creation and the Rise of Modern Natural Science', etc., 'Mind', 1934-36.

GALILEI, G.
'Dialogue Concerning the Two Chief World Systems' (1629), translated Thomas Salusbury (1661), University of Chicago Press, 1953.

GASSENDI, P.
(1) 'Exercitationum paradoxicarum adversus Aristoteleos libri septem', Grenoble, 1624.
(2) 'Opera Omnia', (4 Vols), Lyon, 1658.

GAY, P.
'Deism: An Anthology', edited Peter Gay, Van Nostrand, New York, 1968.

GEACH, P.
(1) 'God and the Soul', London, 1969.
(2) 'Three Philosophers', by G. E. M. Anscombe and P. T. Geach, Oxford, 1961.

GIRILL, T.R.
'Galileo and Platonistic Methodology' 'Journal of the History of Ideas', 1970.

GLANVILL, J.
(1) 'Scepsis Scientifica', London, 1665.
(2) 'Essays', London, 1676.
(3) 'Philosophia Pia', in 'Collected Works of Joseph Glanvill', Goerge Olms Verlag, Hildesheim, 1970, Vol. 5.

GODWIN, W.
'Political Justice', London, 1795.

GOODMAN, D.
(1) 'God and Nature in the Philosophy of Descartes' in 'Towards a Mechanistic Philosophy', The Open University Press, Milton Keynes, 1974.
(2) Editor, 'Science and Religious Belief: A Selection of Primary Sources', Milton Keynes, 1973.
(3) 'Galileo and the Church' in 'The 'Conflict Thesis' and Cosmology', The Open University Press, Milton Keynes, 1974.
(4) 'The Enlightenment: Deists and 'Rationalists' ', in 'Scientific Progress and Religious Dissent', The Open University Press, Milton Keynes, 1974.

GREELEY, A.
'The Persistence of Religion', S.C.M., London, 1973.

GUERRY, H.
'Sommers' Ontological Proof', 'Analysis' 28.2, 1967.

HAMPSHIRE, S.
'Spinoza and the Idea of Freedom' in 'Studies in the Philosophy of Thought and Action' edited P. F. Strawson, Oxford, 1968.

HARRÉ, R.
'Early Seventeenth Century Scientists', Pergamon Press Ltd., Oxford, 1965.

HERBERT OF CHERBURY, Lord E.
'De Veritate' (1624), translated Meyrick H. Carré, Bristol, 1937.

HICK, J.
(1) 'Arguments for the Existence of God', London, 1970.
(2) Editor, 'The Myth of God Incarnate', London, 1977.

HOBBES, T.
(1) 'Leviathan', edited M. Oakeshott, Blackwell, Oxford, 1955.
(2) 'Of Liberty and Freewill', in Raphael, D., (1) below.
(3) 'English Works', edited Molesworth, (11 Vols.), London, 1839-1845.

HOOYKAAS, R.
(1) 'Christian Freedom and the Freedom of Science', Tyndale Press, 1957.
(2) 'Religion and the Rise of Modern Science', Scottish Academic Press, Edinburgh and London, 1972.

HUDSON, W.
'Ethical Intuitionism', London, 1967.

HUME, D.
(1) 'Hume's Enquiries', edited L. Selby-Bigge, Oxford, 1894.
(2) 'Dialogues Concerning Natural Religion', edited N. K. Smith, London, 1935.
(3) 'Treatise of Human Nature', edited L. Selby-Bigge, (reprinted) Oxford, 1951.
(4) 'Essays, Moral, Political and Literary' edited T. H. Green and T. H. Grose, (2 Vols.) London, 1889.
(5) 'The Philosophical Works of Hume', (4 Vols.), edited anon., Boston, 1854.

HURLBUTT, R.
'Hume, Newton and the Design Argument', Lincoln, (Nebraska), 1965.

HUTCHESON, F.
'Illustrations upon the Moral Sense', in Raphael, D., (1) below.

JAKI, S.
'Science and Creation', Scottish Academic Press, 1974.

KANT, I.
(1) 'Fundamental Principles' (Grundlegung), translated T. Abbott, Indianapolis, 1949.
(2) 'Critique of Pure Reason', translated Norman Kemp Smith, Macmillan, London, 1968, (First edition as translated, 1929).
(3) 'Religion Within the Limits of Reason Alone', translated Theodore M. Greene and Hoyt H. Hudson, Harper, New York, 1934.

(4) 'Essays and Treatise', (1791) translated W. Richardson in 'Philosophy of Religion', edited Julius R. Weinberg and Keith E. Yandell, New York, 1971.

KARGON, R.H.
'Atomism in England from Hariot to Newton', Clarendon Press, Oxford, 1966.

KEMSLEY, D.
'Religious Influences in the Rise of Modern Science', 'Annals of Science', 24.3, 1968.

KENNY, A.
(1) 'Descartes, A Study of His Philosophy', Random House, New York, 1968.
(2) 'The Five Ways', London, 1969.

KOYRÉ, A.
(1) 'Metaphysics and Measurement', Chapman and Hall, London, 1968.
(2) 'Newtonian Studies', London, 1965.
(3) 'From the Closed World to the Infinite Universe', Baltimore, 1957.

LA METTRIE, J. Offray de
'L'Homme Machine', Leyden, 1747.

LARSEN, R.
'The Aristotelianism of Bacon's *Novum Organum*', 'Journal of the History of Ideas', 1962.

LEIBNIZ, G.
(1) 'Discourse on Metaphysics' translated Peter Lucas and Lesley Grint, Manchester, 1953.
(2) 'Theodicy', translated E. M. Huggard, edited A. M. Farrer, London, 1951.
(3) 'The Clarke-Leibniz Correspondence', edited H. G. Alexander, Manchester, 1956.
(4) 'Die philosophischen Schriften', edited C. I. Gerhardt, 7 Vols., Berlin, 1875-1890.
(5) 'Leibniz' Philosophical Writings', Everyman's Philosophical Library, London, 1934.
(6) 'Discourse on Metaphysics, Correspondence with Arnauld, and Monadology', translated George R. Montgomery, (2nd edition), Chicago, 1918.

LESSING, G.
'Lessing's Theological Writings', selected and translated Henry Chadwick, London, 1956.

LEVISON, A. and THALBERG, I.
'Essential and Causal Explanations of Action', 'Mind', 1969.

LOCKE, J.
(1) 'Essay Concerning Human Understanding', Everyman, London, 1961. (First published, 1690).
(2) 'Works', London, 1823, reprinted by Scientia Verlag Aalen, Germany, 1963. (10 Volumes).

LOVEJOY, A.
'The Great Chain of Being', Harvard U.P., Cambridge, Mass., 1936.

LUCAS, J.
(1) 'Freedom and Prediction', 'Proceedings of the Aristotelian Society', Supplementary Volume, 1967.
(2) 'The Freedom of the Will', Oxford, 1970.

LUCRETIUS, T. Carus
'De Rerum Natura', Clarendon Press, Oxford, (2nd edition) 1922.

MABBOTT, J.
'The Place of God in Berkeley's Philosophy', 'Philosophy', 1931.

MACINTYRE, A.
'Secularisation and Moral Change', O.U.P., 1967.

MACKIE, J.
'Evil and Omnipotence', Mind, 1955.

MACINTOSH, J.
'Belief-In', 'Mind', 1970.

MALCOLM, N.
'Anselm's Ontological Arguments', 'Philosophical Review', 1960.

MARTIN, D.
'The Religious and The Secular', Routledge and Kegan Paul, London, 1969.

MEDAWAR, P. B.
'The Art of the Soluble', Methuen, London, 1967.

MILLER, L.G.
'Descartes, Mathematics and God', in 'Metameditations', edited Sesonke and Fleming, Wadsworth Publishing Co., Inc., Belmont, California, 1965.

MINTZ, S.
'The Hunting of Leviathan', Cambridge, 1969.

MORE, H.
'Divine Dialogues', London, 1668.

NEWTON, I.
  (1) Correspondence, Vol. I., edited H. W. Turnbull, Cambridge, 1959-61.
  (2) 'Sir Isaac Newton's Mathematical Principles' translated A. Motte (1729) and F. Cajori (1947), Berkeley, California, 1947.
  (3) 'Unpublished Scientific Papers of Sir Isaac Newton', edited and translated A. R. and M. B. Hall, Cambridge, 1962.
  (4) 'Correspondence' Vol. III, edited by H. W. Turnbull, Cambridge, 1961.

PALEY, W.
  (1) 'A View of the Evidences of Christianity', 1794.
  (2) 'The Principles of Moral and Political Philosophy' (1785) in Raphael, D., (1) below.

PALMER, H.
  'Analogy, A Study of Qualification and Argument in Theology', Macmillan, London, 1973.

PARKINSON, G.
  'Logic and Reality in Leibniz's Metaphysics', Oxford, 1965.

PASSMORE, J.
  (1) 'Man's Responsibility for Nature', Duckworth, London, 1974.
  (2) 'Ralph Cudworth, An Interpretation', Cambridge, 1951.

PIKE, N.
  'Divine Omniscience and Voluntary Action', 'Philosophical Review', 1965.

PLAMENATZ, J.
  'The English Utilitarians', (2nd edition), Oxford, 1958.

PLANTINGA, A.
  'The Free Will Defence', reprinted in 'The Philosophy of Religion', edited Basil Mitchell, Oxford, 1971.

PLATO
  'Phaedo', edited J. Burnet, Oxford, 1911.

POPPER, K.
  'Conjectures and Refutations', Routledge, London, 1963.

PRATT, V.
  'Religion and Secularisation', Macmillan, 1970.

PRICE, R.
  (1) As Priestley, J., (1) below.
  (2) 'A Review of the Principal Questions in Morals' (Third edition), London, 1787: also edited D. D. Raphael, Oxford, 1948.
  (3) 'Sermons', London, c. 1790.

PRIESTLEY, J.
(1) 'A Free Discussion of the Doctrines of Materialism and Philosophical Necessity, Etc.', London, 1778.
(2) 'Essay on the First Principles of Government', London, 1768.

PRIOR, A.
'Logic and the Basis of Ethics', Oxford, 1949.

PUCETTI, R.
'Is Pain Necessary?', 'Philosophy', 1975, pp. 259-269.

PURVER, M.
'The Royal Society: Concept and Creation', Routledge, London, 1967.

RANDALL, J.H.
'The Development of Scientific Method in the School of Padua', 'Journal of the History of Ideas', Vol. I, 1940.

RAPHAEL, D.
(1) 'British Moralists, 1650-1800', edited D. D. Raphael, Oxford, 1969.
(2) 'The Moral Sense', Oxford, 1947.

REMNANT, P.
'Kant and the Cosmological Argument', 'Australian Journal of Philosophy', 1959.

RESCHER, N.
'The Philosophy of Leibniz, Englewood Cliffs, New Jersey, 1967.

ROSSI, P.
'Francis Bacon, From Magic to Science' translated by S. Rabinovitch, Routledge, London, 1968.

ROUSSEAU, J-J.
'Émile', translated Barbara Foxley, Everyman, London, 1911.

ROWE, W.L.
'The Cosmological Argument' 'Nous' V, 1971, pp. 49-61.

SHAFFER, J.
'Existence, Predication and the Ontological Argument', 'Mind', 1962.

SHAFTESBURY, Earl of
'Characteristics', edited J. M. Robertson, (2 Vols.), London, 1900.

SMART, N.
'Historical Selections in the Philosophy of Religion', edited N. Smart, London, 1962.

SMITH, N.
'A Commentary to Kant's "Critique of Pure Reason" ', Second edition, London, 1923.

SOMMERS, F.
'Why is There Something and Not Nothing', 'Analysis', 26.6, 1966.

SPINOZA, B.
(1) 'Correspondence', translated and edited A. Wolf, London, 1928.
(2) 'Spinoza Selections', edited John Wild, New York, 1930.
(3) 'The Chief Works', translated R. H. M. Elwes, (2 Vols.), London, 1891.

SPRAT, T.
'History of The Royal Society', edited Jackson I. Cope and Harold Whitmore Jones, Routledge, London, 1959.

STRAWSON, P.
(1) 'Freedom and Resentment', Proceedings of the British Academy, Vol. XLVIII, Oxford, 1962.
(2) 'Individuals', London, 1959.

SUTHERLAND, S.
'Immortality and Resurrection', 'Religious Studies', 1967.

SWINBURNE, R.
(1) 'The Concept of Miracle', London, 1970.
(2) 'Whole and Part in Cosmological Arguments', 'Philosophy', 1969.
(3) 'The Argument from Design', 'Philosophy', 1968.

TAYLOR, A.
'The Ethical Doctrine of Hobbes', 'Philosophy', 1938.

THAYER, H.
'Newton's Philosophy of Nature', Hafner Library of Classics, Columbia, 1952.

URMSON, J.
'Aristotle on Pleasure', in 'Aristotle', edited J. Moravcsik, Macmillan, London, 1968.

VAN LEEUWEN, H. G.
'The Problem of Certainty in English Thought, 1630-90', Nijhoff, The Hague, 1963.

VON WEIZSACKER, C.
'The Relevance of Science', Collins, London, 1964.

WARRENDER, H.
'The Political Philosophy of Hobbes', Oxford, 1957.

WATKINS, J.
'Hobbes' System of Ideas', London, 1965.

WEBSTER, C.
'The Great Instauration', Duckworth, London, 1975.

WILKINS, J.
'Of the Principles and Duties of Natural Religion', London, 1675.

WHITE, L.
'The Historical Roots of Our Ecological Crisis' in 'The Environmental Handbook' edited John Barr, Pan Books Ltd., London, 1971.

WILSON, B.
'Religion in Secular Society', Penguin, London, 1966.

YOUNG, R.
(1) 'Compatibilism and Freedom', 'Mind', Vol. LXXIII, 1974, pp. 19-42.
(2) 'Freedom, Reponsibility and God', Macmillan, London, 1975.

INDEX

Aaron, R., 38, 216.
analogy, 13, 58-59, 189-90, 193-95, 197.
Aquinas, T., 88, 168, 174, 216.
Aristotle, 20-23, 27, 39, 42, 54, 207.
Attfield, D., 177, 216.
authority, 9, 13, 32, 58, 214.
Ayers, M., 103, 216.

Bacon, F., 12, 15-33, 34, 36, 37, 40, 43-45, 47-51, 53, 56, 58, 60, 64-66, 76, 91, 134, 211-12, 216.
Barrow, I., 48, 217.
Bayle, P., 85-86, 108, 124, 199.
Bekker, B., 204, 217.
Bentham, J., 10, 123, 131, 132, 133, 135, 141, 143, 217.
Berkeley, G., 60, 62-64, 70, 217.
Bonhoeffer, D., 9, 12, 31, 124, 217.
Bourke, V., 122-23, 129, 217.
Boyle, R., 38, 54-57, 65, 77, 81, 96, 151, 217.
Bramhall, J., 111, 119.
Brooke, J. H., 64, 217.
Brunton, J., 186, 217.
Butler, J., 89, 199, 217.

Carré, M., 35, 36, 38, 39, 44, 146, 217.
Castañeda, H.-N., 169, 217.
Clarke, S., 73, 76-80, 80-84, 86, 87, 89, 99, 109-13, 119, 151, 168, 170, 217-18.
classification, 19-20, 55-56, 164-66.
Collins, A., 77, 99, 105, 109-12, 119, 218.
Commoner, B., 13, 64, 218.
cosmological argument, 67, 74, 79, 163-81, 191, 195-97, 213.
Cox, H., 10, 12, 218.
creation, 15, 18-19, 25-26, 30-31, 35, 40, 43-49, 57, 59, 60-67, 69, 70, 78-80, 80-84, 86, 121, 141-44, 150, 163-69, 195-97, 198, 213, 214.
Cudworth, R., 81, 108, 109, 111-14, 118, 119, 120, 124-26, 218.

Darwin, C., 69, 184.
Descartes, R., 15, 32-42, 48, 51, 56, 66, 70-72, 83, 85, 96, 97, 107, 112, 121, 124, 134, 149, 151, 155, 156, 199, 202, 218.
determinism, 13, 99-121, 173.
Deutcher, M., 39.
D'Holbach, Paul Dietrich, Baron, 175, 218.
Diderot, D., 37, 69, 129, 185, 188, 213.
dogmatism, 16, 19-23, 30, 37, 48.
dominion over nature, 18, 30, 64, 214.
Durrant, M., 165, 218.

essentialism, 27, 54-57.
Ewin, R., 140, 218.

Farrington, B., 21, 218.
Farrer, A., 68, 87-88, 100-01.
final causes, 22, 34, 37, 57, 75-76, 184-85.
Findlay, J., 153-54.
Foster, M., 31, 62, 218.

Galilei, G., 16, 23, 28, 30, 33, 43, 45, 47, 48, 58, 59, 63, 65, 76, 91, 211, 218.
Gassendi, P., 33-36, 38, 41, 48, 51, 153, 156-58, 163, 219.
Gay, P., 147, 219.
Geach, P., 176, 219.
Girill, T., 44, 219.
Glanvill, J., 16, 41-42, 50, 51, 53, 54, 56, 65, 66, 219.
Godwin, W., 131, 219.
Goodman, D., 41, 46, 57, 69, 75, 219.
Greeley, A., 9, 219.
Guerry, H., 170, 219.

Harré, R., 20, 43, 219.
Hartley, D., 105, 118.
Herbert of Cherbury, Lord E., 122, 146-49, 220.
Hick, J., 148, 186, 187, 194, 214, 220.
Hobbes, T., 33, 34, 36, 38, 41, 42, 48, 51,

INDEX

65, 72, 101, 105, 106, 108-10, 117, 119, 123, 124, 126-29, 141-42, 165, 197, 220.
Hooykaas, R., 23, 41, 220.
Hume, D., 53, 64, 70, 89, 91-94, 106, 117, 118, 125, 131-33, 135, 153-56, 158, 163, 166-75, 177-82, 184-92, 194, 197-208, 210, 212, 213, 220.
Hurlbutt, R., 77, 220.

incompatibilism, 99-101, 119-21.

Jaki, S., 26, 220.

Kant, I., 10, 110, 125, 128, 129, 139, 141, 143, 146, 148, 149, 153-58, 160, 161, 163, 166-82, 191, 197-200, 212, 213, 220.
Kargon, R., 23, 42, 49, 51, 52, 58, 220.
Kemsley, D., 15, 221.
Kenny, A., 40, 107, 168, 174, 221.
Kepler, J., 16, 27, 30, 33, 41, 43, 48, 65.
Koyré, A., 29, 34, 35, 57, 70-72, 74, 107, 221.

La Mettrie, J. Offray de, 37, 109, 221.
Larsen, R., 56, 221.
Leibniz, G., 37, 73, 75, 76-80, 80-84, 86-89, 96, 97, 100, 108, 110, 113, 114, 124, 151, 155, 156, 160-63, 167-69, 173, 198-200, 221.
Lessing, G., 147, 148, 150, 221.
Levison, A., 116, 221.
Locke, J., 38, 50, 55, 62, 124, 135-37, 141, 142, 145-49, 222.
Lovejoy, A., 83, 222.
Lucas, J., 101-03, 118, 120, 222.
Lucretius, T. Carus, 37, 222.

Mabbott, J., 63, 222.
MacIntosh, J., 19, 29, 204, 222.
MacIntyre, A., 10-11, 222.
Mackie, J., 202, 222.
Malcolm, N., 159, 161, 222.
Martin, D., 10-11, 222.
Marx, K., 144.
Medawar, P., 29, 222.
Mill, J. S., 137.
Miller, I., 40-41, 222.
Mintz, S., 111, 222.
miracles, 70, 87, 89-95.
More, H., 72, 74, 107-09, 222.

naturalism, 124-26, 133, 135-36, 141-44.
natural philosophy, 21-22, 37, 43, 49, 51, 55, 68.

natural theology, 26, 66-67, 145-210, 212-14.
necessitarianism, 99-121, 213.
Newton, I., 16, 23, 33, 34, 37, 38, 41, 42, 45, 48, 49, 57-60, 63, 65, 70-74, 75-80, 96, 183, 191, 223.

Oldenburg, H., 58, 62.
ontological argument, 152-63.

Paley, W., 89, 92, 123, 131, 135-37, 141, 142, 184, 223.
Palmer, H., 13, 197, 223.
Passmore, J., 109, 111, 112-13, 118, 223.
physical theology, 23, 39, 68-98, 185.
Plamenatz, J., 130, 131, 133, 136, 139, 223.
Plantinga, A., 200-03, 223.
Plato, 23, 109, 223.
Popper, K., 29, 223.
Pratt, V., 10, 13, 223.
Price, R., 105, 109, 111-14, 124, 125, 134, 138, 140, 223.
Priestley, J., 101, 105-06, 109, 112-14, 117-18, 120, 131-32, 168, 213, 223-24.
Prior, A., 124, 224.
Puccetti, R., 207, 224.
Purver, M., 15, 29, 42, 224.

Randall, J., 44, 224.
Raphael, D., 114, 125, 138, 224.
religion, 9-11, 12, 17-19, 31, 145-52, 214.
Reid, T., 114-15, 117, 119.
revelation, 143, 145-52.
Remnant, P., 160, 224.
Rescher, N., 80, 81, 124, 224.
Rossi, P., 16, 44, 46, 47, 224.
Rousseau, J. J., 148, 149, 151, 224.
Rowe, W., 173, 224.
Royal Society, The, 15, 16, 41, 42, 45, 48, 49-57, 58, 60, 65, 66, 211.
Russell. C., 15.

scepticism, 16, 23-24, 30, 37, 38, 48, 52-54.
scientific method, 15-16, 24-30, 32, 33-49, 49-57, 57-60, 60-67, 68-84, 89-95, 96-98, 190-91.
secularisation, 9-14, 31-33, 34, 37, 42, 43, 50, 57, 64-67, 69, 71, 73, 84, 93, 122-23, 130, 132, 139, 152, 163, 191, 198, 211-15.
secularism, 12, 34, 40, 42, 121, 123, 131, 135, 149, 152, 181, 197, 213-14.
self-determination, 99-121, 193.

Shaffer, J., 157-59, 224.
Shaftesbury, Earl of, 123, 129, 141, 224.
Sommers, F., 170, 225.
Spinoza, B., 42, 53, 60-62, 70, 89, 90-91, 94-97, 101, 102, 105, 106, 123, 124, 127-29, 146-50, 155, 159, 161, 213, 225.
Sprat, T., 29, 50, 225.
Strawson, P., 119-20, 225.
sufficient reason, principle of, 80,-84, 173-88.
Swinburne, R., 90, 92, 172, 177, 178, 184, 185, 187, 188, 190, 193, 225.

Taylor, A., 126, 225.
teleological argument, 26, 67, 98, 182-97.
Thalberg, I., 116, 221.
Thayer, H., 59, 225.
theodicy, 198-210.
theology, 12, 15, 30, 31, 50, 67, 68-98, 121, 124-26, 130, 145, 211-15.

theoretical physics, 21-22, 33-49, 70-74, 80-84.
Tindal, M., 147.
Toland, J., 147.
Torricelli, E., 16, 46-48.

utilitarianism, 123, 130-41, 212.
Urmson, J., 206-07, 225.

Van Leeuwen, H., 16, 51, 65, 225.
Voltaire, J., 199.
Von Weizsäcker, C., 13, 225.

Warrender, H., 126, 225.
Watkins, J., 105-06, 126, 226.
Webster, C., 15, 226.
Wilkins, J., 52, 226.
White, L., 64, 226.
Wilson, B., 9, 226.

Young, R.; 5, 104, 202, 226.